Fiction

Fiction

A Philosophical Analysis

CATHARINE ABELL

OXFORD
UNIVERSITY PRESS

OXFORD
UNIVERSITY PRESS

Great Clarendon Street, Oxford, OX2 6DP,
United Kingdom

Oxford University Press is a department of the University of Oxford.
It furthers the University's objective of excellence in research, scholarship,
and education by publishing worldwide. Oxford is a registered trade mark of
Oxford University Press in the UK and in certain other countries

Published in the United States of America by Oxford University Press
198 Madison Avenue, New York, NY 10016, United States of America

British Library Cataloguing in Publication Data
Data available

Library of Congress Control Number: 2019920870

ISBN 978-0-19-883152-5

To my mother, Lesley Abell

Contents

Acknowledgements

It has taken me a long time to write this book. During the process of doing so, I have benefited from the opportunity to present my ideas about fiction at various stages of their development to audiences at the University of Sussex, the University of Bristol, the University of Nottingham, the London Aesthetics Forum, the University of Hamburg, the University of Southampton, the Scottish Aesthetics Forum, the London School of Economics, the Czech Academy of Sciences, the University of Hertfordshire, the Institut Jean Nicod, the University of Manchester, the University of Keele, the University of Sydney, and the University of Oxford. I am very grateful to the audiences at these presentations for challenging questions and criticisms and for helpful suggestions, all of which have helped me to improve my views in ways that I could not have done alone.

I am also grateful to Julian Dodd, Víctor Durà-Vilà, Anthony Everett, Stacie Friend, Alex Paseau, François Recanati, Nick Shea, and Enrico Terrone for discussion of some of the issues I address in this book, and to Tim Bayne, Stacie Friend, and Enrico Terrone for helpful comments on draft material. Three anonymous referees also provided constructive comments and criticisms that have helped me to improve my argument. Thank you, whoever you are. Kathleen Stock generously read the entire draft typescript and provided invaluable comments and criticisms that have prompted me to clarify my argument, although I know she still will not be persuaded by the views presented here.

Thank you to Peter Momtchiloff from OUP for his help and for the efficiency with which he obtained readers' comments. My thanks to Gagosian and John Currin for permission to use John Currin's painting, *2070*, on the cover of this book. Thanks also to Jim Grant and James Knight and to my colleagues at Queen's, particularly Nick Owen and Ben Sorgiovanni, for helping me to get to grips with a new job while finishing this book. If there is anyone else I ought to have thanked but have forgotten, please forgive me.

The process of writing this book was made much more palatable by my friends and family. Thank you especially to Tim Bayne, Helen Beebee, Cathy Evans, Stacie Friend, Katherine Harrison, Rebecca Hartley, Gayle Impey, Aida Kaisy, Marion and Roger Kinns, Peter Lawler, Roger Liddy,

Luke Russell, Sara Sorial, Jola Shields, Joel Smith, and Ann Whittle, and to Mum, Guy, Min, and Owen. My greatest debt of gratitude is to Rob Knowles, for his steadfast friendship, for always being prepared to talk about fiction with me, for reading drafts of every chapter (in some cases, more than one!) and for probing, intelligent, and insightful comments on the completed typescript.

1

Aims, Scope, and Overview

Introduction

My aim in this book is to provide a unified solution to a wide range of philosophical problems raised by fiction. While some of these problems have been the focus of extensive philosophical debate, others have received insufficient attention. In particular, the epistemology of fiction has not yet attracted the philosophical scrutiny it warrants. There has been considerable discussion of what determines the contents of works of fiction, but there have been few attempts to explain how audiences identify their contents, or to explain the norms governing the correct understanding and interpretation of works of fiction.

However, the metaphysical issue of what determines the contents of works of fiction is closely related to the epistemological issue of how audiences identify those contents. Audiences often succeed in identifying the contents of works of fiction. Any account of what determines their contents must, therefore, explain how audiences are able to identify the determinants of their contents given the resources available to them in the contexts in which they succeed in doing so. There is a danger in attempting to address metaphysical questions concerning the determinants of fictive content in isolation from epistemological questions concerning how audiences identify fictive content. What may seem like satisfactory answers to the former questions given a narrow set of purely metaphysical criteria will not be satisfactory from a broader perspective that takes into account the need for consistency with adequate answers to these epistemological questions.

The account of fiction that I develop in this book avoids the dangers of such an approach. Like Kendall Walton (1990: 8), my aim is to build a 'single comprehensive and unified theory' of fiction with many applications rather than to give a set of independent responses to specific problems. My theory answers a wide range of both metaphysical and epistemological questions

Fiction: A Philosophical Analysis. Catharine Abell, Oxford University Press (2020). © Catharine Abell.
DOI: 10.1093/oso/9780198831525.001.0001

concerning fiction in a way that clarifies the relations between them. The metaphysical questions include: what distinguishes works of fiction from works of non-fiction; what is the nature of fictive utterances; what determines the contents of works of fiction; what kinds of fictive content are there; how broad in scope is fictive content; and what kinds of things are fictional entities? The epistemological questions include: how do audiences identify the contents of authors' fictive utterances; how does understanding a work of fiction differ from interpreting it; and what role do thinking and talking about fiction from an external perspective play in enabling communication through fiction? There is as yet no single theory that can answer all these questions.

The account of fiction I offer is a general one. It is intended to apply to fictional plays, films, operas, paintings, and poems, not merely to novels. Please do not be misled by my use of the terms 'author' and 'utterance' into thinking otherwise. I use 'author' to refer to any person who produces a work of fiction, whatever its medium. I use 'utterance' simply to mean an occasion of use of a representation, whatever the medium of that representation. A fictive utterance can be filmic, theatrical, or pictorial. I have attempted to reflect this generality by using the term 'audience' throughout, in lieu of the narrower term 'reader'. I have also avoided talking of what is 'true in a fiction' or 'true according to a fiction' when talking about the contents of works of fiction, since this presupposes that the contents at issue are propositional. Instead, I will talk throughout of 'fictive content' and of what is 'fictional' in a work. Nevertheless, because the existing philosophical debate about many of the questions that I will address often deals exclusively with the linguistic case, it will often be necessary for me to focus on linguistic works of fiction in order to engage with that debate.

Engagement with the existing debate is necessary in order to defend my own theory. I will argue that the answers it provides to the questions I have identified are superior to those provided by its rivals. Nevertheless, my main aim is to develop the details of my own argument, rather than to provide an overview of the history of the philosophical debate about fiction or critically to assess rival positions. Consequently, I will discuss those positions only when identifying their limitations helps to motivate my own position; when it helps to clarify my own view to contrast it with them; or when it is necessary to address an objection that advocates of rival positions are likely to have to my own. In the next section, I will provide some brief general background to the issues I will discuss for readers who are unfamiliar with the existing philosophical literature that addresses them.

1.1 The Issues to be Addressed

Fictive utterances, like assertions, have context-sensitive/contents. That is, different fictive utterances of the same representation can differ in their contents according to the contexts in which they are made. For example, although both representations have the same literal contents, a fictive utterance of 'he gave up his heart quite willingly' might have one content when used in writing a romance novel, but a quite different content when used in a science-fiction novel. Similarly, in the context of one film, a close-up of worn furniture might have the content simply that the furniture is worn while, in the context of another, it might have the content that the family who owns that furniture is in dire financial straits. This raises the issue of what determines the contents of fictive utterances and how features of the contexts in which they are produced influence their contents.

The dominant view claims that authors' intentions determine the contents of their fictive utterances. On such a view, different fictive utterances of the same representation can differ in their contents because they are made with different intentions. The intentions at issue are generally characterized as Gricean reflexive communicative intentions. Grice (1989: 220) takes the content of an utterance to be determined by an intention to elicit an effect in an audience by means of their recognition of that very intention, where what is meant by the utterance is determined by its intended effect. For example, assertions are made with reflexive, communicative intentions to elicit beliefs in an audience, such that they have the same contents as the beliefs they are intended to elicit. Similarly, Gregory Currie (1990), David Davies (2007), and Kathleen Stock (2017) take the content of a fictive utterance to be determined by an intention to elicit an imagining with a particular content in an audience partly in virtue of their recognition of that very intention, The fictive utterance, they claim, has the same content as the imagining it was intended to elicit. On their view, different fictive utterances of 'he gave up his heart quite willingly' differ in their content according to whether they are produced with a communicative intention to elicit the imagining that a given character fell in love quite willingly or to elicit the imagining that a given character voluntarily relinquished a vital organ.

The dominant view is, therefore, a form of actual intentionalism about the contents of fictive utterances. That is, it claims that actual authors' intentions determine the contents of their fictive utterances. There are stronger and weaker versions of this view. Stock is an *extreme actual intentionalist*: she holds that it is *sufficient* for a fictive utterance to have a certain content that its author communicatively intended to elicit an imagining with that content in her audience. More moderate forms of actual intentionalism claim that this is merely necessary for a fictive utterance to have the content in question. The rivals to both versions of actual intentionalism are *anti-intentionalism* and *hypothetical intentionalism* about the contents of fictive utterances. Anti-intentionalism claims that their contents are determined by factors independent of authors' intentions, such as conventions, and denies that it is necessary for a fictive utterance to have a certain content that its author intended it to have that content. Hypothetical intentionalism (e.g. Levinson 1992) claims that the contents of fictive utterances are determined by appropriate audiences' *hypotheses* regarding authorial intentions, irrespective of whether their hypotheses track actual authors' intentions. It is often considered a moderate, sensible alternative to versions of actual intentionalism, which better accommodates the possibility of authors failing to realize their intentions.

While the dominant view has the virtue of explaining the context-sensitivity of fictive utterances in a manner continuous with that of ordinary assertions, it raises an epistemological problem. Audiences can identify the intentions that determine the context-sensitive contents of assertions by appealing to their knowledge of how the world is, together with the assumption that speakers intend their assertions accurately to reflect the way things are. However, this strategy does not work for fiction, because we do not expect the content of a fiction to reflect how things are in reality. The plausibility of the claim that authors' intentions determine the contents of their fictive utterances depends on the availability of some other explanation of how audiences identify those intentions. The absence of any adequate such explanation suggests that we need a different explanation of what determines the context-sensitive contents of fictive utterances that can accommodate audiences' ability to identify their contents.

Whatever determines the contents of fictive utterances, the contents of works fiction can outstrip those of the fictive utterances by which they are produced. For example, it is fictional in *Middlemarch* (1871) that Dorothea regrets marrying Casaubon, although none of the fictive utterances by which George Eliot produced the novel has the content that she regrets it. This raises the issue of what determines these additional aspects of fictive content.

Although its precise nature is contested, it is widely accepted that there is a general principle by which fictive content is generated indirectly on the basis of the contents of authors' fictive utterances. This principle is usually thought to entail either that a work's fictive content is as much like things really are as is consistent with the contents of authors' fictive utterances; or that it is as much like things are mutually believed to be by the members of the author's community as is consistent with the contents of authors' fictive utterances (Lewis 1983a; Walton 1990). On the former construal, it is fictional in *Middlemarch* that Dorothea regrets marrying Casaubon because, if a woman like Dorothea were to marry a man like Casaubon, she would regret it. On the latter, it is fictional in *Middlemarch* that Dorothea regrets marrying Casaubon because the members of George Eliot's community mutually believed that, if a woman such as Dorothea is described as being were to marry a man such as Casaubon is described as being, she would regret it.

On both these construals, it is part of the content of *Middlemarch* that Dorothea eats regularly, sleeps at night, perspires when she exerts herself physically, and has all of the other characteristics common to ordinary human beings. However, readers of *Middlemarch* do not invariably ascribe all these features to Dorothea. Such principles entail that fictive content is far broader in scope than audiences generally take it to be. Moreover, we do not take audiences' failure to ascribe to works of fiction all the contents generated by such principles as evidence of interpretative failure on their part. One has not failed successfully to interpret *Middlemarch* if one does not ascribe to Dorothea properties such as having a belly button. Neither of the proposed principles reflects our interpretative norms.

The fact that the proposed principles posit fictive content that audiences do not ascribe to works of fiction and that our norms of interpretation do not require audiences to ascribe to them suggests that fictive content is not generated indirectly by such principles. An adequate account of fictive content should reflect our interpretative norms, attributing to works of fiction only those contents the identification of which is required for successful interpretation. Moreover, it should explain how audiences are able to interpret works of fiction, by identifying the resources on which they can draw in order to do so and by explaining how those resources enable them to identify the determinants of fictive content.

I will also address the issue of what distinguishes works of fiction from works of non-fiction. Works of fiction are often thought to bear a distinctive relation to the imagination, by appeal to which one can distinguish works of fiction from works of non-fiction. This view is related to the conception of fictive utterances as illocutionary acts produced with communicative intentions to elicit imaginings in their audiences. Such a construal of fictive utterances is often accompanied by the further claim that works of fiction are distinguished from works of non-fiction by being the products of fictive utterances (Stock 2011, 2017). This claim entails that works of fiction bear the distinctive relation to the imagination of having been produced with communicative intentions to elicit imaginings.

However, it is not clear that this relation distinguishes fiction from non-fiction. First, many works of non-fiction are also intended to elicit imaginings in their audiences. At least some of these intentions are arguably communicative intentions. Secondly, it is not obvious that all works of fiction are produced with communicative intentions to elicit imaginings in an audience. It is arguably possible to produce a work of fiction while remaining indifferent as to whether or not its audience imagines its contents. It is also unclear that works of fiction bear any other distinctive relation to the imagination. Whether or not they are intended to do so, works of fiction generally elicit the imaginative engagement of their audiences, but so too do many works of non-fiction. It is reasonable to expect an adequate account of the nature of works of fiction to illuminate their relation to the imagination. However, this relation need not distinguish works of fiction from works of non-fiction. In the absence of a distinctive such relation, an adequate account of the nature of fiction must identify some other feature that works of fiction invariably possess and works that are not fiction invariably lack.

A further issue concerns the existence and nature of fictional entities. We engage in thought and talk about fictional entities. I can think that Tom Jones is a good-hearted fellow, and can tell anyone who does not already know that Tom Jones is a fictional character created by Henry Fielding while writing his novel *Tom Jones* (1749). This raises the issue of what makes it the case that I think and talk about Tom Jones when I do these things. It is tempting to claim that I do so because my thoughts and utterances refer to Tom Jones. This requires the existence of an entity, Tom Jones, to which they refer and thus raises the question of what kind of thing Tom Jones is. It is difficult to answer this question, because many of the properties we ascribe to Tom Jones are incompatible. It simply is not possible to create a good-hearted fellow just by writing a novel. Moreover, no good-hearted fellow with all the features ascribed to Tom in Fielding's novel has ever existed.

These difficulties in explaining the nature of fictional entities have seemed to many sufficient reason to deny their existence. Anti-realists about fictional entities claim that I do not really refer to anything when I think that Tom Jones is a good-hearted fellow. The most prominent form of anti-realism is the pretence theory, first proposed by Kendall Walton (1990), and subsequently elaborated by Anthony Everett (2013), Stacie Friend (2014), and others. Pretence theorists claim that, when I engage in thought and talk that appears to be about Tom Jones, I engage in the pretence that there is something to which I refer, although there is in fact no such thing. When I think that Tom Jones is a good-hearted fellow, I engage in a pretence according to which my thought refers to a person. By contrast, when I claim that Tom Jones is a fictional entity created by Henry Fielding, I engage in a distinct pretence according to which there are such things as fictional entities and my claim refers to such an entity.

Anti-realists deny that thought and talk apparently about Tom Jones is about something different from thought and talk apparently about Becky Sharp. They deny that there is any object of such thought and talk. However, we often judge our thought and talk to be about one fictional entity rather than another. For example, I take my thought that Becky Sharp is an extremely entertaining creation to be about the same thing as many of the fictive utterances by which Thackeray produced *Vanity Fair* (1847), and not about the same thing as any of the fictive utterances by which Fielding produced *Tom Jones*. Let us follow Friend (2014) in using the term *identification* to talk about object-directedness without implying any ontological commitment. Anti-realists face the difficulty of providing some account of what facts about the real world underpin our judgements of co-identification. This task poses no great difficulty to realists, who can explain co-identification in terms of co-reference. However, they face the difficulty of providing an account of the nature of fictional entities that is compatible with their existence and with the different kinds of properties we ascribe to them.

1.2 A Distinctively Institutional Approach

My chief contention is that satisfactory responses to these issues are to be provided by construing fiction as an essentially social practice. I will argue that our social practice of fiction comprises an institution. This claim is not new. Numerous authors have acknowledged that fiction is an institution (e.g. Carroll 1990: 83; Walton 1990: *passim*; Lamarque and Olsen 1994: 20, 37; Smith 1995; Köppe and Kindt 2011; Zipfel 2011; Matravers 2014: 89). However, there has as yet been no systematic attempt to use theories of institutions from the philosophy of social science to illuminate the nature of fiction. I will draw on philosophical accounts of the nature of institutions and of the determinants of social facts to determine the implications of the claim that fiction is an institutional practice for how the questions identified above are to be answered.

On the face of it, our practice of fiction might not seem much like an institution. One might agree that we have long-standing social practices of writing and reading fiction but deny that these practices are institutionalized. One reason for doing so is that institutions often involve explicitly encoded rules and processes for endowing individuals with special institutional statuses, while the practice of fiction lacks such rules and processes. While there are explicit rules that determine what it takes to be a prime minister, vice-chancellor, CEO, judge, or cardinal, there are no rules that determine what it takes to be an author of fiction. Anyone can pick up a pen and write fiction. If such rules and processes were essential to institutions, there would be no institution of fiction, because one does not require any special institutional status to produce or to consume fiction.

However, one who is persuaded by this line of thought is operating with too narrow and demanding a conception of the nature of institutions. There are informal institutions that do not essentially involve either explicitly encoded rules or attributions of special institutional authority, such as the institution of promising. Fiction is another such institution.

Following Francesco Guala (2016a), I will construe institutions as systems of regulative rules that represent equilibrium solutions to coordination problems. Coordination problems are problems that cannot be solved by agents who act unilaterally, but only by agents who coordinate their actions with one another. On this construal, institutions do not essentially involve either explicitly encoded rules or attributions of authority. Whether or not an institution does so depends on the nature of the coordination problems to which its rules represent equilibrium solutions. It may aid the solution of some such problems but not others to have explicitly encoded rules or to ascribe special statuses to certain individuals.

Guala's account of institutions combines two different approaches to understanding them, one that conceives of them as rules that guide the actions of individuals engaged in social interaction, and another that construes them in game-theoretic terms as equilibria to coordination problems. Guala's distinctive contribution (2016a) is to argue that these two approaches are compatible, and that the insights of both can be accommodated by understanding institutions as systems of rules that people are motivated to follow *because* they are equilibria to coordination problems.

In what follows, I adopt Guala's account of institutions, not only because it is compatible with both these approaches, but also because it avoids the controversial commitments of some other prominent theories of institutions. For example, John Searle (1995, 2010) argues that institutions consist in systems of constitutive rules towards which their participants have psycho-logical attitudes of collective acceptance. The claim that agents can have collective, as opposed to individualistic, intentional states is controversial. Searle also makes very strong assumptions about the necessity of language to social institutions (see Hindriks 2009). The fact that Guala's account is not committed to the existence of attitudes of collective acceptance and does not assume that we must have the vocabulary required linguistically to represent institutional facts in order for there to be such facts provides reason to prefer it to Searle's account.

I agree with Tilmann Köppe and Tom Kindt (2011) that fiction institutions incorporate rules that serve as a link between features of works of fiction and their contents, and that govern how audiences respond to them. If we are to answer the epistemological question of how audiences identify the responses those rules prescribe, however, we need to know more about the nature of the rules in question than Köppe and Kindt tell us. Frank Zipfel (2011: 109) claims that fiction is an institutional practice, but also claims that audiences identify what they are to imagine in response to a work of fiction by identifying authors' intentions. I deny this. The institutional account I develop is more comprehensive and detailed than that provided by either Köppe and Kindt or Zipfel, and very different from Zipfel's approach.

1.3 Summary of the Argument

I will argue that there are compelling epistemological reasons for rejecting a construal of the rules of fiction as prescribing audiences to respond to works of fiction by imagining what their authors communicatively intend audiences to imagine in response to them. Audiences lack the resources to identify the imaginings in which authors communicatively intend them to engage, I will argue, because imaginings lack either a mind-to-world or a world-to-mind direction of fit. That is, unlike beliefs, they do not purport to conform to the way the world is and, unlike desires, they are not satisfied when the world is brought into conformity with the way they represent things as being. Individual imaginings *can* conform to the way the world is or to the way those who engage in them would like the world to be, but imagining something does not carry a commitment to conformity of either type.

Because beliefs have a mind-to-world direction of fit, it is rational for an agent who communicatively intends to elicit a belief in her audience by her utterance to ensure that the belief she intends to elicit reflects the way the world is. Her audience can, therefore, appeal to their knowledge of how the world is to help them to identify that belief. By contrast, I will argue that it follows from the imagination's lack of direction of fit that there are insufficient rational constraints on the nature of the imaginings that an agent communicatively intends to elicit in her audience for audiences' knowledge of how the world is to enable them to identify the imaginings authors communicatively intend to elicit. Consequently, I will argue, audiences lack the resources required to identify agents' communicative intentions to elicit imaginings. This precludes the contents of fictive utterances from being determined by such intentions.

I will argue that the content-determining rules of fiction institutions are *purely conventional*, in the sense that they need not exploit any pre-existing relations between fictive utterances and contents, but rather establish relations that need not exist independently of those rules. Not all rules or conventions are of this kind. Some pick out one among a number of pre-existing relations. For example, a convention according to which one takes as a dance partner the person closest to oneself in height picks out an existing relation (greatest similarity in height) as determining to whom one stands in the relation of dance partner. Purely conventional rules are distinctive in themselves being necessary to the existence of the relations they pick out.

Audiences rely on their grasp of the content-determining rules of fiction institutions to identify the contents of authors' fictive utterances. These are regulative rules that prescribe audiences to engage in certain types of imaginings in response to utterances with certain features. By doing so, they establish relations between utterances with certain features and contents of certain types. This makes it rational for authors with a grasp of those rules to produce fictive utterances with certain features rather than others when they intend to elicit particular imaginings in their audiences. Nevertheless, these rational constraints depend on the existence of the content-determining rules. Consequently, they do not support the claim that audiences identify the contents of fictive utterances by drawing inferences about authors' intentions based on the assumption that they are rational. The *rules* determine the contents of fictive utterances. Although competent authors can intentionally exploit these rules in order to produce fictive utterances with particular contents, the contents of authors' fictive utterances can differ from the contents they intend them to have.

Our institution of fiction incorporates rules that govern fictions in a variety of different media. Depending on the features by which it identifies the utterances whose contents it governs, a given rule of fiction may govern either utterances exclusively in one medium, or utterances in a range of different media. There is one feature that any utterance *must* exhibit if it is to be governed by a content-determining rule of a fiction institution. There must be a practice of fiction to which audiences' responses to the series of utterances of which it is a part are intended to conform. Beyond this, different content-determining rules can pick out utterances of the type whose contents they govern by features of different kinds. Any features to which they appeal must be accessible to audiences. They can include features of the literal or depictive contents of those representations, as well as lexical or syntactic features of linguistic representations, formal or design features of non-linguistic representations, and features of the media in which representations are made or the techniques by which they are produced. A rule that picks out the utterances it governs partly by their syntactic linguistic features will govern only written works of fiction, a rule that identifies utterances by their use of editing will govern only film fictions, while a rule that identifies utterances by features of the contents they have independently of the rules of fiction institutions can govern any works with those content features, whatever their media.

The content-determining rules of fiction institutions can differ, not only in how they pick out the utterances whose contents they govern, but also in the kinds of imaginings they prescribe. Some prescribe audiences to engage in propositional imaginings, while others prescribe imaginings with non-propositional contents. The kinds of utterances in response to which the rules prescribe imaginings of a given kind is determined by the features by which the rules identify those utterances. Nevertheless, if they are to follow the rules in question, audiences must be capable of responding to an utterance with the features in question by engaging in an imagining of the relevant kind. Consequently, linguistic utterances often prescribe propositional imaginings, while cinematic utterances often prescribe imagistic imaginings, although linguistic utterances may prescribe non-propositional imaginings and cine-matic utterances may prescribe propositional imaginings.

The claim that the contents of fictive utterances are determined by rules rather than by intentions raises the problem of how different fictive utterances of the same representation can differ in their contents. I will argue that the context-sensitivity of the contents of fictive utterances has two sources. The first is the features by which the content-determining rules of fiction institutions identify the fictive utterances whose contents they govern. The second is the way in which those rules specify the contents they assign to those utterances.

I have already noted that the content-determining rules of fiction institutions can identify fictive utterances by features of the contexts in which they are produced. Different fictive utterances of the same representation can, therefore, differ in their contents as a consequence of having been produced in different contexts. For example, the rules can identify the utterances whose contents they govern by certain of the intentions with which they were produced. Different fictive utterances of the same representation can, therefore, differ in their contents because they were produced with different intentions. I deny that the contents of fictive utterances are determined by authors' communicative intentions to elicit imaginings with certain contents. Nevertheless, this is consistent with the rules that determine their contents picking out fictive utterances by certain *other* intentions with which they were produced. In particular, the rules can identify the fictive utterances whose contents they govern by the effects their authors intend them to elicit in their audiences, where these effects concern the *manner* in which the utterances convey their contents, rather than the nature of the contents they convey. For example, an author might intend her fictive utterance to make its contents (whatever they are) intelligible to her audience, or to convey them in a way that elicits an aesthetic response. I will argue that audiences can access the resources required to identify these intentions, and therefore that they can identify the contents of fictive utterances that are governed by such rules.

Because the manner in which different fictive utterances of the same representation are intended to convey their contents can differ, different fictive utterances of the same representation can be governed by different rules and can therefore differ in their contents. On this account, although authors' intentions can play a role in determining the contents of their fictive utterances, it does not follow that fictive utterances have the contents they do because their authors intend them to have those contents.

Fictive utterances can exhibit context-sensitivity with the second source because the rules that govern them can specify their contents *indexically*. Those rules can prescribe that, in response to fictive utterances of representations with certain features, audiences imagine what non-fictive utterances of those representations would communicate, if they were made in certain contexts. They can then specify these contexts by appeal to features of the contexts in which authors make the fictive utterances in question. For example, in response to an author's fictive utterance of a representation, a rule could prescribe audiences to imagine what a non-fictive utterance of that representation would communicate, if it were made by a member of that author's own community, or in the fictional context determined by the contents of the author's preceding fictive utterances. Because different fictive utterances of the same representation can be made in different such contexts, their contents can therefore differ.

This account of the form that the rules of fiction can take has certain affinities with Gregory Currie's claim (1990) that identifying the content of a work of fiction involves drawing inferences about what its fictional author believes. The fictional author, Currie claims, is a hypothetical construct whom we are to construe as a member of the author's own community who is recounting matters of fact. Somewhat similarly, I take the contents of fictive utterances of representations to be determined by what non-fictive utterances of those representations would communicate, were they made in certain indexically specified contexts. However, the account I will defend differs from Currie's in two important respects. First, for Currie, appeal to the fictional author functions as a holistic interpretative device that governs our ascriptions of fictive content to works as wholes. He claims:

> Understanding the fictional author is thus like understanding a real person; it's a matter of making the best overall sense we can of his behaviour (and here we are limited to speech behaviour alone). The *belief* set of the fictional author—the set of propositions he believes—is the set of propositions that go to make up the story.   (Currie 1990: 76)

By contrast, on my account, only some fictive utterances are governed by rules that ascribe to them the contents that non-fictive utterances of the same representations would have, were they made in certain indexically specified contexts. Different rules can govern the different fictive utterances by which a single work of fiction is produced, depending on the particular features of each of the utterances in question. Consequently, audiences must interpret them piecemeal. This may require them to understand some such utterances by appeal to one context, others by appeal to a different context, and others by ascribing to them contents that do not depend on any of the features of the contexts in which they are produced.

Secondly, unlike me, Currie takes the contents of fictive utterances to be determined by their authors' communicative intentions to elicit imaginings in their audiences. He does not explicitly address exactly how this aspect of his account fits together with his appeal to the fictional author. The most plausible explanation is that he takes inferences about the fictional author's beliefs to be drawn on assumption that his non-fictive utterances have the same contents as those of the actual author's fictive utterances. Consequently, for Currie, appeal to what the fictional author's utterances reveal about his beliefs functions as a general principle by which fictive content is generated indirectly on the basis of the contents of authors' fictive utterances. It plays no role in determining the contents of authors' fictive utterances.

This points to a more general difference between how I construe the role of background knowledge in understanding fictive content and how rival accounts construe that role. It is usually assumed that our background knowledge that people eat, sleep, and perspire plays a role in our understanding of *Middlemarch* by enabling us to work out that *Middlemarch* has the content that Dorothea eats, sleeps, and perspires. On my account, audiences may need to draw on their knowledge that people do these things in order to understand *Middlemarch* in accordance with the rules of fiction, because some of the rules that govern Eliot's fictive utterances may prescribe audiences to imagine whatever non-fictive utterances of the same representations would communicate in contexts in which what they communicate is determined partly by the fact that people eat, sleep, and perspire. However, this does not make it part of the fictive content of *Middlemarch* that Dorothea does these things. We draw on rich informational resources and engage in complex counterfactual reasoning in order to identify the contents of fictive utterances, but fictive content is finite and tractable.

It is implausible, however, that fictive content consists solely in the rule-governed contents of authors' fictive utterances. Authors often intentionally exploit the content-determining rules of fiction in order to elicit further imaginings whose contents are not among those of their fictive utterances. To use my earlier example, in *Middlemarch*, George Eliot intentionally exploits the content-determining rules that govern her fictive utterances to elicit the imagining that Dorothea regrets marrying Casaubon, although none of Eliot's fictive utterances has the content that Dorothea does so.

I will distinguish two different activities in which audiences engage in response to works of fiction: *understanding* and *interpretation*. If they are correctly and completely to understand a work of fiction, audiences must grasp the rules of fiction, and successfully apply them to that work in order exhaustively to identify the contents of the fictive utterances by which it was produced. Interpretation is a distinct activity that requires audiences to draw inferences about authors' intentions on the basis of the rule-governed contents of their fictive utterances in order to explain why they produced the works they did. This can involve identifying further imaginings that authors intended to elicit by producing those works.

When authors grasp the rules that govern the contents of their fictive utterances and successfully exploit them to produce fictive utterances with the contents they intended them to have, they can succeed in conveying further, *interpretative* fictive content by doing so. Because I deny that authors' intentions to elicit imaginings with certain contents (or, more generally, to produce utterances with certain contents) play a role in determining the contents of their fictive utterances, I am an anti-intentionalist about the contents of fictive utterances. However, I am a moderate actual intentionalist about interpretative fictive content. Unlike extreme actual intentionalists, I deny that interpretative fictive content incorporates *all* the further contents that authors intend audiences to imagine in response to their fictive utterances. Interpretative fictive content consists only in the contents that authors intend their fictive utterances to prompt audiences to engage in and that those fictive utterances are in fact capable of prompting audiences to engage in.

Although I allow a work's fictive content to outstrip the contents of the fictive utterances by which it was produced, my construal of fictive content is nevertheless much more austere than most of its rivals. Moreover, I deny that there are any general principles by appeal to which audiences can identify interpretative fictive content. This is because the authorial intentions that determine interpretative fictive content are not communicative intentions to elicit imaginings in an audience, but ordinary, non-communicative intentions in action. Because they lack the reflexive structure of communicative intentions, authors do not need to rely on resources that are mutually known to both author and audience to be available for use in interpretation in order to realize these intentions. They can instead exploit whichever of the resources available to them provide the best means of realizing their intentions, irrespective of whether audiences are aware of those resources.

Consequently, the means authors employ to prompt audiences to imagine interpretative fictive content are many and various, and there is no general strategy that enables audiences to identify such content. Interpretation involves drawing inferences to the best explanation of why authors produced the works they did. In drawing such inferences, audiences must rely on whatever information is available to them. There is no guarantee that any given audience member will have access to the information required to identify a work's interpretative fictive content. The distinction between understanding and interpretation and the construal of interpretation as an activity that carries a real possibility of failure captures the fact that ordinary audience members often arrive at an adequate understanding of works of fiction without succeeding in interpreting them, and explains how critics can become embroiled in irresolvable debates about the correct interpretation of works of fiction.

I will argue that works of fiction are distinguished from works of non-fiction by the institutional contexts in which they are created, rather than by any distinctive relation they bear to the imagination. What distinguishes a fiction institution from other institutions, I will argue, is the nature of the coordination problems to which its rules represent equilibrium solutions. They represent equilibrium solutions to coordination problems of communicating imaginings. If she is successfully to communicate an imagining to her audience, an author must elicit in that audience an imagining with the same content as her own. The communication of imaginings of different types poses distinct coordination problems, requiring different equilibrium solutions that are provided by different rules. While my focus in this book will be our institution of fiction, any institution whose rules represent equilibrium solutions to such coordination problems is a fiction institution. There need not be just one such institution. A work is fiction, I will argue, if and only if there is an institutional practice of fiction to which audiences' responses to the whole series of utterances by which it was produced are intended to conform and it contains at least one utterance that is in fact governed by the regulative rules of that practice.

On the account I develop, the only distinctive relation works of fiction bear to the imagination is very indirect: works of fiction are distinctive in being at least partly the products of utterances whose contents are governed by institutional rules that represent equilibrium solutions to coordination problems of communicating imaginings. I will argue that these rules need not always be used to communicate imaginings and consequently that authors of fiction need not invariably intend to elicit imaginings in their audiences. While the rules represent equilibrium solutions to coordination problems of communicating imaginings, those who exploit them need not do so in order to solve such problems. Authors may in fact be indifferent to whether or not their audiences imagine the contents of the works of fiction they produce.

It follows from my claim that fictive utterances are governed by institutional rules that they are a type of *declaration* (also known as an 'institutionalized performative'). Declarations are illocutionary acts that are distinctive in their capacity to effect changes to the existence and status of their objects simply in virtue of their successful performance. I will argue that fictive utterances do this by creating fictional entities and making certain things fictional of them, just as the declaration of marrying creates marriages and the declaration of surrendering makes it the case that one is no longer engaged in active combat. The rules of fiction enable the creation of fictional entities by specifying conditions sufficient for their existence. When authors produce fictive utterances that meet these conditions, they create fictional entities.

Once fictional entities have been created, authors and audiences can engage in thought and talk that identifies those entities by referring to them. A fictive utterance identifies Tom Jones rather than Becky Sharp if it refers to the former rather than to the latter. When he refers to Tom Jones by his fictive utterances, Fielding ascribes to him such properties as being an illegitimate son. However, Tom Jones is not in fact an illegitimate son, but an abstract, social entity. Tom Jones has properties such as having been created by Henry Fielding, and being the protagonist of an early English novel. It is merely fictional that Tom Jones is an illegitimate son.

I will argue that this realist account of fictional entities has an advantage over its anti-realist rivals. Some anti-realists have attempted to elucidate the conditions under which we judge two thoughts or utterances to co-identify by appealing to the nature of the information contained in the 'mental files' involved in those thoughts or causally implicated in the production of those utterances. For example, Tim Crane (2013) argues that two thoughts co-identify when they involve mental files containing information that is sufficiently qualitatively similar. Stacie Friend (2014) argues that we judge two utterances of fictional names to co-identify when the information in the mental file each speaker associates with the name she utters is dominantly derived from the same authorial source. I will argue that such approaches fail because they cannot accommodate the fact that we often judge two thoughts or utterances to co-identify even when one implicates a mental file that contains information exclusively about properties it is fictional that the entity possesses, while the other implicates a mental file containing information exclusively about properties attributable to that entity only from a perspective external to that work of fiction (that is, properties of the kind that I claim fictional entities actually possess).

We ascribe properties of this latter type to fictional entities when we engage in external thought and talk about works of fiction. When we engage in external thought and talk, we think and talk about works of fiction *qua* works of fiction. For example, we might say or think such things as that a certain character is derivative, that a given plot device unifies a novel, or that a film would have been better if it had employed a different means of indicating its characters' poverty. As these examples suggest, external thought and talk are important to our evaluation of works of fiction. I will argue that they can also play three further important roles. First, they are essential to our ability to interpret works of fiction, because they play a crucial role in enabling us to draw inferences to the best explanation concerning why authors produced the works they did. Second, they can improve the stability of fiction institutions by making participants in fiction institutions aware of the preferences of other participants and by helping to bring about a coincidence in participants' preferences. Finally, I will argue that external thought about the merits of various ways of responding imaginatively to utterances with certain features can enable participants to coordinate, on the fly, on equilibrium solutions to novel coordination problems of communicating imaginings.

1.4 The Limits to my Explanatory Aims

My account provides a unified set of answers to a wide range of philosophical questions about fiction. However, there are various philosophical issues about fiction that I will not attempt to address. While I think my account has possible implications for how issues such as the puzzle of imaginative resist-ance are to be resolved, I will not explore that possibility here. Moreover, there are various philosophical problems, such as the paradoxes of fiction and of tragedy, that I think are to be solved entirely independently of my account of fiction. Because my account has no bearing on how they are to be solved, I do not discuss those problems here.

There are two issues that have attracted considerable philosophical atten-tion about which one might think I should have more to say than I do. The first is the question of whether there is a distinctive kind of audience response that is appropriate to works of fiction but not to works of non-fiction and, if so, what that response is. Many philosophers have claimed that works of fiction are distinctive in prescribing imaginative responses. Indeed, Derek Matravers (2014) calls this 'the consensus view'. For example, because Stock thinks that works of fiction are distinctive in being produced with communicative inten-tions to elicit imaginings in an audience, she holds a version of the consensus view. The view has also been ascribed to Kendall Walton (1990), although Matravers argues against such a construal.

The second question that I do not attempt to answer is that of the nature of the imagination. If one thought, like Stock, that there is an imaginative response uniquely appropriate to fiction, one would then have to explain what it is about the nature of those responses that makes them inappropriate responses to works of non-fiction. This is likely to require one to say something about the nature of the imagination. Indeed, Stock (2011, 2017) provides a functional account of the imagination that is designed to explain why imaginative responses are uniquely appropriate to works of fiction).

Although my account entails that works of fiction prescribe imaginative responses, I am not committed to works of fiction being *distinctive* in prescribing such responses and am therefore not committed to there being any kind of audience response that is appropriate to works of fiction but not to works of non-fiction. One can accept my account even if one denies, like Friend (2008) and Matravers (2014),that there are imaginative responses that are uniquely appropriate to works of fiction. What distinguishes works of fiction from works of non-fiction, on my account, is the *source* rather than the nature of their prescriptions to respond imaginatively to them. Works of fiction prescribe imaginative responses because at least some of the utterances by which they are produced are regulated by institutional rules that represent equilibrium solutions to coordination problems of communicating imaginings. Because I am not committed to there being an imaginative response uniquely appropriate to fiction, I do not need to furnish an account of the imagination that can make good on such a commitment.

I say very little about the nature of the imagination in what follows, and rely largely on a pre-theoretical understanding of what it is to imagine something. I rely only on the claims that one can engage in imaginings with both propositional and non-propositional contents, and that imaginings lack either a mind-to-world or a world-to-mind direction of fit. These are widely accepted and not contentious.

There is one further limit to my explanatory aims. To justify my claim that the contents of fictive utterances are determined by the regulative rules of fiction institutions, I need to say enough about the forms those rules can take to make it plausible that they govern the contents of *all* fictive utterances. To do this, I need to describe some of the different kinds of relations between fictive utterances and contents that the rules establish. This requires me to identify how certain such rules pick out the fictive utterances whose contents they govern, and how they characterize the contents they ascribe to them. To do so, I will give examples of particular fictive utterances, describe the rules that govern them, and explain how those rules account for their contents. However, my account should not be expected to provide, for every fictive utterance, a specification of its content and an explanation of why it has that content. *No* philosophical account of fiction does this. My account can help to resolve questions regarding the contents of particular fictive utterances and the determinants of their contents insofar as it suggests a general methodological approach to answering such questions. They are to be answered by looking for widespread, stable correlations between features of fictive utterances and features of the contents we ascribe to them, by identifying rules that can explain those correlations, and by ascribing to particular fictive utterances with the features in question the contents that those rules assign to them. My account entails that such questions are not to be answered by trying to identify the intentions with which particular fictive utterances were produced.

1.5 Chapter Summaries

I will develop the argument summarized here over the course of the following five chapters. In Chapter 2, I will explain what fiction institutions are and what it is for a work to be fiction rather than non-fiction. I will outline Guala's account of institutions as systems of regulative rules that represent equilibrium solutions to coordination problems. I will then characterize fiction institutions as those institutions whose rules represent equilibrium solutions to coordination problems of communicating imaginings. I will explain both why the communication of imaginings poses a coordination problem, and why the coordination problem it poses is distinct from that posed by the communication of beliefs. By elucidating the relation between works of fiction and the institution of fiction, I will then explain both the relation between fictive utterances and works of fiction and what distinguishes works of fiction from works that are not fiction. Finally, I will explain what makes a certain feature of a work of fiction a good or a bad feature of that work, considered as fiction.

In Chapter 3, I will examine the nature of fictive utterances and explain what determines their contents. I will argue that fictive utterances are declarations. Although such a construal is compatible with the claim that their contents are determined by authors' intentions, I will argue, contrary to rival accounts, that their contents are not determined by authors' intentions to elicit imaginings. I will then argue that the rules of fiction institutions determine the contents of fictive utterances by *purely conventional* means. That is, they enable authors and audiences to coordinate on ways of communicating imaginings that would not have been available at all without those rules. Finally, I will identify various forms those rules can take, such that the contents they assign to fictive utterances are sensitive to the contexts in which those utterances are made.

In Chapter 4, I will address the structure of fictive content. I will begin by outlining one common construal, according to which fictive content has a two-level, hierarchical structure, with some fictive content being generated *directly*, independently of any other fictive content, and the rest being generated *indirectly*, on the basis fictive content that is directly generated. I will argue that one apparent problem for such a construal can be remedied by recognizing that the contents the rules of fiction assign to fictive utterances can be sensitive to certain of the effects authors intended those fictive utterances to produce in their audiences. I too will argue that fictive content has a two-level, hierarchical structure, albeit one that construes fictive content as much more limited in scope than most of its rivals. I will argue that the first level comprises the contents of authors' fictive utterances, while the second consists in further contents that authors intentionally convey by making those fictive utterances. I will argue that audiences grasp these further contents by drawing inferences to the best explanation about authors' intentions.

In Chapter 5, I will address the existence and nature of fictional entities. I will begin by explaining how the regulative rules of institutions enable the creation of social entities. I will then identify two distinct conditions sufficient for the existence of fictional entities, each of which is described by a reference-fixing rule of fiction institutions. One of these rules describes conditions sufficient for the existence of fictional entities that are not constituted by anything, while the other describes conditions sufficient both for the existence of fictional entities and for them to be constituted by other things. I will then identify what these rules reveal about what the existence of fictional entities is metaphysically dependent on, and will argue that this does not include anything metaphysically mysterious. I will then describe the nature of fictional entities and their identity and individuation conditions. Finally, I will compare my account of fictional entities with that of Amie Thomasson and will argue that, despite obvious similarities, there are fundamental differences between our accounts.

In Chapter 6, I will address two issues concerning external thought and talk about works of fiction and fictional entities. First, I will examine the onto-logical implications of the various ways in which we can think and talk about fictional entities. I will argue that those who deny the existence of fictional entities are unable to accommodate the ways in which we are able to think and talk about fictional entities from an external perspective, and that our ability to engage in such thought and talk gives us good reason to accept them into our ontology. I will argue, however, that analogous considerations do not compel us to embrace the existence of mythical entities and failed scientific posits. Secondly, I will examine the roles that external thought and talk about fiction can play in the institution of fiction. I will argue that external thought and talk about fiction can play a crucial role in enabling us to draw inferences about authors' intentions. It is therefore important to the identification of interpretative fictive content. I will also argue that it can play an important role in improving the stability of the content-determining rules of fiction institutions, and that it can help participants in fiction institutions to coordinate on rules that provide equilibrium solutions to novel coordination problems of communicating imaginings.

2

Fiction Institutions

Introduction

There are many, well-established social practices of both producing and consuming fiction. These include those of writing works of fiction in particular genres, of particular lengths, and featuring certain types of characters, such as heroines and heroes. They also include that of reading works of fiction to children, of consuming paperback novels while on holiday, and of watching detective dramas on television. In this chapter, I will argue that fiction is *essentially* a social practice. That is, if the multiple agents involved in the practice of fiction had not jointly developed various social practices governing the production and consumption of fiction, there would be no such thing as fiction and no such things as works of fiction. In this respect, fiction is like money, rather than like eating. While there are many social practices of producing and consuming food, we would still eat if there were no such practices. By contrast, without certain social practices, such as that of using certain kinds of things as media of exchange and stores of value, there would be no such thing as money. These practices are *constitutive* of the institution of money. The practices at issue may change over time and may vary across different societies, but without some such practices, there can be no money. Similarly, I will argue, certain social practices are constitutive of the institution of fiction.

I noted in Section 1.2 that fiction is widely acknowledged to be an institution. However, few have seriously considered the implications of this fact for the nature of fiction. In order to identify these implications, it is important to begin with a clear understanding of what an institution is. When philosophers of art appeal to the notion of an institution, as they do most famously when discussing institutional theories of art such as that advocated by George Dickie (1969, 2000), they tend to assume that institutional social practices are inherently arbitrary. Consequently, they assume that, if art is a social institution, anything whatsoever can be art. This assumption frequently leads to the criticism that institutional theories of art cannot explain its value (e.g. Goldman 1995: 2). As we will see, there is some link between the notion of

Fiction: A Philosophical Analysis. Catharine Abell, Oxford University Press (2020). © Catharine Abell.
DOI: 10.1093/oso/9780198831525.001.0001

arbitrariness and that of an institution. Nevertheless, it is not the case that an institutional account of some phenomenon is incompatible with that phenomenon exhibiting value of a distinctive kind. Indeed, in this chapter, I will argue that fiction institutions are distinguished from institutions of other kinds by the kinds of goals they help us to achieve.

In Section 2.1, I will outline Francesco Guala's account of institutions. It shows that, although institutional practices are inherently arbitrary, in that they provide solutions to problems that could always have been solved in other ways, they are valuable because they enable us to coordinate on solutions to the problems at hand. In Section 2.2, I will argue that fiction institutions are distinguished from social institutions of other kinds by the nature of the problems they enable us to solve. Fiction institutions have a distinctive value because they help us to solve problems of communicating imaginings.

When philosophers investigate the nature of fiction, they are often interested in identifying criteria that distinguish works of fiction from works of non-fiction. By itself, the account of fiction institutions that I develop in Section 2.2 does not provide such criteria. To identify them, we need to know more about how works of fiction are related to fiction institutions. In Section 2.3, I explain the nature of this relation. To be fiction, I argue, there must be some practice of fiction to which a work's author intends audiences' responses to it to conform. Moreover, the contents of some of the utterances by which she produces that work must be governed by the rules of that fiction institution.

Fictive utterances, I argue, are those utterances whose contents are governed by the rules of a fiction institution. It is a consequence of my account that works of fiction need not be produced entirely by fictive utterances. This might seem to suggest that whether or not a work is fiction depends on the proportion or number of fictive utterances involved in its production, with the unacceptable result that the notion of a work of fiction is inherently vague. In Section 2.4, I will argue that such a construal is misguided. On my account, a work is fiction only if its author has certain intentions regarding the whole series of utterances by which it is produced. Whether or not she does so is not a matter of degree.

In Section 2.5, I will argue that whether a given feature of a work of fiction is a good or a bad feature in that work, considered as fiction, depends on whether or not it works, either alone or in conjunction with other features, readily and reliably to elicit the imaginings its author intended it to elicit in the members of its intended audience. I demonstrate this by discussing the significance of

both accuracies and inaccuracies in works of fiction to how we evaluate them
as works of fiction.

2.1 The Nature of Institutions

Institutions are widely held to consist in systems of rules (e.g. Searle 1995,
2010; Guala 2016a). The existence of a rule does not, on its own, guarantee that
people are motivated to follow it. There are plenty of ineffective rules. For
example, several years ago, a rule was introduced at the university at which
I then worked, requiring members of staff to be present in their departments
three days a week during semester, whether or not they had teaching commitments on three different days, unless they were on sabbatical. This rule
proved ineffective because most staff preferred to work at home on those days
they did not have teaching, and continued to do so because they knew that
their attendance at the university was not sufficiently well monitored for
anyone to know with certainty that they were violating the rule.

Guala argues that people are motivated to follow the systems of rules
comprising institutions because those rules are equilibrium solutions to
games of coordination. A game is simply any situation of strategic interaction
between two or more agents, in which the consequences of each agent's actions
are not entirely under her own control but depend on the actions of the other
agents. *Coordination* games are situations of interactive decision-making in
which agents need to achieve some goal together, but there is more than one
way of achieving that goal, each of which involves a different division of
labour. More formally, they are situations of interdependent decision-making
involving two or more agents, in which there is a coincidence of agents'
interests and in which there are two or more Nash equilibria. A Nash equilibrium is a profile of agents' strategies, such that no agent has an incentive to
change her strategy unilaterally. In a Nash equilibrium, each agent's strategy is
the best available to her, given the actions of other agents.

For example, consider a game in which two agents approach one another on
a road with two lanes. Each must decide on which side of the road to drive.
The decision each agent makes depends on which decision the other makes.
An agent is better off driving on her left only if the other agent also drives on
his left. If the other agent drives on his right, she is better off driving on her
right. This is a coordination game. Both agents share the goal of driving
unimpeded and avoiding collision. Moreover, there are two Nash equilibria.

	L	R
L	1,1	0,0
R	0,0	1,1

Figure 1. Driving game

If both agents drive on their left, or both drive on their right, each agent's strategy is the best available to that agent, given the strategy of the other agent.

Games can be modelled as payoff matrices that represent agents' strategies. The numerical values assigned to the various possible strategies in the payoff matrix for a coordination game represent how well the outcomes satisfy agents' subjective preferences, with higher numbers representing outcomes that satisfy agents' interests better than outcomes represented by lower numbers. The individual rows and columns of such matrices represent the strategies of each individual agent. Agent 1 is always Row and Agent 2 is always Column. In simple two-by-two matrices, the agents choose from two possible actions. The numbered cells represent the outcomes of the different strategies in the format [Agent 1, Agent 2], with higher numbers representing better outcomes. For example, Figure 1 represents the payoff matrix for the driving game just described. In this game, there are two equilibrium strategies: both agents drive on the left (LL), or both drive on the right (RR). The matrix represents the fact that neither agent prefers one strategy to the other by assigning the same numbers to the outcomes of both strategies.

In order successfully to achieve a Nash equilibrium, each agent needs to be confident that the other agents will do their part in performing the collective task. Only if they believe that others will do this will they perform their own part. If she is successfully to solve the coordination problems that such games present, each player must develop a strategy that comprises the best possible response to the actions of other players.

Coordination problems therefore raise an epistemological problem. Which strategy it is in one agent's interest to adopt depends on what strategy she believes the other agents will follow. But which strategy each of the other agents employs also depends on what strategy they believe she will follow. Since their decision regarding which strategy to adopt is contingent on hers, it looks as if she cannot know which strategy they will employ until she herself has decided to follow a particular strategy. This makes it look very difficult to ensure that one acts in one's own interest.

Correlation devices help to solve this problem. They are devices external to the initial coordination games, which assist coordination by enabling agents to form expectations about the behaviour of other agents and thus to converge on equilibrium solutions to coordination problems. *Correlated equilibria* are achieved when agents make their strategies conditional on an external device accessible to all players. For example, agents in the Driving Game may adopt a strategy that is conditional on the existence of a law prescribing driving on one particular side of the road. If each agent adopts the strategy: *drive on the left if the law prescribes doing so, drive on the right if it prescribes doing so*, they are more likely to succeed in coordinating their actions, because the law is accessible to both agents and guides the expectations of each about how the other will act. By facilitating agents' coordination, correlated equilibria improve the stability of the equilibrium solutions that agents achieve.

Guala argues that institutions consist in systems of regulative rules with the conditional form 'if X, then do Z', which represent equilibrium strategies in coordination games. These may be formal rules that are explicitly stated, or they may be informal rules that agents represent only mentally. In either case, these rules are *prescriptive*: they play an action-guiding role (Guala 2016a: 54). Consequently, they constitute external correlation devices that enable agents to form expectations about the behaviour of others and thereby to converge on equilibrium solutions to coordination problems. The fact that the rules represent equilibrium strategies is what motivates people to follow them. No agent can do better by deviating from the rules unilaterally. The fact that the equilibrium strategies take the form of rules is what enables players to converge on them. Institutions help to achieve stable equilibria by incentivizing participants to act so as to maintain those equilibria.

For example, we can understand the institution of money as consisting in a system of rules such as 'If a bill has been issued by The Bureau of Engraving and Printing, then use it to purchase commodities or save it for the future' (Guala 2016a: p. xxvii). Such rules guide agents' actions, and enable them to coordinate on equilibrium solutions to the coordination problem of identifying a medium of exchange, store of value, and unit of accounting (Guala 2016a: 35). Without these rules to assist coordination, this task is likely to prove difficult, because one cannot use something as a medium of exchange or store of value unless other agents also accept it as such.

Guala does not address the issue of *how* participants in institutions must mentally represent the regulative rules of institutions in order for them to serve as external correlation devices that guide their actions in ways that enable them to coordinate on equilibrium solutions to coordination problems. It is possible for the rules of fiction institutions to play this role even when participants in those institutions have *tacit*, rather than explicit, knowledge of the rules. To see this requires some understanding of what it is to have tacit knowledge of such rules. That one's behaviour conforms to a rule, such that one behaves in the manner prescribed by the rule in response to the relevant stimulus, does not suffice for knowledge of the rule. One's knowledge of a rule is supposed to *explain* one's conformity to that rule. If there is a common information processing structure, whether a mechanism, module, or processor, that causally mediates all the mental transitions from one's representation of the stimulus through to one's representation of one's intended behavioural response, then one can be said to know the rule.

Whether one's knowledge of the rule is explicit or tacit depends on whether or not one can make one's knowledge of the rule explicit by means of a verbal statement. If one can do so, one has explicit knowledge of the rule. This requires one to possess the concepts required to specify the rule. It also requires the common causal information processing structure that can explain one's conformity to the rule to involve accessing a stored representation that encodes the rule. However, this alone does not suffice for explicit knowledge of the rule, since the stored representation may be contained in a module and therefore inaccessible to consciousness. In such a case, one has only tacit knowledge of the rule. One's knowledge of the rule is also tacit when the common causal information-processing structure does not involve a stored representation of a rule but consists solely in a computational procedure. That is, it could be part of the processing itself, rather than a representation that is processed (M. Davies 2015; see also M. Davies 1987, 1995).

Agents who have tacit knowledge of a rule need neither grasp nor possess the concepts that a theorist would use to specify the rule of which they have tacit knowledge. Nevertheless, their tacit knowledge of the rule can serve as an external correlation device that guides their actions and enables them to coordinate on equilibrium solutions to coordination problems. While such agents cannot explicitly verbally represent the rules that guide their actions, and therefore cannot share the rules that enable them to coordinate their actions by telling one another the rules, they can nevertheless communicate those rules by processes of performance and imitation whereby they learn from example (M. Davies 2015).

This account reveals the sense in which institutional social practices are arbitrary. Any equilibrium solution to a coordination game, including the correlated equilibria comprising institutions, is arbitrary in the sense that there is always some other available equilibrium solution that agents could have adopted instead. It does not follow from this either that the regulative rules of institutions can take any form whatever, or that practices governed by these rules do not exhibit distinctive forms of value. They cannot take just any form, because institutional rules must provide equilibrium solutions to the coordination problems posed by the situations of interdependent decision-making that give rise to those institutions. Moreover, this entails that all institutions have at least one form of value. That is, they enable agents to coordinate on equilibrium solutions to those problems with low effort and high reliability and therefore make agents better off than they would be if they failed to coordinate their actions (Guala 2016a: 71). They provide solutions to those coordination problems that are the best available to each agent, given the actions of the others.

2.2 Fiction Institutions

Equipped with this understanding of what an institution is, we now need to address the question of what makes an institution a *fiction* institution. The social practices of writing and reading fiction have changed over time and can differ at a given time from society to society. What is interesting for the purposes of developing a general philosophical theory of fiction is what unites these different practices, not what distinguishes them. To understand this, we do not need to identify the rules of particular fiction institutions, but rather to identify the distinctive type of coordination problem to which the rules of fiction institutions provide equilibrium solutions. Different token fiction institutions may consist in different systems of rules, but the distinctive type of coordination problem to which the rules that make up the different systems all represent equilibrium solutions are what make those systems fiction institutions.

Different fiction institutions at different times and places are united in consisting in rules that represent equilibrium solutions to coordination problems of communicating imaginings. The contents of these imaginings may be propositional in form, but they may also be non-propositional. Because different imaginings have contents of different types, the communication of different imaginings poses distinct coordination problems, requiring different kinds of solutions. For example, some imaginings might be such that they can be communicated only by the utterance of linguistic representations, whereas others might be such that they can be communicated only by the utterance of imagistic representations.

For present purposes, we can construe communication as a process involving two agents, in which the first agent modifies the physical environment of the second and, as a result, the second agent constructs a mental representation similar to one possessed by the first (Sperber and Wilson 1995: 1). All forms of communication pose coordination problems. If two agents want to communicate with one another, each wants her own mental representation to resemble that of the other agent. Consequently, how the communicating agent modifies the physical environment of the other in order to get the other agent to construct a mental representation similar to her own depends on what mental state she thinks that agent will construct in response to her modifications. Similarly, what mental state the other agent constructs depends on what mental state she thinks prompted the communicating agent to make those modifications. Consequently, all successful communicative practices can be understood as equilibrium solutions to coordination problems.

We can construe the coordination problem of communicating an *imagining* with a certain content as requiring one to modify one's audience's environment in a way that will lead them to engage in an imagining with that content. An agent communicates an imagining to her audience if she succeeds in getting her audience to engage in an instance of that imagining. Agents modify their audiences' environments in order to communicate imaginings to them by producing utterances. Fiction institutions help authors and audiences to coordinate to achieve equilibrium solutions to the problem of communicating imaginings because they include rules that serve as external correlation devices. These rules have the conditional form 'If an agent produces an utterance of type Z, imagine X'.

One might question whether the goal of communicating imaginings really poses a coordination problem distinct from that posed by the goal of communicating beliefs. There are two reasons why it does. First, the methods by which audiences identify communicating agents' beliefs will not always enable them to identify communicating agents' imaginings. There are two models of how audiences identify the mental states agents communicate. According to the code model of communication, agents communicate mental states to audiences by producing utterances that encode the contents of those mental states, which audiences then decode. By contrast, according to the inference model of communication, agents communicate their mental states to audiences by producing utterances that serve as evidence that they possess certain mental states, and audiences then infer from this evidence that they possess those mental states. The inference and decoding processes are importantly different: inferential processes start from sets of premises and result in conclusions that are justified by those premises, whereas decoding processes start from utterances and result in the recovery of representations associated with those utterances by an underlying code (Sperber and Wilson 1995: 12–13).

Different utterances of the same sentence or image can be used to communicate beliefs or imaginings with different contents. For example, distinct utterances of 'It's raining cats and dogs' can be used to communicate beliefs with very different contents. On some occasions of use, an utterance of that sentence might be used to communicate that it is raining very heavily, while, on a very different occasion, it might be used to communicate that cats and dogs are falling from the sky. The context-sensitivity of the contents of utterances seems easier to accommodate on the inference than on the code model of communication. The code model seems to suggest that different utterances of the same representation are always to be decoded in the same way, whereas the inference model allows audiences to treat a communicating agent's utterance of a sentence or image as evidence for their possession of a mental state, and to appeal to their background knowledge to draw inferences about what that mental state is. Depending on the different contexts in which those utterances are made, audiences will appeal to different background knowledge and therefore draw different inferences about the mental states at issue.

Knowledge of the way the world is plays a crucial role in enabling audiences to infer that a communicating agent possesses a belief with a certain content. It does so because the way the world is constrains the contents of agents' beliefs independently of the utterances they produce. Beliefs have a mind-to-world direction of fit: they aim to reflect the way the world is. With enough knowledge of the world, therefore, we are able to form plausible hypotheses about the contents of agents' beliefs by assuming that their beliefs reflect the way the world is, even when the sentences or images they utter do not encode the contents of their beliefs. When someone utters the words 'it's raining cats and dogs', during a torrential rainstorm with nary a cat or dog in sight, we infer that she is trying to communicate the belief that it is raining heavily, because such a belief conforms to the way things are.

By contrast, imaginings have neither a mind-to-world nor a world-to-mind direction of fit: they do not purport to represent the way things are, and they are not satisfied if the world reflects the way they represent things as being. They have propositional content without any commitment that they represent with either direction of fit (Gaut 2003; Searle 2010: 15). This is true even if, as Kathleen Stock (2017: 22) claims, 'imagining that *p* necessarily involves thinking of *p* as being the case'. That imagining *p* involves thinking of *p* as having a direction of fit does not entail that imagining p in fact has a direction of fit. One who imagines that p can think of p as being the case without in fact being committed to p being the case. Knowledge of the way the world is therefore cannot enable audiences to infer that a communicating agent possesses an imagining with a certain content in the same way as it enables them to infer that she possesses a belief with that content. The way the world is affords no purchase on the contents of others' imaginings. That it is raining torrentially and that there are no cats or dogs in sight does not justify the inference that one who communicates an imagining by uttering 'it's raining cats and dogs' is entertaining the imagining that it is raining very heavily rather than the imagining that there are cats and dogs falling from the sky.

The explanation of how agents can communicate imaginings with different contents by different utterances of the same sentence or image therefore cannot be the same as that of how they can communicate beliefs with different contents by different utterances of the same sentence or image. The communication of imaginings in ways that are sensitive to the context of utterance therefore poses coordination problems that cannot be solved by adopting the solutions we have developed to the coordination problems posed by the context-sensitive communication of beliefs.

In Chapters 3 and 4, I will explain how the rules of fiction institutions solve the coordination problems posed by the context-sensitive communication of imaginings. I will argue that fiction institutions incorporate content-determining rules that enable authors to communicate imaginings in ways that are sensitive to the contexts of their utterances. They do so in two ways. First, which rule governs a given utterance of a certain representation can depend on features of the context in which that utterance was made. Secondly, different utterances of a given representation can be governed by a single rule that prescribes audiences to engage in different imaginings, depending on the different contexts in which those utterances were made. All successful communicative practices can be understood as equilibrium solutions to coordination problems. Nevertheless, the communication of imaginings through fiction differs from other communicative practices. It relies on rules that provide equilibrium solutions to distinctive problems posed by the communication of imaginings.

The second reason why the communication of imaginings poses coordination problems over and above those posed by the communication of beliefs is that specific beliefs that purport to refer to particular entities usually do refer to particular entities, whereas specific imaginings that purport to refer to particular entities frequently do not. When one has a specific thought about an entity or entities, one has a particular entity or entities in mind) rather than thinking of an entity or entities merely as bearing certain properties. Tim Crane argues that we can have specific thoughts about non-existent entities. Whether or not a thought is specific, he claims, depends on its cognitive role rather than on there being some specific thing or things to which it refers (Crane 2013). Specific thoughts purport to refer to a specific object or plurality of objects, even if there is no individual or plurality to which they refer. One can have specific imaginings that refer to particular entities. However, it is also very common to have specific imaginings that do not refer to anything. For example, I can imagine that there is a malevolent fairy, Bruce, who does his best to ensure that all my tights have snags. When I extract yet another pair of snagged tights from my drawer, I can imagine that Bruce is responsible. This is a specific imagining: it purports to be about Bruce in particular, not about anything whatever that happens to bear the properties of being malevolent, being a fairy, and snagging tights. Although it purports to refer to a particular malevolent fairy, there is no malevolent fairy to which it refers.

One can also have specific beliefs that lack referents. For example, Le Verrier believed that there was a particular planet, Vulcan, that orbited between Mercury and the Sun. Although his belief purported to refer to a particular planet, there was in fact nothing to which it referred. When we have specific beliefs that lack referents, that is often because, like Le Verrier, we are mistaken about how things are. Le Verrier thought that there was a particular planet to which his belief referred, but there was not. Sometimes, however, we have true specific beliefs that lack referents. For example, one can have the true specific belief that Vulcan does not exist.

The communication of specific thoughts that lack referents poses a problem because, to communicate a specific thought to an audience, one must modify that audience's environment so as to elicit in them a specific thought, such that we would legitimately judge it to identify (in the ontologically neutral sense identified in Section 1.1) the same entity or entities as one's own thought. When our specific thoughts have referents, this condition is met so long as the two thoughts refer to the same entity. When they lack referents, however, it is not clear what could justify our judgements of co-identification. It is, therefore, unclear how one could succeed in communicating such thoughts.

Our interest in communicating beliefs is usually in communicating beliefs that reflect an accurate understanding of how things are. Some specific beliefs that lack referents meet this criterion. However, the vast majority of the specific beliefs that meet it refer to particular things. A general solution to the coordination problems posed by the communication of beliefs could therefore be adequate to the vast majority of our ordinary communicative projects (or at least seem to us to be adequate), even if it did not enable the communication of specific beliefs that lack referents. By contrast, because specific imaginings that lack referents are common and are not defective, solutions to coordination problems of communicating specific imaginings would not be adequate unless they enabled the communication of such specific imaginings. The communication of specific imaginings therefore poses coordination problems not generally posed by the communication of specific beliefs.

In Chapters 5 and 6, I will examine how the rules of fiction institutions solve the problem posed by the communication of specific imaginings that lack referents. I will argue that they do so by enabling authors to communicate specific imaginings that are *similar*, but not identical, to their non-referring specific imaginings. They do so by supplying referents for their imaginings, when there would otherwise be nothing to which those imaginings referred. The rules of fiction include reference-fixing rules that enable authors to create fictional entities by their fictive utterances. While my imagining that Bruce is responsible for snagging my tights lacks a referent, the reference-fixing rules of fiction are such that, if I produce a fictive utterance of the representation 'Bruce is responsible for snagging my tights', I create a fictional entity, Bruce, to which my audience's subsequent imagining that Bruce is responsible for snagging my tights can refer. Once an author has created a fictional entity, she too can engage in imaginings that refer to the entity she has created. For example, consider Muriel Spark's novel *The Prime of Miss Jean Brodie* (1961). Once she had produced the initial fictive utterance by which she created the fictional entity Miss Jean Brodie, Muriel Spark was then able to engage in the specific imagining that Miss Jean Brodie believed herself to be in her prime, and to communicate this imagining to her audience by making further fictive utterances that ascribe to Miss Jean Brodie the attribute of believing herself to be in her prime. Had she not created the fictional entity Miss Jean Brodie, Spark could have engaged in qualitatively similar imaginings, but there would have been nothing to which those imaginings referred. Because her subsequent imaginings *do* refer to Miss Jean Brodie, however, Spark can communicate those imaginings to her audience by prompting them to engage in specific imaginings that refer to the same fictional entity.

The value of fiction institutions lies in their enabling us to coordinate on equilibrium solutions to these two problems. By doing so, they extend the scope of the imaginings in which their participants can engage. One does not require any institutional infrastructure to engage in imaginings. A socially isolated individual can imagine many things. However, some people have more creative imaginations than others. Moreover, what one is apt to imagine is influenced by one's experiences, such that those with different experiences will tend to imagine quite different things. Fiction institutions help us to imagine things that we otherwise could not have imagined, by assisting us to engage in imaginings informed by the experiences and imaginative capacities of others. They break down the limits of experience and ability that would otherwise impede our imaginings. By doing so, they take us beyond our own limited perspective on the world.

2.3 Works of Fiction

I have proposed an account according to which fiction institutions are distinguished from other institutions, such as those of money and language, by the distinctive goals they help us to achieve. Fiction institutions alone help us to achieve goals of communicating imaginings. When philosophers investigate the nature of fiction, however, they are usually concerned predominantly with answering the question of what determines whether a given *work* is fiction or non-fiction. To understand this distinction, we need an account of the relation works of fiction bear to fiction institutions.

Works of fiction are produced by series of utterances. The rules of fiction institutions enable these utterances to perform the function of communicating imaginings. In the previous section, I distinguished between the content-determining and the reference-fixing rules of fiction institutions. In Section 5.2, I will argue that the reference-fixing rules of fiction institutions determine the referents of authors' utterances, without determining their contents. The content-determining rules of fiction institutions are what determine the contents of their utterances. They have the following, conditional form:

If an agent produces an utterance of type Z, imagine X.

These rules function to enable authors to communicate the imagining X by producing an utterance of type Z. They determine the contents of fictive utterances by determining the contents of the imaginings they communicate.

Let us call those utterances that are governed by such content-determining rules *fictive utterances*. In virtue of being governed by such rules, fictive utterances give their contents special institutional status. In particular, they make their contents *fictional*.

To be governed by a given content-determining rule of a fiction institution, a fictive utterance must be of the type Z, described by that rule. Different content-determining rules can pick out the utterances whose contents they govern by features of different kinds. In Sections 3.5 and 4.3, I will discuss the differing features by which different content-determining rules of fiction institutions can pick out the utterances whose contents they govern. Nevertheless, there is one feature to which every content-determining rule of any fiction institution appeals in characterizing the type of utterance whose contents it governs. There is, therefore, one feature that any utterance *must* possess in order to be a fictive utterance. In particular, there must be a practice of fiction to which audiences' responses to the series of utterances of which it is a part were intended to conform. This feature is necessary, but not sufficient, for an utterance to be a fictive utterance.

It is important to note two things about this feature. First, an author need not intend audiences' responses to an individual utterance to conform to a practice of fiction in order to intend their responses to the series of utterances of which it is a part to conform to such a practice. The intention at issue applies to the series of utterances by which works are produced as wholes. It involves an intention that, whenever an utterance in the series is of a type to which the relevant practice of fiction prescribes a certain response, audiences should respond to it in that way. It does not involve an intention that audiences' responses to every utterance in the series conform to a practice of fiction. To possess such an intention, an author must believe that some utterances in the series are of a type to which the relevant practice of fiction prescribes certain responses and have produced those utterances precisely because she believed this to be the case.

This is compatible with some utterances in the series not being of a type to which that practice prescribes certain responses, and not being intended by their author to be of such a type. It is also compatible with the author being mistaken about the nature of the practice of fiction at issue. That is, an author might believe a practice of fiction to prescribe certain imaginative responses to some of her utterances, and intend audiences to respond to the series of utterances she produces in the manner prescribed, although the practice of fiction does not in fact prescribe the responses she believes it to. It is a consequence of this account of what it is for an utterance to be governed by a content-determining rule of a fiction institution that, so long as it is part of a series of utterances produced with the relevant intention, if it possesses the further features required for it to be governed by that rule, its contents will be determined by the rule, whether or not its author intended it to have the content the rule assigns to it.

Secondly, it is important to note that the intention by appeal to which this feature is characterized refers *de re* rather than *de dicto* to a particular practice of fiction. For an author to produce a series of utterances with such an intention, there must be a practice of fiction such that she intends audiences' responses to conform to it. This does not require her to have the concept of a practice of fiction. This is important to the psychological plausibility of the account, since not every author of fiction has the concept of a practice of fiction, especially construed as I have elaborated it here, as an institutional social practice regulated by rules that provide correlated equilibrium solutions to coordination problems of communicating imaginings. All that an author requires, in order to have an intention of the type at issue, is the capacity to refer, *de re*, to a practice that, whether she knows it or not, has the features that I have identified as distinctive of fiction institutions.

> This explains how my account is able to provide a reductive explanation of what it is for a work to be fiction rather than non-fiction partly in terms of such an intention.
>
> A work is fiction if and only if:
>
> 1. there is a practice of fiction such that audiences' responses to the series of utterances by which that work was produced are intended to conform to it; and
> 2. at least one utterance in the series by which it was produced is governed by a content-determining rule that regulates that practice.

As it is presented here, this account appeals to the notion of a practice of fiction to explain what it is for a work to be fiction. However, one can obtain a genuinely reductive account of what it is for a work to be fiction by replacing the reference to a practice of fiction with reference to an institution whose rules provide correlated equilibrium solutions to coordination problems of communicating imaginings.

This account construes a work's being fiction as a matter of its bearing a certain relation to a fiction institution. Consequently, a group of agents who solve the coordination problem of communicating their imaginings to one another without the help of rules to serve as external correlation devices does not produce fiction, because they do not engage in an institutional practice. One does not produce fiction merely by communicating imaginings. This seems counter-intuitive only if one assumes that the institutional infrastructure required to produce works of fiction is more complex than it need in fact be. For proto-fiction to yield fiction proper does not require a formalized institutional structure with explicitly encoded rules. It requires only that agents succeed in communicating imaginings to one another in part because their actions are regulated by rules prescribing certain imaginative responses to utterances with certain features. This requires that they represent those rules mentally but does not require that they do so explicitly. They may instead do so tacitly.

When a work fails to meet the requirements for fictionality, it is not fiction. Since my purpose here is to explain what it is for a work to be fiction, and not to explain what it is for a work to be non-fiction, I will remain neutral regarding whether there are further features, other than not being fiction, a work must possess in order to qualify as non-fiction and, if so, what those features are. This account of what distinguishes works of fiction from works that are not fiction is compatible with some of the utterances involved in the production of works of non-fiction being regulated by the rules of fiction institutions. Norman Mailer's 'non-fiction novel' *The Armies of the Night* (1968) is divided into two parts, the first of which is arguably fiction while the second is not. Let us assume that parts of works can themselves qualify as works and that the first part of Mailer's book does so. In this case, if the series of utterances by which Mailer produced it meets the requirement for fictionality identified here, it is a work of fiction. Nevertheless, this does not entail that the book as a whole is fiction. The series of utterances by which Mailer produced the first part of the book can have been produced with the intention required for some of its constituent utterances to be governed by the rules of a fiction institution without this being true either of the series of utterances by which he produced the second part of the book or of the entire series of utterances by which he produced the book.

This account of what it is for a work to be fiction has implications for the relation between a work's fictionality and the truth values of its contents. Some have claimed that one cannot intentionally produce a work of fiction the contents of which are true (Currie 1990). Others have claimed that, while one can do so, this is possible only if one's choice of content is governed by some constraint other than fidelity to the facts (see D. Davies 2007: 48, although he later disavows this view). I disagree on both fronts. An author can intentionally produce a work of fiction whose contents she knows to be entirely true, and can do so precisely because they are true. Helen Garner's novel *The Spare Room* (2008) is purportedly a factual account of the time she spent nursing a friend who was dying of cancer (Legge 2008). One of the reasons Garner presented the story as fiction rather than non-fiction was reportedly to protect her from legal action by the clinics that exploited her vulnerable friend by offering expensive treatments of dubious medical benefit. Let us suppose that Garner's novel is entirely factually correct and that its accuracy was Garner's primary concern in writing it. This alone does not impugn its fictionality. Let us assume that at least some of the utterances by which she produced it satisfy the further requirements for being governed by the content-determining rules of a fiction institution, or would do if her work had been produced with the requisite intention. Consequently, what is at issue in determining whether or not it is fiction is whether or not she intended audiences' responses to the series of utterances by which she produced the work to conform to a practice of fiction. If the work was produced with such an intention, *The Spare Room* is fiction. However, if she merely retrospectively pretended to have produced it with this intention, it is not.

Another implication of this account concerns the relation between works of fiction and the imagination. Many philosophers take works of fiction to be distinctive in prescribing imaginative responses. As we saw in the previous chapter, Matravers (2014) labels this 'the consensus view'. On the account I have proposed, while works of fiction do bear a distinctive relation to the imagination, it is much more indirect than advocates of this view take it to be.

Gregory Currie (1985, 1990) and Kathleen Stock (2011, 2017) claim that works of fiction are distinctive in being communicatively intended to elicit imaginative responses in their audiences. However, works of fiction are not distinctive either in prescribing imaginative responses or in being intended to do so. Works of non-fiction may also prescribe imaginings, sometimes explicitly. Stacie Friend gives the following example from Simon Schama's *A History of Britain* (2009):

> Take a look at [Disraeli's] Buckinghamshire country house, Hughenden Manor, with its stupendous over-decoration (unerringly like Osborne House); imagine its terraces full of peacocks, and the sense of Disraeli the sorcerer—or 'magician', as his friends and enemies liked to say—becomes more plausible.   (Schama, as quoted in Friend 2012: 183)

This passage prescribes imagining terraces full of peacocks. Moreover, it plausibly does so because Schama communicatively intended to elicit this response in his readers.

Moreover, it is not necessary for a work to be fiction that it be intended to elicit such responses. The rules of fiction institutions have developed because they provide equilibrium solutions to coordination problems of communicating imaginings and because they can, therefore, help agents to realize their goals of communicating imaginings. It does not follow that one must have such a goal in order to produce a series of utterances with the intention that audiences' responses to it conform to a practice of fiction. Once the rules have been developed, they can be intentionally exploited in the pursuit of a variety of goals, which need not include the communication of imaginings. Consequently, although works of fiction are *typically* intended by their authors to elicit imaginative responses in their audiences, they are not *necessarily* intended to do so.

It is necessarily the case that there is a practice of fiction to which authors intend audiences' responses to the series of utterances by which they produce works of fiction to conform. It does not follow from this that authors always intend to elicit imaginings in their audiences by means of those utterances. Such intentions refer *de re*, not *de dicto*, to the practices in question. That an author has such an intention therefore does not entail that she conceives of the practice in question as one of eliciting imaginings. For example, a disaffected author of Mills and Boon novels might dash off five new works in order to fill his contractual obligation to the publisher, intending that audiences' responses to them conform to a practice of fiction, but without intending audiences to engage in imaginings in response to his utterances. He might be utterly indifferent whether or not they do.

Works of fiction differ from works of non-fiction only in respect of the *source* of their prescriptions to imagine. Works of fiction alone prescribe imaginings as a consequence of the institutional contexts in which they are produced. That is, they prescribe imaginings because the contents of at least some of the utterances by which they are produced are governed by institutional rules that represent equilibrium solutions to coordination problems of communicating imaginings. Works of non-fiction do not prescribe imaginings in virtue of institutional social practices to which audiences' responses to the series of utterances by which they are produced are intended to conform. This is consistent with them prescribing imaginative responses because they are intended to do so. If a work is intended to elicit imaginings in its audience, but none of the contents of the utterances by which it was produced is governed by such rules, it may prescribe imaginings, but it is not fiction.

2.4 Works of Fiction and Fictive Utterances

The proposed account of works of fiction also has implications for the relation between works of fiction and fictive utterances. It construes fictive utterances as necessarily involved in the production of works of fiction. In this regard, I am in agreement with Currie (1990), D. Davies (2007), and Stock (2011,

2017), who define works of fiction as works that are produced by fictive utterances. However, my account of the relation between fictive utterances and works of fiction avoids a problem with their accounts.

The series of utterances involved in producing a work of fiction can include ordinary, non-fictive illocutionary acts such as assertions. This raises the question of how many non-fictive illocutionary acts can be involved in the production of a work before it ceases to be a work of fiction. Currie (1990: 49) claims that this question is 'bad' and that,

> if we wanted to, we could define a numerical degree of fictionality, but it would be artificial and unilluminating. What is illuminating is a precise account of the fictionality of statements. For in some perhaps irremediably vague way, the fictionality of works is going to depend upon the fictionality of the statements they contain.

This response is unsatisfactory, because our concept of a work of fiction is not in fact vague in the way it would be if a work's being fictional depended in a vague way on the proportion of fictive utterances involved in its production. Stock (2011) has a better response to this problem. She notes that, just as an utterance of 'it's hot in here' can be both an assertion and an indirect request to open a window, so, too, an utterance can be both an assertion and a fictive utterance. Consequently, she argues that works of fiction are works that are produced entirely by fictive utterances.

Consider Muriel Spark's *The Comforters* (1957), a novel about a literary scholar, Caroline Rose, who is at work on a monograph, *Form in the Modern Novel*, but suffering from writer's block. It is fictional in the novel that Caroline starts to hear tapping at a typewriter, together with a voice recording her own thoughts and actions, and occasionally commenting on them. This leads her to recognize that she is a character in a fiction:

> 'But the typewriter and the voices—it is as if a writer on another plane of existence was writing a story about us.' As soon as she had said these words, Caroline knew that she had hit on the truth. After that she said no more to him on the subject.   (Spark 1963: 63)

Caroline responds to this realization by issuing the following challenge to her author:

> She raised her voice a little, and said, 'And if anyone's listening, let them take note.'   (Spark 1963: 68)

Caroline's author then responds by writing:

> As this point in the narrative, it might be as well to state that the characters in this novel are all fictitious, and do not refer to any living persons whatsoever.
>   *Tap-tappity-tap. At this point in the narrative* . . .   (Spark 1963: 69)

In this last passage, Spark asserts, truly, that the characters in her novel are fictitious. In so doing, she also performs a fictive utterance with the same content. That she does so is demonstrated by the fact that her utterance makes it fictional in the novel that Caroline is a fictional character.

I agree with Stock that a given utterance can be *both* a fictive utterance *and* an assertion. When an utterance both falls under the scope of a rule of a fiction institution *and* constitutes an ordinary illocutionary act such as an assertion, question, or request, it licenses dual interpretation: it is to be understood both in the way that ordinary illocutionary acts of the type at issue are understood, and according to the content-determining rule of fiction under whose scope it falls. However, it is not the case, *pace* Stock, that every utterance involved in the production of a work of fiction must qualify as a fictive utterance. This is obvious in the case of authorial interjections. Consider the following passage from John Fowles's *The French Lieutenant's Woman* (1969):

> You may think novelists always have fixed plans to which they work, so that the future predicted by Chapter One is always inexorably the actuality of Chapter Thirteen. But novelists write for countless different reasons: for money, for fame, for reviewers, for parents, for friends, for loved ones; for vanity, for pride, for curiosity, for amusement: as skilled furniture-makers enjoy making furniture, as drunkards like drinking, as judges like judging, as Sicilians like emptying a shotgun into an enemy's back. I could fill a book with reasons, and they would all be true, though not true of all. Only one same reason is shared by us all: *we wish to create worlds as real as, but other than the world that is.* Or was. This is why we cannot plan. We know a world is an organism, not a machine. We also know that a genuinely created world must be independent of its creator; a planned world (a world that fully reveals its planning) is a dead world. It is only when our character and events begin to disobey us that they begin to live. When Charles left Sarah on her cliff-edge, I ordered him to walk straight back to Lyme Regis. But he did not; he gratuitously turned and went down to the Dairy.
>   (Fowles 2012: 104–5)

This passage is partly the product of assertions, including Fowles's assertion that excessive planning stymies authors' attempts to create fictional worlds. Fowles interrupts the story he is telling to draw attention to the fact that Sarah and Charles are in fact fictional characters. However, unlike Muriel Spark in *The Comforters*, he does not thereby make it fictional in *The French Lieutenant's Woman* that they are fictional characters. As he emphasizes, he intends the fictional world he creates to be independent from him. Authorial interjections are not usually fictive utterances. Fowles's authorial interjection is merely an assertion and is to be interpreted, not by appeal to the rules of any fiction institution, but solely in the manner appropriate to ordinary assertions.

Although I hold that works of fiction need be produced only in part by fictive utterances, my account does not suggest that it is a vague matter whether or not a work is fiction. So long as a work is produced by a series of utterances at least one of which falls under the scope of some rule of a fiction institution, that work is fiction. This requirement is not artificial or unilluminating, because, in order for any of the utterances in the series by which it is produced to meet this requirement, the series as *a whole* must by intended, by its author, to be regulated by the rules of the relevant fiction institution. A work's being fiction depends, not just on conditions that are met by only some of the individual utterances involved in its production, but on the intentions with which the work as a whole was produced.

2.5 The Evaluation of Works as Fiction

The concepts of fiction and non-fiction are descriptive, rather than evaluative. In other words, to classify a work as fiction is not to imply anything about its value. Works of fiction, like works of non-fiction, can be either good or bad. Nevertheless, features that we consider good in works of fiction we may consider bad in works of non-fiction, and vice versa. An account of what it is for a work to be fiction should help to explain what makes a certain feature of a work a good or a bad feature of that work, considered as a work of fiction.

While we expect works of non-fiction to be accurate, and tend to think of accuracy as a good feature of a work *qua* work of non-fiction and inaccuracy as a bad feature of a work *qua* work of non-fiction, we do not generally consider accuracy a particular merit in a work of fiction, nor do we consider inaccuracy a particular demerit. Features that are generally considered merits in works of non-fiction may strike us differently in works of fiction. Similarly, features that we consider unproblematic in works of fiction may strike us as problematic in works of non-fiction. Consider the following passage from Edward St Aubyn's *Never Mind* (1992):

> *'Come up here immediately!'*
> Now Patrick knew where the voice was coming from. He looked up and saw his father leaning over the balcony.
> 'What have I done wrong?' he asked, but too quietly to be heard. His father looked so furious that Patrick lost all conviction of his own innocence. With growing alarm, he tried to work backwards from his father's rage to what his own crime might be.
> By the time he had climbed the steep stairs to his father's bedroom, Patrick was ready to apologise for anything, but still felt a lingering desire to know what he was apologising for.   (St Aubyn 2012: 98)

How we evaluate this passage varies significantly, depending on whether we read it as fiction or as non-fiction. In fact, the novel is heavily autobiographical fiction. Reading the passage as fiction, we do not consider its privileged access to Patrick's mental states to be problematic. By contrast, if we were to read it as non-fiction, the viewpoint of the passage would strike us as perplexing, because we would take the passage to purport accurately to represent actual events. We might ask ourselves how St Aubyn knew what was going on inside Patrick's head. Did Patrick tell St Aubyn how he felt in the situation described? If so, what is St Aubyn's relationship to Patrick? Even if we read it as autobiography, and take Patrick to be St Aubyn himself, questions arise that do not arise when we read it as fiction. For example, is St Aubyn's memory of events reliable? Does he really recall his 'lingering desire' or 'growing alarm', or has he embellished his memories? Can we trust him to be sufficiently impartial to have represented things as they actually occurred? If these questions could not satisfactorily be answered, we would consider the work's viewpoint a flaw.

One account of fiction purports to explain how evaluating works as fiction differs from evaluating works as non-fiction. Friend (2012) argues that fiction and non-fiction are categories relative to which various features of a work are either standard (they tend to place that work in that category), variable (they have no bearing on the work's membership of that category), or contra-standard (they tend to exclude the work from that category) for works in that category. Moreover, she argues, these categories are such that knowledge that a work belongs to one of them plays a role in its correct interpretation and evaluation. She claims that accuracy is especially salient in works of fiction because it is contra-standard in fiction. By contrast, it is less salient in works of non-fiction because it is standard in non-fiction. Likewise, free indirect speech is striking in non-fiction, but not in fiction, because it is contra-standard in the former, but standard in the latter. Because different features of a work are salient to us when we read it as fiction than when we read it as non-fiction, we are likely to cite different features of a work in explaining our evaluation of it when we read it as fiction than when we read it as non-fiction.

Appealing to the distinction between those features that are standard, variable, and contra-standard for fiction and those that are standard, variable, and contra-standard for non-fiction may help to explain the differences in which features are evaluatively salient when we read a work as fiction and when we read it as non-fiction. However, it does not help to explain why we evaluate them in the specific ways we do. A feature's status as standard, variable, or contra-standard for fiction does not determine whether we evaluate it positively or negatively. That accuracy is contra-standard for fiction does not tell us whether it is a good or a bad feature in a work *qua* work of fiction.

Whether a feature is standard, variable, or contra-standard relative to the category of works of fiction is in fact irrelevant to whether it is a good, bad, or indifferent feature in a work, considered as fiction. Although accuracy is a contra-standard feature and inaccuracy a standard feature, whether each is a good or a bad feature in a work, considered as fiction, is determined by its role in enabling the work to perform the function of communicating imaginings. A feature of a work is a good feature of that work, considered as fiction, to the extent that it is an effective means of communicating imaginings. It is a bad feature of that work, considered as fiction, to the extent that it is an ineffective means of communicating imaginings or it impedes the effective communication of imaginings. Inaccuracy is not in general a flaw in works of fiction, because inaccuracy does not, in general, impede the effective communication of imaginings. The imaginings a fiction communicates can depart significantly from the facts and, when they do, works communicate those imaginings most effectively by being inaccurate. However, accuracy and inaccuracy alike are demerits in works of fiction when they impede the effectiveness with which works communicate imaginings.

For a feature of a work of fiction to comprise the means by which an imagining is communicated, the work's author must have intentionally produced the work with that feature because she entertained that imagining and intended to elicit it in her audience. In addition, the work must succeed in eliciting the imagining in question in at least some of its audience in virtue of possessing that feature. A given feature of a work of fiction comprises an *effective* means of communicating an imagining to the extent that it works, either alone or in conjunction with other features, readily and reliably to elicit the imagining its author intended it to elicit in the members of its intended audience. A feature comprises an *ineffective* means of communicating an imagining when it works, either alone or in conjunction with other features, to elicit that imagining in at least some of its audience, but not readily and reliably to do so in the members of its intended audience. A feature of a work impedes the effective communication of an imagining when it causes the work to elicit that imagining in its intended audience less readily and reliably than it would otherwise do.

There are two ways in which a feature of a work of fiction can serve to communicate an imagining. First, it can do so when the content-determining rules of the relevant fiction institution prescribe audiences to engage in a certain imagining in response to utterances with that feature. When this is the case, the work's author can intentionally produce an utterance with that feature and rely on her audience both grasping the content-determining rule that governs that utterance and engaging in the imagining prescribed by that rule. So long as some of her audience both grasp and conform to the rule, the feature will communicate the imagining in question. A feature of a work of fiction is effective at communicating an imagining in this way when the author's intended audience readily and reliably both grasp the content-determining rule in question and engage in the imagining it prescribes.

The historical novelist James Forrester (2010) provides a good example of how a work of fiction that communicates imaginings in this way can fail to do so effectively. He writes:

> The path a historical novelist has to tread is clearly beset by dangers. There is an inherent tension between trying to do something new and something old at the same time. One cannot have medieval characters using correct period language because no one would find the speech readable.

The members of an audience can readily and reliably grasp the content-determining rule that governs an utterance with a certain feature but fail readily and reliably to engage in the imagining it prescribes. An audience that grasps a rule prescribing its members to engage in an imagining of a particular type in response to an utterance with a certain feature might, in general, be able to respond to utterances with that feature by engaging in an imagining of the type prescribed without invariably being capable of doing so. For example, our fiction institution incorporates a rule prescribing audiences to respond to certain utterances that represent words within quotation marks by imagining characters to have uttered the very words represented. Consequently, this feature of utterances can serve to communicate many imaginings effectively. For example, it enables St Aubyn to communicate both the words Patrick and his father utter and their contents. However, in the case Forrester mentions, it is not an effective means of communicating the contents of characters' speech, because most audiences are not able to identify the contents of medieval speech from verbatim representations of it. The accurate representation of medieval characters' speech would therefore be a flaw in a work of fiction intended to communicate imaginings about the contents of their speech to such an audience, because it does not enable that audience readily and reliably to imagine the contents of the characters' speech.

In Section 4.3, I will argue that the rules of our fiction institution enable authors to communicate imaginings in ways that are sensitive to their audiences' epistemic limitations. The rules of fiction do not prescribe audiences to imagine characters to have uttered the very same words as those represented within quotation marks in response to *every* utterance that represents words within quotation marks. This is precisely because authors sometimes intend to communicate imaginings about the contents of characters' speech to audiences who are not able to identify the contents of speech from verbatim representations of it. I will argue that the rules prescribe audiences to imagine different things in response to such utterances, depending on whether or not they are produced with the intention of making content that might otherwise be inaccessible intelligible to them. In response to utterances that are so intended, the rules prescribe imagining only that characters uttered words with the same contents as those represented, not that they uttered the very words represented. This is what enables authors to communicate the contents of medieval characters' speech by representing that speech in contemporary English, without thereby communicating that the characters spoke the very words by which their speech is represented.

There are other reasons for which features that serve to communicate imaginings in virtue of content-determining rules that prescribe audiences to engage in certain imaginings in response to utterances with that feature can fail to do so effectively. Authors can produce utterances that are unintentionally polysemous. An author might produce an utterance that intentionally has one content, and unintentionally has a further content. The two contents need not be compatible. In such a case, the feature in virtue of which the utterance possesses the second content is a flaw in the work. It undermines the readiness and reliability with which audiences imagine the first content. Instances of unintentional polysemy are to be distinguished from cases in which authors intentionally produce polysemous utterances in order to communicate imaginings with disjunctive contents to their audiences. Intentionally polysemous utterances can be a very effective means of communicating disjunctive imaginings.

In Section 4.5, I will distinguish two types of content that works of fiction can have. *The content of fictive utterances* is determined by the content-determining rules of fiction institutions. By contrast, *interpretative fictive content* is determined by authors' intentions to elicit imaginings. The second way in which a feature of a work of fiction can serve to communicate an imagining is by providing evidence that enables its audience to infer that it was intended to elicit a certain imagining and thus that it has a certain interpretative fictive content. Unlike the first, this method does not rely on the existence of a content-determining rule that prescribes engaging in the relevant imagining.

Audiences identify a work's interpretative fictive content by drawing inferences to the best explanation about its author's intentions on the basis of all the evidence available to them. This evidence includes information about the various features of the fictive utterances by which the work was produced, as well as whatever background knowledge they have concerning its broader context of production. A given feature of a work therefore need not work alone to communicate interpretative fictive content, but may do so only in conjunction with other features and only to audiences who are in possession of certain background knowledge. A given feature serves, alone or together with other features, as an *effective* means of communicating interpretative fictive content and is therefore a good feature in the work, *qua* fiction, to the extent that it works, either alone or together with other features, readily and reliably to prompt the members of its intended audience to imagine that content. It is a bad feature in a work, considered as fiction, to the extent that it fails to do so.

Forrester (2010) also provides good examples of how a work of fiction that communicates imaginings in this second way can fail to do so effectively. He continues:

> an accurate portrayal of a world in which most dutiful and conscientious fathers will regularly beat their sons is likely to alienate readers. If one was to write a novel about the real woman baptised in Dartmouth in 1737 as Constant Sex, it would have all sorts of double entendres and more basic entendres than she herself would have understood (the word 'sex' having little or no connection with the sexual act in 1737).

It need not always be a flaw in a work of historical fiction to represent a father as both dutiful and conscientious and as regularly beating his sons. However, if an author's intention is to communicate the interpretative fictive content that he is fundamentally sympathetic, it may be a flaw in the work, considered as fiction, to represent him as regularly beating his sons. This is because doing so is likely adversely to affect the readiness and reliability with which her audience identifies her intention to elicit the imagining that he is fundamentally sympathetic. Accuracy in the representation of historical social practices can be a demerit in a work, considered as fiction, when it impedes the effective communication of interpretative fictive content.

Similarly, accuracy in the naming of real historical individuals is a flaw in a work, considered as fiction, when it impedes the effective communication of interpretative fictive content. Authors fairly frequently use the naming of their characters as a means of communicating such content. For example, Charles Dickens conveys the hypocrisy of the architect Mr Pecksniff in *Martin Chuzzlewit* (1844) partly by giving him a name that suggests he sniffs the air haughtily, purporting to higher moral motivation, while in fact pecking at the ground in pursuit of his own profit. Audiences who are familiar with this practice are therefore liable to ascribe significance to any name that could be taken to indicate particular qualities on the part of its bearer, whether or not it is intended to do so. This leads David Lodge (1992: 36) to joke that 'one of the great mysteries of literary history is what exactly the supremely respectable Henry James meant by calling one of his characters "Fanny Assingham"'.

If an author were to write a novel about a historical personage named Constant Sex, audiences might mistakenly take its author to have intentionally named her thus as a means of prompting them to imagine that she has certain properties or proclivities. Whether or not naming a character in this way constitutes a flaw in a work, considered as fiction, depends on whether or not it is to the detriment of the effectiveness with which the work prompts its intended audience to imagine its interpretative fictive content. If its author intended her audience to imagine that Constant Sex conformed to Georgian sexual mores, naming her thus would be a flaw in the work, considered as fiction.

These examples are all cases in which accuracy is a flaw in a work, considered as fiction. Inaccuracy, too, can be a flaw in a work, considered as fiction. For example, in the crime novel *A Certain Justice* (1997), P. D. James writes:

the front row in the public gallery was the place from which the only photograph of a defendant being sentenced to death had been taken.

The people in the dock had been Crippen and his mistress, Ethel Le Neve. The photograph had been printed in a daily paper and it was this that had led to the new law that there could be no photography in court.

(P. D. James 2010: 461)

This is false. Hawley Harvey Crippen was indeed sentenced to death for the murder of his wife. However, the only known photograph of a defendant being sentenced to death in the UK is of Frederick Seddon. Moreover, while a photograph of Crippen and Le Neve in the dock was published in a newspaper in 1910, it did not lead immediately to a ban on photography in court. Several further such photographs were published before the ban was introduced fifteen years later.

Fictionally, this passage is part of a letter of confession in which its author describes the information imparted to her by a certain Mr Froggett. It is fictional that Mr Froggett told the letter's author that Crippen and Le Neve were photographed being sentenced to death. The purpose of the passage is to help convey the interpretative fictive content that Mr Froggett has extensive knowledge of matters of the law. The inaccuracy of the quoted passage is therefore a flaw in James's novel, because it impedes the effectiveness with which the novel communicates this content. Readers who are aware of its inaccuracy will imagine that Mr Froggett is knowledgeable about the law less readily and reliably than they would have done had he not been represented as imparting inaccurate information.

William Golding's novel *The Lord of the Flies* (1954) provides another example in which inaccuracy is a flaw in a work, considered as fiction. Only concave lenses can correct myopia, whereas only convex lenses can be used to start a fire. However, it is fictional in *The Lord of the Flies* both that Piggy is too short-sighted to see without his glasses and that his glasses are used to start a fire. This inaccuracy is a flaw in the novel because Piggy's glasses play an important role as symbols of his intelligence and rationality. Golding communicates the diminishing effectiveness of Piggy's reason as a means of maintaining civilization and order on the island partly by representing his glasses as being first broken and then stolen. The representation of Piggy's glasses as performing two incompatible functions is a flaw in the novel, considered as fiction, because it diminishes the effectiveness with which the novel communicates its interpretative fictive content. Piggy's glasses are less effective symbols of intellectual clear-sightedness than they would otherwise have been because they are represented as performing functions that no actual pair of glasses could perform.

Inaccuracies are not always flaws in works, considered as fiction. Consider Tolstoy's famous utterance in *Anna Karenina* (1878):

All happy families resemble one another, but each unhappy family is unhappy in its own way.   (Tolstoy 1965: 1)

Suppose, for the sake of argument, that not every unhappy family is unhappy in its own way. The inaccuracy of Tolstoy's utterance is not a flaw in *Anna Karenina* considered as fiction, because it does not impede the effectiveness with which the work communicates imaginings. Rather, it helps Tolstoy to communicate interpretative fictive content concerning the distinctive sources of Anna's own unhappiness. It does so by providing a thematic statement that focuses audiences' attention first on the infidelity that is the source of unhappiness in Anna's brother's marriage, then on the contribution that Anna's infidelity makes to her own unhappiness, and encourages readers to reflect on the differences between the two cases.

This is compatible with the falsity of Tolstoy's utterance being a flaw in *Anna Karenina*. If Tolstoy's utterance were both a fictive utterance and an assertion, its falsity would be a demerit in the work, without being a demerit in the work *qua* fiction. It would be a demerit for the same reason that Aristotle's assertion that 'men are good in but one way, but bad in many' would be a flaw in his *Nichomachean Ethics* if men are good in a variety of different ways. Assertions aim at truth. False assertions are flawed because they violate the norms of assertion. Although flawed *qua* assertion, Tolstoy's utterance is not a flaw in *Anna Karenina* considered as fiction because it does not impede the effectiveness with which the work communicates imaginings.

Conclusion

In this chapter, I have presented Guala's account of social institutions as systems of regulative rules that provide correlated equilibrium solutions to coordination problems. I have argued that we can distinguish fiction institutions from other social institutions by appeal to the distinctive type of coordination problems to which their rules provide equilibrium solutions. In particular, fiction institutions are distinctive in helping agents to coordinate their actions in order to achieve equilibrium solutions to coordination problems of communicating imaginings. The communication of imaginings poses distinctive coordination problems not generally posed by the communication of beliefs, both because the context-sensitive communication of imaginings poses coordination problems that are not posed by the context-sensitive communication of beliefs, and because the communication of specific imaginings poses coordination problems that are not generally posed by the task of communicating specific beliefs.

I have argued that a work is fictional if and only if there is an institutional practice of fiction to which audiences' responses to the whole series of utterances by which it was produced are intended to conform and at least some of the utterances in that series are governed by the rules of a fiction institution. Unlike rival accounts that construe works of fiction as produced by fictive utterances, this account does not construe a work's fictionality as a matter of degree, since whether or not the series of utterances by which it was produced was intended to conform to such a practice is an all-or-nothing affair. This account also differs from many of its rivals in its construal of the relation between works of fiction and the imagination. It holds that works of fiction are distinctive, not in prescribing imaginative responses, but only in the source of their prescriptions to imagine. Works of fiction alone prescribe imaginings in virtue of the institutional contexts in which they are produced.

On the account I have proposed, the rules of fiction institutions are arbitrary in the sense that the solutions they provide to coordination problems of communicating imaginings could always have been solved in different ways. I have argued that this is entirely consistent with fiction institutions performing a valuable function. Fiction institutions are valuable because they enable their participants to coordinate on solutions to problems of communicating imaginings that are the best available to each participant, given the actions of the others. Fiction institutions perform the function of enabling the communication of imaginings. This function plays an important role in determining how we evaluate works, considered as fiction. A feature of a work is a good feature of that work, considered as fiction, only to the extent that it is an effective means of communicating imaginings.

3

Fictive Utterances

Introduction

Fictive utterances are those utterances involved in the production of works of
fiction whose contents play a role in determining what is *fictional* in those
works. In the previous chapter, I argued that the contents of fictive utterances
are determined by the content-determining rules of fiction institutions. My
aim in this chapter is to elaborate on this claim to develop a more comprehensive understanding of the nature of fictive utterances by answering two
questions: what kind of speech act is a fictive utterance; and how do the rules
that govern fictive utterances determine their contents? In answering this
second question, I will also address the question of what role, if any, authors'
intentions to elicit imaginings play in determining the contents of their fictive
utterances.

In Section 3.1, I will argue that it follows from my argument in the previous
chapter that fictive utterances are *declarations* (also known as 'institutionalized performatives'). Declarations are illocutionary acts that are governed by
the rules of extra-linguistic institutions, and that therefore depend on the
existence of such institutions. They are distinctive in effecting changes to the
existence and status of their objects simply in virtue of their successful
performance. I will argue that fictive utterances affect the status of their
contents by making those contents fictional.

Knowing that the contents of fictive utterances are determined by the rules
of fiction institutions does not tell us very much about how their contents are
determined. This requires that we know more about the nature of the content-
determining rules of fiction institutions. In Section 3.2, I will consider the
proposal that the rules prescribe audiences to imagine what the authors of
fictive utterances communicatively intend them to imagine in response to
their utterances. I will reject this proposal on epistemological grounds. An
adequate account of what determines the contents of fictive utterances must
explain what rational grounds audiences have for ascribing to them the
contents they do. I will argue that the resources available to audiences do
not enable them to draw justified inferences about the imaginings in which

Fiction: A Philosophical Analysis. Catharine Abell, Oxford University Press (2020). © Catharine Abell.
DOI: 10.1093/oso/9780198831525.001.0001

authors intend them to engage. In Section 3.3, I will consider several responses the intentionalist might make to my argument and argue that they fail.

In Section 3.4, I will argue that the rules of fiction institutions determine the contents of fictive utterances by purely conventional means. They enable authors and audiences to coordinate on ways of communicating imaginings that need not have been available to them at all without those rules. I will explain what justifies audiences' attributions of contents to fictive utterances. The resultant account conforms to the code, rather than the inference model of communication. That is, it construes fictive utterances as communicating imaginings by encoding their contents in ways that audiences then decode, rather than providing evidence of authors' imaginings, on the basis of which audiences then draw inferences about what those imaginings are.

In Section 3.5, I will explain how the rules of fiction institutions can allow the context-sensitive communication of imaginings. I will argue that different fictive utterances of the same representation can differ in their contents because which rule governs a fictive utterance of a given representation can depend on features of the context in which that utterance was made. Moreover, I will argue that different fictive utterances of a given representation can differ in their contents even when they are governed by the same content-determining rule, because some of these rules are both counterfactual and indexical in form. In response to fictive utterances of representations, they prescribe audiences to imagine what non-fictive utterances of those representations would have communicated, were they produced in certain contexts. The non-fictive contexts specified by the rule can be characterized indexically, by appeal to features of the either author's own context of utterance or of the internal, fictive context of utterance.

3.1 Fictive Utterances Are Declarations

Two rival accounts dominate contemporary discussions of the nature of fictive utterance. The first denies that fictive utterances are illocutionary acts of any kind, maintaining instead that they are *pretended* performances of ordinary illocutionary acts such as assertion (Searle 1979: 65; Lewis 1983a: 266; Thomasson 2003c). On this account, fictive utterances are neither deceptive nor insincere because the pretence at issue is overt. Authors make it plain to readers that they do not believe the contents of their fictive utterances, but are merely pretending to do so. Searle, who provides the most detailed exposition and defence of this view, claims that fictive utterances consist in pretended illocutionary acts that are possible due to the existence of a set of 'horizontal', non-semantic conventions that suspend the normal operation of the 'vertical', semantic conventions responsible for determining the meanings of the words authors utter, such that they are able to use those words with their ordinary meanings, but without undertaking any commitment that the world is the way their words describe it as being (Searle 1979: 66–7).

The second account construes fictive utterances as illocutionary acts characterized by a reflexive, communicative intention to elicit imaginings, rather than beliefs, in an audience. This view is the most widely endorsed and thoroughly defended in the recent literature (e.g. Currie 1985, 1990; D. Davies 2007; Stock 2011, 2017). On this account, authors of fiction are generally neither deceptive nor insincere, because fictive utterances are not intended to induce beliefs, and making a fictive utterance does not commit one to believing its content.

By contrast, my construal of fictive utterances as utterances governed by the content-determining rules of fiction institutions suggests that they are to be construed as declarations (also known as 'institutionalized performatives'). These are illocutionary acts of the same kind as acts of marrying, canonizing, abdicating, decreeing, and surrendering. Declarations are illocutionary acts that depend on the existence of extra-linguistic institutions (such as those of marriage, the Catholic Church, the monarchy, or war), because they are governed by the rules of these institutions. For example, for an act of canonization to be successfully performed, a pope must perform an action that conforms to a rule of the Roman Catholic Church specifying what a pope must do in order to canonize someone. Fictive utterances are distinguished from other declarations by the nature of the institution on whose existence they depend. They alone depend on the existence of institutions whose rules represent correlated equilibrium solutions to coordination problems of communicating imaginings.

Declarations are distinctive among illocutionary acts in affecting the status of their objects simply in virtue of their successful performance (Searle 1979: 17). So long as the speech act of marrying or of canonizing is successfully performed, the mere performance of the act guarantees that the couple is married and that the person at issue is a saint. Acts of marrying change the status of relationships, acts of canonizing make saints of people, acts of abdicating make it the case that one no longer reigns, and acts of surrendering make it the case that one is no longer at war. Declarations have these effects because the institutional rules that govern them do not merely determine what it takes to perform a declaration of a certain type, but also determine its effects. Those rules ensure that, so long as a declaration of a certain kind is successfully performed, certain effects are thereby achieved. Fictive utterances affect the status of their contents by giving those contents a special institutional status. In particular, they make their contents *fictional*. They do so because they are governed by rules that prescribe audiences to imagine those contents.

Most illocutionary acts have sincerity conditions, such that one can perform acts of that type sincerely only if one has certain mental states. For example, one can sincerely assert only what one believes, and sincerely request only what one desires. However, declarations do not, because they bring about new matters of fact, rather than reporting on independent matters of fact. They therefore do not purport to express the beliefs, desires, or intentions of those who perform them (Searle 1979: 20). This explains why fictive utterances are not routinely insincere. They are not insincere, because declarations do not have sincerity conditions. Moreover, like its rivals, this account explains why fictive utterances are not deceptive. Although the contents of fictive utterances frequently do not reflect the facts, there is no deception involved in performing a fictive utterance because the mere performance of a declaration suffices to bring about an alteration to the status of its content. That is, making a fictive utterance with a certain content suffices to make that content fictional.

This construal of fictive utterances is consistent with the fact that they need not be linguistic. One can perform fictive utterances by writing a novel, but also by making a film or staging a play. Paradigm examples of declarations include such non-linguistic acts as surrendering by waving a white flag, disqualifying a player in a game of football by showing a red card, and knighting someone by tapping the flat of a sword on their shoulders. While some of the rules of fiction institutions may be general enough to govern fictive utterances in a variety of different media, fiction institutions also incorporate rules that govern fictive utterances in specific media.

One might object to this construal of fictive utterances on the grounds that, while declarations such as marrying and canonizing are heavily ceremonial and explicitly rule-bound, fictive utterances are not. Fictive utterances can be performed by almost anyone. It is true that one often requires a special institutional status in order to perform a declaration. One must be a judge to pass a guilty verdict, a pope to canonize, and a minister of religion or a marriage celebrant to perform the act of marrying. However, not all declarations must be performed by individuals to whom a special institutional status has been assigned. As Brian Epstein (2015: 267) notes, certain institutional rights and tasks may be assigned, not to individuals, but to sets of roles that a variety of different people can then fill. For example, the act of giving is a form of declaration. By giving someone something, one changes the status of that thing, making it the case that it belongs to the person to whom one has given it. To give something successfully, one must own that thing. This does not require one first to obtain a special status in the institution of property, but merely to occupy the role of owner of the item in question. Likewise, promising is a declaration whereby one places oneself under an obligation to perform a certain action. To make a promise, one need not first acquire any special status within the institution of promising, but need merely occupy the role of promiser. Similarly, to perform a fictive utterance, one need merely occupy the role of author of fiction. Anyone who occupies that role can make fictive utterances.

Whether or not an individual requires special institutional status to perform a certain kind of declaration depends on the nature of the coordination problems to which the rules of the relevant institution represent equilibrium solutions. For example, legal institutions provide equilibrium solutions to coordination problems of regulating the actions of individuals to ensure the common good. As I will argue in Section 6.5, some equilibrium solutions to a coordination problem may be better than others. Although every equilibrium solution provides the best solution that any agent can achieve by acting unilaterally, some equilibrium solutions satisfy all agents' preferences better than others. A system of rules provides a better solution to the coordination problem to which legal institutions provide solutions if it results in individuals being sanctioned for certain actions only if they have actually performed those actions than if it sometimes results in individuals being punished for actions they have not performed. Legal institutions generally attempt to ensure that people are sanctioned only for actions they have actually performed by granting the authority to pass verdicts and impose punishments only to individuals who have the epistemic aptitudes and experience required accurately to determine the facts. This is achieved by granting special institutional status to such individuals.

By contrast, equilibrium solutions to the coordination problem of communicating imaginings are not better if the authority to communicate imaginings is granted only to certain individuals. The range of imaginings that fiction institutions enable to be communicated is vastly expanded by allowing the role of author to be occupied by anyone whomever. By assigning the task of communicating imaginings to the role of author and enabling anyone to occupy that role, fiction institutions enable readers to engage in imaginings informed by the experiences of a wide range of different people.

One might also object to my construal of fictive utterances that declarations must be performed locution-specifically or at least (in the case of linguistic declarations) literally, but fictive utterances need not be. P. F. Strawson (1964: 458) claimed that a declaration is 'identified as the act it is just because it is performed by the utterance of a form of words conventional for the performance of that act'. He claims, therefore, that, when they are linguistically performed, declarations must be performed by the utterance of specific forms of words. Kent Bach and Robert Harnish (1979: 118) allow that linguistic declarations need not be performed by the utterance of specific forms of words, but claim instead that declarations

> must be performed literally, since the conventions that govern them specify what must be *said*, not meant. However, in locution-specific cases, it is irrelevant whether or not the utterance is literal. All that matters is that the right words be used.

However, *pace* Strawson and Bach and Harnish, it is not an essential feature of declarations that they be performed either literally or locution-specifically. I can give you some wine by saying 'I hereby give you this glass of wine', but saying 'Please accept this glass of wine', or, in an appropriate context, 'This will help you to unwind', can be equally effective. As Bach and Harnish (1979: 117) note, utterances are frequently both declarations and ordinary illocutionary acts such as assertions. By uttering the words 'This will help you to unwind' in a context in which I have reason to suspect that you are less than perfectly relaxed, I can make an assertion with the conversationally implicated content that the wine is yours to drink. In making such an assertion, I can simultaneously indirectly perform an act of giving that shares the content of that assertion, and which makes it the case that the wine is yours to drink. There is no reason why the institutional rules that govern declarations could not allow their contents to be determined by the contents of the ordinary illocutionary acts speakers simultaneously perform when they make those declarations, when they do simultaneously perform such acts.

Again, the ways in which declarations of a given kind can be performed depend on the nature of the coordination problems to which the institution whose rules govern them provides equilibrium solutions. Legal institutions provide better solutions to coordination problems of regulating the actions of individuals to ensure the common good if they ensure that verdicts and sentences are communicated clearly, so that the punishments ultimately imposed accord with those verdicts and sentences. An obvious way of maximizing clarity is by requiring verdicts and sentences to be performed either literally or locution-specifically. By contrast, equilibrium solutions to the coordination problem of communicating imaginings are better if they *do not* require imaginings to be communicated literally or by the utterance of particular representations. Restricting the means by which fictive utterances can communicate imaginings in either way would only serve to restrict the range of imaginings that they can communicate. It would thereby limit the range of coordination problems of communicating imaginings to which the content-determining rules of fiction institutions can provide equilibrium solutions.

3.2 The Role of Intentions in Determining the Contents of Fictive Utterances

My construal of fictive utterances as declarations is therefore compatible with their being governed by content-determining rules that accommodate a role for inference in the communication of their contents. As I argued in Section 2.2, audiences must sometimes draw on their background knowledge to draw inferences about the contents of authors' fictive utterances. This raises the question of *how* the rules of fiction institutions accommodate such a role.

One suggestion is that they do so because they stipulate that fictive utterances have the contents their authors *intended* them to have. That is, the rules specify that, in response to authors' utterances, audiences are to imagine whatever the authors of those utterances intended them to imagine in response to those utterances. The rules therefore require audiences to infer what authors intended them to imagine. On this suggestion, the rules of fiction institutions defer to authors' intentions to communicate imaginings with certain contents. It is authors' intentions, rather than the rules, that ultimately determine the contents of fictive utterances. So long as audiences have some means of drawing justified inferences about authors' intentions, authors and audiences could reasonably be expected to coordinate on such a solution without recourse to rules. On such a construal, therefore, the rules of fiction institutions serve merely to improve the stability of the equilibrium solutions that agents achieve, facilitating authors' and audiences' coordination, without being essential to it.

It is important to distinguish the question of what determines which institution of fiction regulates an author's fictive utterances from the question of what determines the content of a particular fictive utterance regulated by the rules of that institution. In Section 2.3, I argued that an utterance is a fictive utterance only if there is a practice of fiction to which audiences' responses to the series of utterances of which it is a part are intended to conform. An author's intention that audiences' responses to the series of utterances by which a work is produced conform to a practice of fiction determines which institution of fiction regulates her fictive utterances and therefore which content-determining rules govern those utterances. However, it does not follow that authors' intentions determine the contents of their fictive utterances. Consider an analogy with language: my intention to write in English determines that I write in English. Given that I am writing in English, however, the rules of English impose conventional constraints on the contents of my utterances. These constraints are such that, no matter how hard I intend my utterance of the words 'That is a shoe' to have the content that I am a bear, in most contexts it cannot have that content.

Contrary to the suggestion being considered, fictive utterances never have the contents they have because their authors intend them to elicit imaginings with those contents. In Section 2.3, I denied that works of fiction must invariably be intended by their authors to elicit imaginative responses. Even if they were, it would be implausible that authors' intentions to elicit imaginings with certain contents determine the contents of their fictive utterances. This is because an adequate account of what determines the contents of fictive utterances must be consistent with the facts concerning the conditions under which audiences are able to identify their contents. That is, it must be consistent with the following epistemological constraint:

If fictive utterance u *has content* c *iff* p, *any audience who is able to identify the content* c *of* u *must have access to the resources required justifiably to infer that* p.

If the contents of authors' fictive utterances are determined by their intentions to elicit imaginings with certain contents, audiences who are in fact able to identify the contents of authors' fictive utterances must have access to the resources required to draw justified inferences about authors' intentions to elicit imaginings with certain contents. In the remainder of this section, I will argue that this is not the case.

Those who argue that authors' intentions to elicit imaginings with certain contents determine the contents of their fictive utterances generally construe the intentions at issue as communicative intentions. Following H. P. Grice (1957), we can characterize a communicative intention as a reflexive intention to elicit a certain mental state in one's audience, for them to recognize this intention, and for their recognition of this intention to function as a reason for the relevant mental state being elicited in them. On the face of it, an account according to which authors' communicative intentions determine the contents of their fictive utterances looks likely to meet this epistemological constraint. This is because speakers with reflexive, communicative intentions that their intentions be recognized are bound to cooperate with their audiences by making their intentions recognizable to them.

This account also has the advantage of construing the interpretation of fictive utterances as involving an inferential process similar to that which is often taken to be involved in interpreting ordinary illocutionary acts, such as assertions. Assertions are often construed as being communicatively intended to elicit beliefs in an audience, and their contents as being determined by the contents of the beliefs they are communicatively intended to elicit. The proposed account holds that fictive utterances are communicatively intended to elicit imaginings in an audience, and that the contents of those utterances are determined by the contents of the imaginings they are communicatively intended to elicit.

The proposed account coheres with my observation in Section 3.2 that the institutional rules that govern declarations can take their contents to be determined by the contents of ordinary illocutionary acts that speakers perform simultaneously with those declarations. Moreover, it construes the contents of fictive utterances as being determined by intentions of the very same kind as those that Currie, Davies, and Stock take to characterize fictive utterances. If the rules of fiction institutions took authors' communicative intentions to elicit imaginings to determine the contents of their fictive utterances, therefore, my account of fictive utterances would not be a genuine rival to theirs, but would be compatible with it.

This would not make my institutional account redundant. First, as already noted, the content-determining rules would still serve as external correlation devices and would therefore help to explain the stability of the equilibrium strategy of communicating imaginings by the inferential identification of communicative intentions. Secondly, while the rules would not be essential to explaining why fictive utterances have the contents they do, they would still have a role to play in explaining what distinguishes works of fiction from works that are not fiction. As I argued in Section 2.4, for a fictive utterance to be governed by a content-determining rule of a fiction institution, there must be a practice of fiction to which its author intends audiences' responses to the series of utterances to which it belongs to conform. The fact that the rules appeal to such an intention enables the institutional account to accommodate the fact that works of fiction need not be produced entirely by fictive utterances, while avoiding the implausible consequence that it is a matter of degree whether or not a work is fiction.

Nevertheless, the content-determining rules of fiction do not defer to authors' communicative intentions. The claim that authors' communicative intentions determine the contents of their fictive utterances violates the epistemological constraint identified above. To see this, we need to consider both which resources are available to audiences to help them identify authors' communicative intentions to elicit imaginings and how those resources could enable them justifiably to infer that an author communicatively intended them to engage in an imagining with a certain content in response to her fictive utterance.

In Section 2.2, I argued that background knowledge about the way the world is cannot play the same role in the inferential communication of imaginings as it does in the inferential communication of beliefs. This is because beliefs have a mind-to-world direction of fit, while imaginings lack any direction of fit. On the view under consideration, the communication of imaginings, like that of beliefs, involves inferences about authors' communicative intentions. This account is plausible only if the resources available to audiences who are able to identify the contents of fictive utterances enable them to draw justified inferences about authors' communicative intentions to elicit imaginings. This is compatible with background knowledge about the way the world is playing a different role in the inferential communication of imaginings than it does in the inferential communication of beliefs. However, it requires the existence of *some* mechanism by which audiences can justifiably infer, on the basis of the background knowledge available to them, that authors communicatively intend to elicit particular imaginings by their fictive utterances.

Grice claims that audiences identify speakers' communicative intentions to elicit beliefs by assuming that speakers conform to the *cooperative principle* and its associated maxims. The cooperative principle is a normative requirement: 'Make your conversational contribution such as is required, at the stage at which it occurs, by the accepted purpose or direction of the talk exchange in which you are engaged' (Grice 1989: 26). If we assume that the purpose of the talk exchange is the maximally effective exchange of accurate information (Grice 1989: 28), this principle yields the following specific conversational maxims:

Quantity: Make your contribution as informative as is required (and no more informative than is required) for the current purposes of the exchange.

Quality: Do not say what you believe to be false or for which you lack adequate evidence.

Relation: Be relevant.

Manner: Be brief and orderly and avoid ambiguity and obscurity of expression.

Grice's cooperative principle derives from the norms of practical rationality. He assumes that speakers and their audiences share a common goal or mutually accepted direction (Grice 1989: 26). This makes it rational for speakers to conform to the cooperative principle. If that common goal is the maximally effective exchange of accurate information, it is also rational for speakers to conform to Grice's maxims, which describe rational means of pursuing it. There are other possible goals that are not rationally pursued by conforming to Grice's maxims (for example, it is not rational to pursue to goal of filibustering by conforming to *Manner*). Because the norms of rationality apply invariably, in all circumstances, audiences are justified in assuming that speakers who share this common goal will conform to these maxims, and can therefore appeal to them to draw justified inferences about speakers' communicative intentions.

Although speakers sometimes flout the maxims, doing so is an effective way of indirectly conveying their communicative intentions to elicit beliefs precisely because the invariable application of the maxims enables audiences to recognize indirection as interpretatively significant. When the hypothesis that the literal contents of speakers' utterances capture the contents of the beliefs they communicatively intend to elicit is inconsistent with the assumption that their actions conform to these maxims, Grice claims, audiences draw on their background knowledge to identify alternative intentions to elicit beliefs that are compatible with the assumption that speakers conform to the maxims, and infer that speakers communicatively intend to elicit beliefs with those contents.

Grice is clear that the background knowledge to which audiences can legitimately appeal to draw inferences about speakers' communicative intentions must be commonly known by both speaker and audience (or assumed to be known) to be available. He writes that

> the hearer will rely on the following data: (1) the conventional meaning of
> the words used, together with the identity of any references that may be
> involved; (2) the [cooperative principle] and its maxims; (3) the context,

linguistic or otherwise, of the utterance; (4) other items of background knowledge; and (5) the fact (or supposed fact) that *all relevant items falling under the previous headings are available to both participants and both participants know or assume this to be the case.*

(Grice 1989: 31; emphasis added)

Data of any of the kinds (1) to (4) can help audiences to identify speakers' communicative intentions to elicit beliefs only when they are is commonly believed by audiences to be available for use in interpretation. For present purposes, we can understand two agents as having the common belief that *p* if and only if each knows or assumes that *p* and each thinks the other knows or assumes that *p*. This is essential to explaining how speakers are able to convey their communicative intentions to audiences. Speakers expect audiences to use those resources to help identify their communicative intentions, and therefore shape their utterances to make them suitable vehicles for conveying those intentions given the availability of those resources. The existence of commonly known mechanisms for communication that speakers can deliberately exploit is what enables them successfully to communicate with audiences.

The claim that the contents of authors' fictive utterances are determined by *communicative* intentions to elicit imaginings is supposed to ensure that the account meets the epistemological constraint identified here, by enabling audiences to draw inferences about authors' communicative intentions by means similar to those Grice describes. However, it will do so only if three conditions are met. First, the goal of communicating imaginings must be a common goal. Secondly, there must be constraints on how this common goal is pursued that provide a role for audiences' background knowledge in drawing inferences about authors' communicative intentions to elicit imaginings. Finally, the resources available to help audiences to identify those intentions must be commonly believed by authors and their audiences to be available.

If the goal of communicating imaginings is not a common goal, audiences may lack the motivation to identify the imaginings authors intend to elicit. Moreover, even if they recognize that authors intend to get them to engage in certain imaginings, their recognition of this fact need not prompt them to engage in those imaginings. Consequently, authors will not be able reasonably to expect to elicit imaginings by getting their audiences to recognize their intention to elicit such imaginings. If author and audience do share the common goal of communicating imaginings, but there are no constraints on how it is pursued that provide an inferential role for audiences' background knowledge, audiences will be unable to draw on their background knowledge to identify the contents of authors' fictive utterances. If authors and their audiences share a common goal and there are such constraints, but the resources available to audiences to help them identify authors' communicative intentions are not commonly believed by authors and their audiences to be available, authors will not be able to identify which utterances would provide an effective vehicle for conveying their communicative intentions. This is because they will not know what utterances would comprise an appropriate means of doing so, given the resources available to audiences. Moreover, audiences will not know what resources authors intentionally exploited as a means of conveying their communicative intentions, and therefore will not know what significance to ascribe to their utterances.

The first of these conditions is clearly met. Authors of fiction and their audiences generally share the common goal of communicating imaginings. The adequacy of the proposed account of the determinants of fictive content therefore depends on whether or not the remaining two conditions are also met. Because authors and audiences share the common goal of communicating imaginings, it is reasonable to expect authors to conform to Grice's cooperative principle. However, it is not reasonable to expect them to conform to all four of Grice's maxims, and indeed they do not. Authors often communicatively intend readers to imagine things that are false, violating *Quality*. Background knowledge, therefore, cannot help audiences to draw inferences about authors' communicative intentions to elicit imaginings by enabling them to determine whether or not certain hypotheses regarding their intentions are consistent with the assumption that they conform to *Quality*.

This raises the question of what constraints there are on how authors pursue the common goal of communicating imaginings that provide a role for audiences' background knowledge in drawing inferences about authors' communicative intentions to elicit imaginings. Grice's four maxims invariably constrain how speakers pursue the goal of exchanging information because they describe rational means of pursuing that goal. Arguably, it is rational for authors pursuing the goal of communicating imaginings to conform to *Manner*. In addition, there are cognitive and practical limitations on what most people can imagine, from which there flow rational constraints on what imaginings an author can reasonably expect to succeed in communicating. However, the existence of such rational constraints does not provide a role for audiences' background knowledge in enabling them to draw justified inferences about what authors communicatively intend them to imagine. The problem is that, as I noted in Section 2.2, imaginings have neither a mind-to-world nor a world-to-mind direction of fit. It is perfectly rational for authors communicatively to intend to elicit in readers imaginings that reflect neither the way things are, nor the way they would like them to be. There are no rational constraints on how the imaginings authors intend to elicit are related to the way the world is. Consequently, it is not clear what role audiences' background knowledge could play in enabling them to draw inferences about the imaginings authors communicatively intend to elicit. The proposed account violates the second of the conditions identified above. Stipulating that the intentions to elicit imaginings that determine fictive content are communicative therefore does not help to meet the epistemological constraint.

3.3 Intentionalist Responses

Contrary to the argument I have just provided, Stock (2017) argues that readers *can* work out what authors communicatively intend them to imagine. Which strategy of interpretation readers are to employ to draw inferences about authors' communicative intentions depends, she claims, on which strategies authors intend them to employ. Authors sometimes intentionally appeal to readers' grasp of Grice's maxims to convey their communicative intentions, as they do when they use fictions in order to communicate their actual beliefs (Stock 2017: 33). However, not all authors intend readers to use the same strategies of interpretation. Consequently, there are many legitimate such strategies available to readers, none of which is appropriately employed to understand all fictions (Stock 2017: 45). She claims:

> For every application of a given strategy, we need to assume implicitly, or in some cases explicitly look for, a prior sanction offered by the author's intentions.   (Stock 2017: 45)

According to Stock, readers can identify such prior sanction by reasoning about authors' goals. She argues that their goals (for example, to write in a given genre, to sell lots of copies, to improve their skill as a writer, to explore a theme, to make a moral point, to establish their reputation, to express their feelings) can lead them communicatively to intend readers to imagine particular things as a way of achieving those goals (Stock 2017: 76–7). Readers should, therefore, appeal to authors' goals when interpreting their fictive utterances, since some hypotheses regarding fictive content will fit well with those goals, while others will not. To identify these goals, she claims, readers can legitimately appeal to a range of extra-textual evidence from such sources as holograph drafts, interviews, letters, diaries, and authors' other works (Stock 2017: 81).

Stock gives few further details about how this interpretative process is supposed to work. The process she describes differs from Grice's account in important ways. First, whereas Grice takes the rational constraints on how speakers pursue the goal of information exchange to enable audiences to pursue a single, invariable interpretative strategy, Stock denies that there is a single strategy that audiences can employ to identify authors' communicative intentions to elicit imaginings. This raises the question of what, on Stock's account, gives audiences' background knowledge a role to play in drawing inferences about authors' intentions.

She claims that audiences appeal to authors' goals to identify which strategy of interpretation they are supposed to pursue. *Prima facie*, it is plausible that appeal to such goals should help audiences identify the imaginings authors communicatively intend to elicit. There are constraints on how it is rational to pursue such goals as expressing one's feelings or exploring a theme. For example, it is rational for an author whose goal it is to express her feelings to express those feelings she actually possesses, rather than feelings she does not. Consequently, if audiences have access to background knowledge about what that author's feelings actually were, that knowledge can help them to draw inferences about what she communicatively intended them to imagine. When the literal contents of the utterances authors produce do not conform to the assumption that they are pursuing their goals rationally, therefore, it seems reasonable to expect audiences to recognize those utterances as intended indirectly to convey some other content that does conform to this assumption.

However, it is not in fact plausible that audiences identify the contents of authors' fictive utterances in this way. The goals that are supposed rationally to constrain the contents of authors' fictive utterances are not common goals shared by both author and audience and known by both to be shared. Rather, they are authors' personal goals. Consequently, authors do not conform to any cooperative principle in their pursuit of those goals. Instead, they pursue them in whatever way seems to them most likely to result in their achievement.

Authors' intentions to achieve these goals are ordinary, non-communicative *intentions in action* (Lepore and Stone 2015: 206). That is, they are intentions that commit authors not just to the performance of particular concrete actions, such as making utterances with certain features, but to the performance of whichever concrete actions are necessary to advance those broader goals. We identify agents' ordinary, non-communicative intentions in action by drawing inferences to the best explanation concerning what desirable ends agents' actions might enable them to achieve, and attributing to them the intention to achieve those ends. We may need to appeal to a very wide range of information in order to do so. As Ernie Lepore and Matthew Stone (2015: 229) note:

> Part of recognizing someone's intentions in action is to make sense of a specific choice she has made. But another part is to explain how her choices fit into an anticipated network of cause and effect, respecting her background beliefs and desires, supported where necessary by further commitments about what to do and what will result.
>
> Clearly, such inference is widely variable in its scope. For one and the same action, you may recognize some of the agent's commitments by superficial cues and simple inference. You may recognize other commitments only after you notice subtle connections between what she is doing, what you know about her, and what you would expect anyone to do in her shoes. And there may be key commitments that shape what she has chosen to do and how she has chosen to do it, about which you have no evidence at all.

I agree with Stock that authors often seek to realize certain personal goals by producing fictive utterances that they intend to elicit certain imaginings in their audiences. However, I disagree with her claim that audiences can identify the contents of authors' fictive utterances by reasoning about these goals. It is implausible that audiences who are able to identify the contents of fictive utterances invariably have the evidence required to identify those goals.

It does not help to argue that audiences achieve knowledge of authors' communicative intentions and knowledge of the personal goals that their fictive utterances comprise an instrumental means of achieving hermeneutically, with knowledge of both kinds emerging together, inflected by each other. As Robyn Carston (2002: 44) notes, the standard pattern of inference from behaviour to identification of desirable outcome to intention cannot be used to identify communicative intentions to elicit effects. The desired effect cannot be achieved without the audience's prior recognition of the communicative intention to achieve that effect. Until audiences know what imaginings authors communicatively intend to elicit by their fictive utterances, therefore, those utterances cannot provide them with evidence of authors' goals, and audiences need knowledge of authors' goals to identify their communicative intentions to elicit imaginings. Knowledge of authors' personal goals must, therefore, do all the heavy lifting here. It is the rational constraints on how authors pursue those goals that provide a role for audience's background knowledge in their inferences about the contents of authors' fictive utterances.

Consequently, there are two problems with Stock's account. First, to identify authors' non-communicative intentions to achieve certain goals, audiences need access to information that there is no guarantee they possess. To draw correct inferences to the best explanation regarding these goals, audiences will often require access to a wide range of information, including information about the particular beliefs, desires, and commitments that lead authors to pursue one goal rather than another, and about peculiarities of their particular circumstances that affect which concrete actions will advance their goals. It is, therefore, a matter of luck whether or not audiences have access to the information required to enable them to identify those goals. Stock's account therefore violates the epistemological constraint just identified because audiences in fact frequently succeed in identifying the contents of fictive utterances in circumstances in which it is implausible that they have access to the information that would be required to enable them successfully to identify authors' personal goals. For example, consider the opening line of Jane Austen's novel *Pride and Prejudice* (1813):

It is a truth universally acknowledged, that a single man in possession of a good fortune, must be in want of a wife.   (Austen 2014: 1)

Austen's fictive utterance is ironic, and does not make it fictional that a single man in possession of a good fortune must be in want of a wife, but rather that single women in search of a husband are apt to *hope* that a single man in possession of a good fortune is in want of a wife. Audiences can recognize this even when they know very little about Austen's circumstances and lack the grounds on which to ascribe to her any goal that would be rationally pursued by means of an utterance with this content. Similarly, consider the following passage from Raymond Chandler's novel, *The High Window* (1942):

In and around the old houses there are flyblown restaurants and Italian fruit-stands and cheap apartment houses and little candy stores where you can buy even nastier things than their candy. And there are ratty hotels where nobody except people named Smith and Jones sign the register and where the night clerk is half watchdog and half pander.   (Chandler 1984: 62)

Chandler's fictive utterance has the content that people go to the ratty hotels at issue to engage in illicit activities of which they want no record, not that the hotels at issue are frequented by a proliferation of Smiths and Joneses, or that the night clerk is half canine. Audiences can recognize this, even when they do not know enough to ascribe to Chandler a goal that would rationally be pursued by means of an utterance with this content.

The second, more fundamental problem is that, even when audiences do have access to the information they require to identify authors' goals, doing so will not help them to identify authors' communicative intentions to elicit imaginings unless there is a match between the knowledge authors believe to be available to their audiences, and the knowledge that is actually available to audiences. Only if there is such a match will authors know which utterances would provide an effective vehicle for conveying their communicative intentions. Similarly, only if audiences know what resources authors intentionally exploited in pursuit of their goals will they know what significance to ascribe to authors' utterances. Grice's account ensures that there is such a match by requiring the resources available to audiences to help them identify authors' communicative intentions to be commonly believed by authors and their audiences to be available. However, this is implausible when the goals at issue are not common goals, but personal goals that authors rationally pursue in whichever way they think most likely to result in their achievement, given their background beliefs and desires and other commitments. The required match will be very unlikely to occur. If it does occur, it is a matter of luck.

Characterizing authors' intentions to elicit imaginings as communicative does not help to explain how audiences are able to identify the imaginings they intend to elicit. Moreover, it does not help to characterize the intentions at issue instead as ordinary, non-communicative intentions to elicit imaginings in an audience. Such a view also violates the epistemological constraint identified here. Because authors pursue their ordinary, non-communicative intentions in action in whatever way they think most likely to result in their achievement, audiences must rely on inference to the best explanation to identify those intentions. However, they frequently succeed in identifying the contents of fictive utterances in circumstances in which it is implausible that they have access to the information that would be required successfully to infer authors' non-communicative intentions to elicit imaginings.

The positive role I have ascribed to authors' intentions in determining the contents of their fictive utterances does not violate this epistemological constraint. Audiences who succeed in identifying the contents of authors' fictive utterances are able to work out, by drawing inferences to the best explanation, that their responses to the series of utterances to which they belong are intended to conform some practice of fiction. This enables them to determine that the content-determining rules of an institution of fiction regulate authors' utterances. One does not need to know very much about Austen's or Chandler's specific goals or circumstances to work out that it is more likely that they intended their audiences to respond the relevant series of utterances in conformity with a practice of fiction than to respond to them in any other way. The information on the dust jacket of one's copy of *Pride and Prejudice* or the fact that one is assigned *The High Window* to read in a class on detective fiction may suffice to enable one to draw such an inference. However, this intention plays a categorial rather than a semantic role. That is, it helps to determine both whether or not individual utterances in the series by which a work is produced are fictive utterances and whether that series produces a work of fiction, but it does not determine the contents of authors' fictive utterances.

The contents of authors' fictive utterances cannot be determined by their intentions to elicit imaginings with certain contents, whether those intentions are communicative or not. Accounts of fictive utterances as illocutionary acts characterized by a reflexive, communicative intention to elicit imaginings in an audience therefore fail. They do so quite independently of the account of fictive utterances as declarations that I am defending here.

One might respond to the argument just presented that the common goal of authors and readers is narrower than I have suggested. It is not merely the communication of imaginings, but that of imaginings of a particular kind. Depending on how one specifies the kind of imaginings at issue, one may then be able to derive more stringent constraints on how it is rational for authors to pursue this goal. Searle (1979: 72–3) notes:

> In part, certain fiction genres are defined by the nonfictional commitments involved in the work of fiction. The difference, say, between naturalistic novels, fairy stories, works of science fiction, and surrealistic stories is in part defined by the extent of the author's commitment to represent actual facts, either specific facts about places like London and Dublin and Russia or general facts about what it is possible for people to do and what the world is like.

An advocate of the view that the contents of fictive utterances are determined by authors' communicative intentions to elicit imaginings might, therefore, claim that authors of works of naturalistic fiction and their audiences share the common goal of communicating imaginings that are consistent with the way the world is in certain respects. Authors of fairy stories also share with their audiences the common goal of communicating imaginings that are consistent with the way the world is in certain respects, although the respects at issue are more limited than in the case of naturalistic fiction.

This suggestion differs from Stock's. Whereas goals of the kind to which Stock appeals are not plausibly pursued in cooperation with audiences, the goal of communicating imaginings that are consistent with the way things are in certain respects is plausibly a shared goal pursued cooperatively by authors and their audiences. It is plausible that, when audiences recognize the genre to which a work belongs, they come to share its author's goal of communicating imaginings that are consistent with the ways things are in the respects characteristic of that genre. If particular authors and their audiences do share such goals, there are constraints on how it is rational to pursue those goals that provide a role for audiences' background knowledge in drawing inferences about authors' intentions. Moreover, if they do so, authors and their audiences will have common beliefs about the resources to which audiences can appeal to draw such inferences. Under such conditions, it seems plausible that audiences identify those intentions in the manner suggested.

On this proposal, if the author of a work of naturalistic fiction makes a fictive utterance the literal content of which is not consistent with the way things are in the respects characteristic of naturalism, audiences will ascribe an alternative content to her utterance that is compatible with the assumption that its content reflects the way things are in the relevant respects. The proposed explanation has the advantage of construing the process by which audiences identify the contents of authors' fictive utterances in a manner continuous with that by which we grasp the contents of speakers' assertions.

Let us assume, for the sake of argument, that audiences always need to know a work's genre in order to identify the contents of the fictive utterances by which it was produced. This assumption must be true if the proposed explanation of how audiences identify the contents of fictive utterances is to be plausible. Let us ignore the difficulties this assumption raises for the explanation of how audiences interpret genreless works or works that violate generic constraints. The main problem with the proposal is that the constraints on how it is rational to communicate imaginings that exhibit the relevant respects of consistency with the ways things are do not generally suffice to enable audiences to identify which imaginings authors communicatively intend to elicit. The proposal is most plausible in the case of naturalistic genres such as those to which *Pride and Prejudice* and *The High Window* belong. On the assumption that *Pride and Prejudice* belongs to a genre committed to consistency with the facts regarding how people of various types think and behave, it can explain why audiences take Austen's utterance cited earlier to be ironic rather than literal. Similarly, it can explain why audiences do not take it to be part of the content of Chandler's fictive utterance that the night clerk is half canine.

However, the proposed account cannot explain how audiences identify what the authors of works in non-naturalistic genres communicatively intend them to imagine in response to their fictive utterances. For example, works in fantasy genres are committed to consistency with how things are in far fewer respects than works in naturalistic genres. Consequently, there are fewer rational constraints on how authors of works in fantasy genres communicate imaginings by their fictive utterances. Used in the production of a work of fantasy, a fictive utterance of 'she dropped her head' could be used to communicate either that someone lowered her head, or that someone was holding her head in her hands and dropped it. The production of works of fantasy is not constrained by the ways things are tightly enough to explain how audiences are able to determine that a fictive utterance of these words is to be assigned one of these contents rather than the other.

The correct interpretation of a fictive utterance is often inconsistent with the way things are. Consider the opening of Kafka's *The Metamorphosis* (1915):

> As Gregor Samsa awoke one morning from uneasy dreams he found himself transformed in his bed into a gigantic insect. He was lying on his hard, as it were armour-plated, back and when he lifted his head a little he could see his dome-like brown belly divided into stiff arched segments . . .   (Kafka 1961: 9)

Although it is not the case that people can transform into vermin overnight, Kafka's fictive utterance has the content that Gregor Samsa has done so. Advocates of the claim that the contents of fictive utterances are determined by authors' communicative intentions to elicit imaginings might attempt to accommodate this by claiming that the common goal of authors and audiences is instead the communication of *a coherent set of imaginings*. It coheres well with the rest of the fictive utterances by which Kafka produced *The Metamorphosis* to construe his utterance of its opening words as having the content that Gregor Samsa had transformed into a vermin overnight, but not, for example, the content that Gregor Samsa woke up with a terrible hangover.

This suggests that the contents of fictive utterances are identified holistically. It gives readers' background knowledge about authors' preceding and subsequent fictive utterances a clear role to play in their inferences about the content of any particular fictive utterance. However, there are several problems with this proposal. It suggests implausibly that audiences' hypotheses about the contents of authors' fictive utterances always remain provisional until they have finished reading or viewing a work. It is plausible that some such hypotheses remain provisional, but not that all do. It is also difficult to see how the process of assigning contents to authors' fictive utterances could get going, given that the content audiences assign to every fictive utterance depends on those they assign to all the other fictive utterances involved in producing the same work.

Even if it were possible to answer these objections, this proposal suffers from a similar problem to the previous proposal. The rational constraints on how authors pursue a common goal of communicating a coherent set of imaginings will not always be sufficient to explain why audiences assign one content rather than another to a fictive utterance. The internal, *fictive* context created by authors' fictive utterances is very indeterminate in comparison to the background knowledge about the world on which we draw to identify the contents of speakers' assertions. For any fictive utterance, there is likely to be more than one hypothesis regarding its content that is consistent with authors and audiences sharing the common goal of communicating a coherent set of imaginings.

It would be question-begging for one who takes the contents of authors' fictive utterances to be determined by their intentions to elicit imaginings with certain contents to argue that, because audiences in fact regularly succeed in identifying the contents of fictive utterances, there must be some way of identifying the intentions that govern them. The failure of the accounts considered in this and the previous section to explain how audiences identify authors' intentions to elicit imaginings with certain contents show that the contents of fictive utterances are not determined by such intentions.

3.4 The Role of Rules in Determining the Contents of Fictive Utterances

Rather than deferring to authorial intentions as determining the contents of fictive utterances, the rules of fiction institutions themselves determine their contents. They do so by prescribing audiences to imagine X in response to utterances of type Z, where there need be no connection whatever between utterances of type Z and imaginings with content X independently of the rules themselves. By doing so, the rules determine that fictive utterances of type Z have content X.

On this account, the rules of fiction institutions do not merely serve as external correlation devices that improve the stability of the equilibrium solutions to the problem of communicating imaginings that authors and audiences could have arrived at without the help of those rules. Instead, they enable authors and audiences to coordinate on new ways of communicating imaginings by adopting strategies that are conditional on the rules. Sometimes, external correlation devices enable agents to coordinate on equilibrium solutions that would not otherwise be available to them. For example, consider a game in which two agents driving towards one another along different axes of a traffic intersection must decide whether to stop at the intersection, or to continue driving. This game is represented in Figure 2. It has two different Nash equilibria: the first agent continues driving, while the second stops (DS), or the second keeps driving, while the first stops (SD). In neither case can either player achieve a better outcome by changing her strategy unilaterally.

However, if each agent adopts a response that is conditional on the operation of the external correlation device of a set of traffic lights that is red for the same proportion of the time as it is green, both can adopt a strategy: *drive if the light is green and stop if it is red*. The operation of the traffic lights is not represented in the initial game and serves to enlarge the number of equilibrium strategies available to agents (Guala 2016a: 48). This strategy is a Nash equilibrium of an expanded game represented in Figure 3, which is achieved by representing the conditional strategy.

	D	S
D	0,0	4,2
S	2,4	2,2

Figure 2. Traffic intersection

	D	D	S if R, D if G
D	0,0	4,2	2,1
S	2,4	2,2	2,3
S if R, D if G	1,2	3,2	3,3

Figure 3. Traffic intersection with lights

By enabling agents to adopt strategies that are conditional on their rules, fiction institutions enlarge the number of available equilibrium solutions to problems of communicating imaginings. In Section 2.1, I argued that any equilibrium solution to a coordination game is arbitrary, because there is always some other equilibrium solution available that agents could have adopted instead. On the account I am defending, the rules of fiction institutions are also arbitrary in the stronger sense that they need not exploit any pre-existing relations between authors' fictive utterances and audiences' imaginings. That is, those rules are *purely conventional*: the relations they establish between fictive utterances and contents need not exist independently of the rules themselves.

One might wonder how rules that are arbitrary in this strong sense emerge in the first place. There is nothing in the practical logic of the situation that favours one such set of rules over another. Consequently, we cannot explain how agents come to adopt one such set of rules rather than another by appeal to their rationality and their preferences. Which set of rules emerges need not initially depend on agents' reasoning, or on their thinking strategically about others' actions. Agents may simply adopt whichever strategy seems the most salient, without having any particular reason to do so, other than that it is salient.

In general, the salience of a given strategy could be due to the fact either that arbitrary human psychological mechanisms make it stand out more than other strategies, or because all agents explicitly agree to adopt that strategy, or because it is a strategy that agents have adopted in the past. Fiction institutions are comprised of informal, rather than formal rules. Unlike formal rules, informal rules are not explicitly codified, but are manifested largely through the behaviour of individual agents (Guala 2016a: 7). Those rules therefore acquire salience through precedent, rather than because they are strategies that agents have explicitly agreed to adopt. As the rules acquire increasing weight of precedence, they become more and more salient, until agents expect one another to adopt them.

It is important to note that there is no scope for intentionalists about the contents of fictive utterances to insist that what stands out about salient strategies is that they are the strategies that are most likely to prescribe us to imagine *p* on occasions on which the author intends us to imagine *p*. My argument in the previous two sections shows that there are no such strategies. It follows from the imagination's lack of any direction of fit that there are no general strategies that it is rational for authors to pursue in order to communicate their intentions to elicit imaginings, and therefore no general strategies that audiences can pursue in order to identify the imaginings they are intended to engage in. Fiction institutions do not consist in systems of rules that maximize our chances of imagining in accordance with authors' intentions. Rather, authors who grasp the rules can intentionally exploit those rules to get audiences to engage in the imaginings they intend them to engage in. They can do so because the rules encode salient relations between utterances with certain features and imaginings with certain contents.

I will return to the issue of how participants in fiction institutions succeed in coordinating on rules that provide equilibrium solutions to problems of communicating imaginings in Section 6.5, where I will argue that their artistic judgements can play a role in enabling them to do so. For present purposes, we can understand the rules of fiction institutions as emerging gradually, with agents at first succeeding in coordinating on the strategies those rules provide through salience and good luck, without relying on any understanding of which strategies other agents will follow. While this is satisfactory as a causal story about how the rules emerge, however, it does not explain what justification audiences have for engaging in certain imaginings in response to certain utterances. An audience who, solely through salience and good luck, conforms to a rule that prescribes engaging in an imagining with content Y in response to an utterance of type Z has no rational grounds for entertaining such an imagining. Its members are not intentionally engaged in a communicative project.

Authors' and audiences' common interest in communicating imaginings and common beliefs about one another give them reason to adopt the salient strategies represented by the rules of fiction institutions. We can understand the rules of fiction institutions as conventions of the kind described by David Lewis (1969, 1975). He writes (1975: 4–5):

> Conventions are regularities in action, or in action and belief, which are arbitrary but perpetuate themselves because they serve some sort of common interest. Past conformity breeds future conformity because it gives one a reason to go on conforming; but there is some alternative regularity which could have served instead, and would have perpetuated itself in the same way if only it had got started.

Lewis (1975: 22) assumes that conventions must be limited to regularities in action or belief because it is essential to conventionality that others' conformity gives one a reason to conform, and these reasons must be either practical reasons for action or epistemic reasons for belief. The rules of fiction institutions represent regularities in authors' utterances and audiences' imaginings. The latter are not regularities in *physical* action. Nevertheless, we can construe regularities in audiences' acts of imagining as conventions. Given a common interest in communicating imaginings, audiences have a practical reason to conform to regularities in imagining in response to certain kinds of utterances, so long as authors conform to regularities of producing certain kinds of utterances in response to certain kinds of imaginings. Although acts of engaging in imaginings are mental, not physical acts, they are nonetheless acts in which audiences can have practical reasons to engage.

As we have seen, authors and audiences with a common interest in communicating imaginings are involved in a situation of interdependent decision-making in which the strategy each adopts depends on what strategy they think the other will adopt. Each has reason to conform to the salient regularity because they have common beliefs about one another that give each reason to believe that the other will conform to the salient regularity. According to Lewis (1975: 6), they have reason to believe this because they have the common beliefs that:

1. they conform to the regularity and believe the others to do so;
2. the fact that they believe the others to do so gives them decisive reason (practical or epistemic) to conform to that regularity themselves;
3. they prefer general conformity to the regularity to less-than-general conformity; and
4. the regularity at issue is not the only possible regularity conformity to which would give them a reason to conform to it and a preference for general conformity to it.

Lewis acknowledges that such common beliefs may be merely potential (that is, they would be available to agents if they were to think hard enough). Nevertheless, he claims, it is rational for agents to conform to the regularity because, if they were to replicate the reasoning of other agents, their expectation of conformity to that regularity would be reinforced, rather than undermined.

As Lepore and Stone (2015: 243) note, Lewis makes very strong assumptions about the common beliefs required to give agents decisive reasons to conform to conventions. Nevertheless, let us assume that he is right, and that authors and audiences must have common beliefs of these kinds if they are to have reason to conform to the rules of fiction institutions.

These common beliefs are of a very general kind. Unlike the knowledge of authors' personal goals to which Stock thinks audiences appeal to identify their communicative intentions to elicit imaginings, they do not involve knowledge of the particular goals that influence authors' fictive utterances on particular occasions, but only knowledge of the goals and preferences that guide their actions in general, and of the general behavioural regularities they exhibit. It is, therefore, plausible that authors and audiences have common beliefs about these goals, preferences, and regularities, even though, as I argued in Section 3.2, they often lack the knowledge of authors' goals of the kind to which Stock appeals.

On this account, authors and audiences must, in general, share the goal of communicating imaginings in order for the rules of fiction institutions to emerge in the first place, since their emergence is due to their providing equilibrium solutions to coordination problems of communicating imaginings. Nevertheless, it does not follow that authors and audiences can succeed in the communication of imaginings only if both parties share this goal. My account can accommodate successful communication in the absence of a common goal.

Several of Grice's critics have pointed out that communication can succeed even when speaker and audience are not cooperating in pursuit of a common goal (e.g. Searle 1969: 46). A speaker whose job it is to promote toothpaste to shoppers in a mall by making announcements over a tannoy can succeed in communicating the features of the toothpaste to shoppers, even though he does not care whether or not anyone pays any attention to him and they would prefer not to be disrupted by his announcements. Grice cannot accommodate this possibility, because it is not possible to recognize a speaker's communicative intentions unless we cooperate with speakers in pursuit of a common goal. Even if we share with speakers common beliefs about the resources available to help us to identify their intentions, those resources will not help us to identify their intentions unless speakers deliberately exploit those resources to convey their intentions, and they will not do this unless they know that we are cooperating with them in pursuit of a common goal.

Authors, too, can succeed in communicating with readers by their fictive utterances even when, like the disaffected Mills and Boon novelist mentioned in Section 2.3, they do not care whether or not audiences imagine anything in response to their utterances and their audiences do not care whether or not they engage imaginatively with those utterances. So long as both authors and audiences have common beliefs about the goals, behavioural regularities, and preferences that, in general, authors and audiences manifest, the author will communicate her imaginings to her audience, even though, in the particular case at issue, both author and audience conform to the rules of fiction institutions out of habit rather than because they have any reason to do so.

3.5 How the Rules Accommodate Context-Sensitive Contents

In Section 2.2, I noted that the fact that different fictive utterances of the same representation can differ in their contents appears to support the inference model, rather than the code model of communication. The code model seems to suggest that different utterances of the same representation are always to be decoded in the same way. By contrast, on the inference model, depending on the different contexts in which those utterances are made, audiences will appeal to different background knowledge and therefore draw different inferences about authors' imaginings. However, I have rejected the inference model in favour of a code model of the communication of imaginings. This raises the question of how my account can accommodate the context-sensitivity of the contents of fictive utterances.

There may be limits to this context-sensitivity. It is not obvious that different fictive utterances of any representation whatsoever can differ in their contents. It is an empirical question whether or not this is the case. It is, therefore, possible that fictive utterances of some representations are governed by rules that ascribe the same content to every fictive utterance of a given representation. We can remain neutral regarding whether or not this is the case. What is important for present purposes is that not all the content-determining rules of fiction institutions can be of this kind. Some rules must allow different fictive utterances of the same representation to differ in their contents.

They can do so in different ways depending on how we elaborate rules with the basic form:

If an author produces an utterance of type Z, imagine X.

Content-determining rules with this form take the reference of the utterances they govern to be fixed, and determine their contents, given their reference. In Section 5.2, I will identify the reference-fixing rules of fiction and explain how they fix the reference of fictive utterances.

As I noted in Section 2.3, there is one feature that any utterance *must* exhibit if it is to be governed by a content-determining rule of a fiction institution. Audiences' responses to the series of utterances of which it is a part must be intended to conform to that institutional practice. The content-determining rules of fiction institutions invariably appeal to this feature in specifying the types of utterances they govern. I will, therefore, ignore this feature in my discussion of the nature of the rules both here and in subsequent chapters, since I am interested in the different forms the rules can take, not in what is common to all of them. Readers should take it for granted that, in addition to the other features I mention, all the rules appeal to this feature in their specification of the type of utterances whose contents they govern.

The context-sensitivity of the contents of fictive utterances can have two distinct sources. First, different fictive utterances of the same representation can differ in their contents because the rules need not identify the utterances whose contents they govern solely by features of the representations of which they are utterances. They will usually appeal to some features of those representations. Any such features to which they appeal must be accessible to audiences, but there is otherwise no restriction on the features in question. They can include features of the literal or depictive contents of those representations, as well as lexical or syntactic features of linguistic representations, design features of imagistic representations, and features of the media in which they are made or the techniques by which they are produced. However, the rules can also pick out the utterances they govern partly by features of the contexts in which they were made. For example, a content-determining rule can pick out the utterances it governs partly by appeal to the genre of the works they are used to produce. Such a rule has the following form:

If an author utters representation R in the production of a work belonging to genre G, imagine X.

Let us suppose that Kafka's fictive utterance of the opening lines of *The Metamorphosis* is governed by a rule of this form. In particular, suppose it is governed by a rule that prescribes imagining that things are as they are literally represented as being in response to utterances of representations of a certain kind that are used in the production of non-naturalistic works. This is compatible with a *different* rule governing fictive utterances of the same representation when they are used in the production of works belonging to naturalistic genres. The rule that governs them might prescribe imagining whatever a reliable inhabitant of the real world would communicate by a non-fictive utterance of the relevant representation. Because such a person would not communicate that Gregor Samsa woke to find himself changed into a vermin by her non-fictive utterance of Kafka's lines, audiences would therefore imagine something different in response to a fictive utterance of that representation if it were used in the production of a naturalistic work.

The plausibility of the claim that Kafka's utterance is governed by a rule that identifies his utterance partly by appeal to the genre of *The Metamorphosis* depends on whether or not it is consistent with the epistemological constraint identified in Section 3.2. That is, it depends on whether or not audiences who are in fact able to identify the content of his fictive utterance have access to the resources required justifiably to infer that *The Metamorphosis* belongs to a non-naturalistic genre. While they must be able to do so independently of their grasp of the content of that fictive utterance, they need not be able to do so independently of their grasp of the contents of every fictive utterance involved in producing *The Metamorphosis*. Not every one of the fictive utterances by which Kafka produced *The Metamorphosis* need be governed by a rule that identifies the utterances whose contents it governs by appeal to the genre of the work they are used to produce. Audiences can therefore legitimately rely on their grasp of the contents of those of Kafka's fictive utterances that are not governed by rules of this kind to work out that his novella is non-naturalistic. Once they know this, they will be in a position to identify the rule that governs Kafka's fictive utterance of its opening lines, and thus to identify the content of that utterance.

The process of identifying the contents of the fictive utterances by which a work was produced may, therefore, be holistic in the sense that, in order to identify the content of a particular fictive utterance, audiences may first need to grasp the contents of some of the other fictive utterances involved in producing that work. This may be necessary in order for them to work out that the context in which that utterance was produced is such that it is governed by one content-determining rule rather than another.

However, in contrast to the holistic appeal to coherence considered in Section 3.3, holism of this kind does not make it difficult to understand how the interpretative process gets started in the first place. It is not the case that the content audiences assign to *every* fictive utterance depends on those they assign to all the other fictive utterances involved in producing the same work. Some content-determining rules of fiction institutions identify the utterances whose contents they govern independently of the contexts in which they were produced, while others do so by appeal to features of those contexts that audiences can grasp without knowing the contents of any other fictive utterances.

Nor does it imply that audiences' hypotheses about the contents of any fictive utterances must remain provisional until they have finished reading or watching a work. For example, as soon as audiences have grasped enough of the content of a work to determine that it is naturalistic, they can non-provisionally ascribe content to those of the utterances by which it was produced that are governed by rules that identify them partly on the basis of the work's naturalism. This is consistent with experimental works sometimes surprising audiences by revealing, late on, that they belong to genres other than those to which they had seemed to belong, and thus forcing audiences to revise the contents they ascribe to earlier fictive utterances.

I have focussed on the example of genre. However, the content-determining rules of fiction institutions can pick out the utterances whose contents they govern by a wide variety of other features of the contexts in which they are produced. The only in principle limit to the features of those contexts to which they can appeal is set by the epistemological constraint identified earlier. For any proposed specification of a content-determining rule of fiction to be plausible, the features of context by which it picks out the fictive utterances whose contents it governs must be accessible to audiences who can in fact grasp the contents of the fictive utterances in question. In Section 4.3, I will argue that some rules of fiction pick out the fictive utterances whose contents they govern by certain of the intentions with which those utterances were produced, although these are not intentions to elicit imaginings with certain contents. The important point for present purposes is that the code model can accommodate the context-sensitivity of the contents of fictive utterances by taking different codes or rules to govern fictive utterances of the same representation, depending on the contexts in which those utterances are made.

The second source of the context-sensitivity of the contents of fictive utterances is the way in which the content-determining rules specify the contents they assign to fictive utterances of a given representation. Even when all fictive utterances of a given representation are governed by a single rule, their contents can vary, because the rule that governs them can specify the imaginings it prescribes in response to them in ways that are both counterfactual and indexical. Such rules have the following form:

If an author utters representation R, imagine X, where X is the content that a non-fictive utterance of R would communicate if it were made in context C.

The fact that rules with this form specify the contents of the imaginings they prescribe counterfactually does not alone enable them to ascribe different contents to different fictive utterances of R. It is merely a convoluted way of specifying the contents of those imaginings. They can do so only if they also specify context C indexically, by appeal to features of contexts in which the fictive utterances they govern are made. For example, such a rule may appeal to a context in which the speaker is a member of the author's own community. Different fictive utterances of the same representation governed by such a rule can differ in their contents if the beliefs prevalent in the communities in which they are produced differ. For example, Austen's fictive utterance of the opening lines of *Pride and Prejudice* makes it fictional that single women in search of a husband are apt to hope that a single man in possession of a good fortune is in want of a wife. It plausibly does so because it is governed by a rule that ascribes to it the content that a non-fictive utterance of that sentence would communicate, if a member of Austen's community made it. No matter how obsessed with marriage the members of Austen's community were, a non-fictive utterance of that sentence by a member of her community would still have been ironic. However, the same rule would assign a different content to a fictive utterance of the same sentence, made by an author the members of whose community did believe it to be universally true that unmarried men of ample means must wish to marry.

Indexical rules of this form can also specify context C by appeal to the internal, fictional context established by the author's preceding fictive utterances. For example, a rule might specify the relevant context as one in which a non-fictive utterance of R is made *by a person of the type who narrates the fiction, in the fictional context at issue* (although such a rule could govern only the contents of fictive utterances used in the production of works that have internal narrators). So long as some of the author's preceding fictive utterances are governed by rules that serve to determine both what type of person the internal narrator is and the nature of the internal, fictional context, there is no circularity involved in the contents of other fictive utterances being determined by rules of this form. Chandler's fictive utterance cited earlier plausibly has the content it does because it is governed by such a rule. In *The High Window*, the internal narrator, Philip Marlowe, is a cynical, hard-boiled private detective, who inhabits a world in which vice and deception are rife. The same rule might assign a different content to a fictive utterance of the same sentence, made in a different internal, fictional context by a different kind of narrator.

While rules with this counterfactual, indexical form conform to the code model, they nevertheless incorporate a role for inference in the communication of imaginings. By prescribing audiences to imagine the contents that non-fictive utterances of those representations would communicate in certain contexts, they exploit audiences' ability to identify speakers' communicative intentions by appeal to Gricean interpretative mechanisms of the kind discussed in Section 3.2. To work out what content such a rule assigns to Chandler's utterance, audiences need to reason about what a man such as, fictionally, Marlowe is would communicate by uttering the words Chandler utters in the fictional context established by Chandler's previous fictive utterances. To do this, they assume that, in that context, such a man conforms to Grice's maxims, including *Quality*. They then reason counterfactually about what such a man would mean by uttering those words in that fictional context. This will generally require them to draw on their background knowledge of the world to work out what else would be the case if things were as they are in that fictional context. If the literal contents of the words uttered do not conform to the assumption that such a man conforms to *Quality* in that fictional context, they will assign a different content to that utterance that is consistent with this assumption.

Rules of this kind can describe the contents of the utterances they govern by appeal to a range of further features of the contexts in which those utterances are made. Again, the only in principle limit to the features of those contexts to which these counterfactual, indexical rules can appeal is set by the epistemological constraint identified earlier. Whether any proposed specification of such a rule is plausible depends on whether the features of context it uses to describe the contents of the fictive utterances it purports to govern are accessible to those audiences who can in fact grasp the contents of those utterances.

There is a further constraint that any proposed specification of a content-determining rule of fiction must meet, which restricts the form of the rule rather than the features to which it appeals: the regularities described by the rules must be salient to authors and audiences. As I argued in Section 3.4, conventions require the existence of salient regularities to which agents each have reason to conform because they have common beliefs about one another that give each reason to believe that the others will conform to the salient regularity. Without such salience, therefore, purely conventional rules of the kind I have described cannot provide equilibrium solutions to coordination problems of communicating imaginings. This restricts the complexity of the rules. I have described two ways in which the content-determining rules of fiction institutions can accommodate the context-sensitivity of the contents of fictive utterances: by picking out the utterances whose contents they govern by features of the contexts in which they are produced; and by specifying the contents of the utterances they govern counterfactually, by appeal to features of those contexts. A given rule could do both these things. However, no rule can be so convoluted that it cannot be salient to both authors and audiences.

Conclusion

In this chapter, I have argued that fictive utterances are declarations whose contents are determined by the rules of fiction institutions, and which affect the status of their contents by making those contents fictional. On this account, fictive utterances are neither insincere nor deceptive, because they bring about new matters of fact, rather than reporting on independent matters of fact. The successful performance of a fictive utterance with a certain content makes that content fictional.

I have considered various ways in which the rules of fiction institutions can accommodate the fact that different fictive utterances of the same representation can differ in their contents. I have rejected, on epistemological grounds, the suggestion that these rules ascribe to fictive utterances the contents of the imaginings that authors intend to elicit in their audiences by those utterances. Audiences who are able to grasp the contents of fictive utterances do not do so by drawing inferences about either authors' non-communicative or their communicative intentions to elicit imaginings with certain contents, because they often lack the resources required to enable them to do so.

I have argued instead that the rules of fiction institutions determine the contents of fictive utterances by establishing arbitrary connections between utterances with specific features and imaginings of certain kinds. The account I defend is thus a version of the code model of communication. I have argued that this account can accommodate the context-sensitivity of the contents of fictive utterances because some of the content-determining rules of fiction institutions pick out the utterances whose contents they govern by appeal to features of the contexts in which they are produced. Different fictive utterances of the same representation made in different contexts can therefore differ in their contents.

In addition, some rules describe the contents they ascribe to utterances of a given representation indexically, by appeal to aspects of the contexts in which those utterances are made. Because different fictive utterances of those representations are made in different contexts, they can therefore differ in their contents. Moreover, these rules ascribe to fictive utterances of representations the contents that non-fictive utterances of those representations would have if they were made in certain contexts. Consequently, understanding the contents of those fictive utterances involves the same kind of the reasoning about speakers' communicative intentions as understanding the contents of ordinary assertions. However, contrary to the intentionalist hypothesis I have rejected, audiences do not use such reasoning to identify the intentions with which authors produced their fictive utterances. The contents of fictive utterances are determined by the rules of fiction institutions rather than by authors' intentions.

4

The Structure of Fictive Content

Introduction

One might think that the contents of the fictive utterances by which a work is produced cannot exhaust what is fictional in that work. For example, one might take it to be fictional in *Middlemarch* that Dorothea eats regularly, sleeps at night, and does all the other things ordinary people ordinarily do, although this is not part of the contents of Eliot's fictive utterances. My aim in this chapter is to explain what determines the totality of a work's fictive content.

It is often claimed that fictive content exhibits a two-level, hierarchical structure, with some of what is fictional in a work being generated *directly*, independently of any other fictive content, and the rest being generated *indirectly*, on the basis of fictive content that is directly generated (Walton 1990: 140). On such a construal, the task of identifying the determinants of fictive content divides into the two tasks of identifying the determinants of directly generated fictive content, and identifying the determinants of indirectly generated fictive content. Most discussion of fictive content relies on an intuitive, pre-theoretical understanding of what the directly generated contents of fictions are, and focuses on the task of identifying principles of indirect generation.

On the view I will defend, although fictive content exhibits a two-level hierarchical structure, the distinction between directly and indirectly generated fictive content is of no theoretical importance. The important distinction is that between the contents of fictive utterances and *interpretative fictive content*. Together, these comprise the totality of a work's fictive content. I will argue that identifying content of each form involves fundamentally different practices. *Understanding* a work of fiction involves grasping the contents of the fictive utterances by which it was produced by appeal to the content-determining rules of a fiction institution. By contrast, *interpreting* it involves relying on one's grasp of the contents of those fictive utterances together with other background knowledge in order to draw inferences to the best explanation about the intentions with which it was produced. This can

Fiction: A Philosophical Analysis. Catharine Abell, Oxford University Press (2020). © Catharine Abell.
DOI: 10.1093/oso/9780198831525.001.0001

result in the identification of fictive contents that audiences do not grasp merely as a result of having understood it. I will deny that there are any general principles by which interpretative fictive content is generated on the basis of the contents of authors' fictive utterances.

In Section 4.1, I will discuss two prominent approaches to indirect generation, both of which take it to be fictional in *Middlemarch* that Dorothea eats, sleeps, and perspires. In Section 4.2, I will discuss a problem with both approaches. They appear to give rise to what Walton (1990: 176) calls 'silly questions': questions about fictive content that would be perfectly legitimate if the principles of indirect generation were correct, but are in fact illegitimate.

In Section 4.3, I will argue that such questions are illegitimate because they result from the misidentification of the contents of authors' fictive utterances. They show that we need to recognize a role for authors' intentions to elicit certain effects in their audiences in determining which rules govern their fictive utterances, and thus in determining the contents of their fictive utterances. Recognizing that authors' intentions can play such a role shows that silly questions do not threaten to undermine the principles of indirect generation.

Nevertheless, I will argue in Section 4.4 that these principles are to be rejected. It is widely recognized that they over-generate fictive content, ascribing to fictions contents that are intuitively irrelevant to understanding them. Moreover, we need not endorse such principles to explain the role that background information plays in enabling us to understand works of fiction. The account of fictive utterances that I provided in the previous chapter shows that audiences may need to draw on their knowledge that people eat, sleep, and perspire to interpret *Middlemarch* in accordance with the rules that govern Eliot's fictive utterances, because some rules of fiction prescribe audiences to imagine what non-fictive utterances would communicate in certain contexts, and this depends on facts about the contexts in question. Nevertheless, it is not part of the content of *Middlemarch* that Dorothea eats, sleeps, and perspires. We often draw on rich informational resources and engage in complex counterfactual reasoning in order to understand authors' fictive utterances, although their contents are finite and tractable.

Nevertheless, there is good reason to deny that what is fictional in a work is limited to the contents of the fictive utterances by which it was produced. A complete grasp of fictive content often requires audiences to draw further inferences on the basis of the contents of those fictive utterances. In Section 4.5, I argue that these inferences are not governed by general principles, but are instead inferences to the best explanation about authors' intentions, based on a grasp of the contents of their utterances, together with other available background information. Interpreting a work of fiction involves drawing such inferences. Although authors' intentions do not determine the contents of their fictive utterances, they nevertheless play a role in determining what is fictional in the works they produce.

4.1 Accounts of Indirect Generation

In this section, I will examine the influential accounts of indirect generation proposed by Kendall Walton and David Lewis. These are not the only accounts of indirect generation available (see, e.g., Currie 1990). Nor are they generally uncritically accepted. Various problems with them have been identified and several attempts made to overcome them (see, e.g., Byrne 1993; Phillips 1999). However, my purpose here is not the exhaustive assessment of Lewis's or Walton's accounts. Rather, my aim in discussing them is to help motivate my own account of the structure of fictive content and of the role of authors' intentions in determining fictive content.

Walton proposes two alternative principles of indirect generation, *the reality principle* and *the mutual belief principle*. According to the former, what is fictional in a given work incorporates everything that would be true, were its directly generated content true (Walton 1990: 147). According to the latter, what is fictional in a work incorporates everything that would be true, according to the mutual beliefs of its author's society, were the work's directly generated content true (Walton 1990: 152). A community's mutual beliefs are those beliefs that most of its members hold, most believe one another to hold, most believe one another to believe one another to hold, and so on. The notion of mutual belief is therefore similar to, although not exactly the same as, the notion of common belief introduced in the previous chapter.

Each of Walton's principles of indirect generation resembles one of Lewis's accounts of the determinants of fictive content. On Lewis's first account, what is fictional in a given work of fiction incorporates everything that would be true, were it told as known fact, rather than as fiction (Lewis (1983a: 270) cashes out what would be true in such a situation by appeal to his possible worlds account of modality and method of evaluating counterfactuals, but the details of this analysis need not concern us here). Lewis (1983a: 273) also offers an alternative account, on which what is fictional in a given work incorporates whatever would be true, *according to the mutual beliefs of its maker's community*, were it told as known fact. Although Lewis does not explicitly recognize the distinction between directly and indirectly generated fictive content, we can see the resemblance between his accounts and Walton's principles if we assume that, on his accounts, the directly generated content of a fiction is what is told as known fact in the situations he takes to determine what is fictional.

Both Walton's reality principle and Lewis's first account have the consequence that fictive content includes facts about the world unknown to either author or audience. For example, it will be fictional in Jane Austen's *Emma* that the invention of the telephone is less than a century away, because, were the events recounted in *Emma* told as known fact, the telephone would be invented some time in the coming century. It is anachronistic, though, to suppose that telephones feature in the contents of Regency novels. By contrast, Walton's mutual belief principle and Lewis's second account provide a more restricted construal of what is fictional in a work, according to which what is fictional in *Emma* excludes future innovations in telecommunication, because Jane Austen's community held no mutual beliefs about them.

Although both Walton and Lewis see some reason to construe what is fictional in the work an author produces as dependent on the mutual beliefs of the members of her community, neither construes it as dependent on her intentions. It does not follow from the fact that a certain belief is mutual among the members of an author's community that the author herself holds that belief. Even if she does hold the belief in question, this does not entail that she intended it to be fictional that things are as they are mutually believed to be. Even on Walton's and Lewis's more restrictive accounts, what is fictional in a given work will usually outstrip what its author intended to be fictional.

The most significant difference between Walton's and Lewis's approaches concerns the role of an internal narrator. Lewis takes what is fictional in a given work to be determined by counterfactual situations in which it is told as known fact. Consequently, it is fictional in every work, on both of Lewis's analyses, that it has a narrator. This is counter-intuitive, given the conceptual possibility of works in which it is fictional that certain events occur although there are no witnesses to, or records of, them. Walton's principles have an advantage here, because they make no reference to narrators. Unlike Lewis, he can therefore accommodate fictions without internal narrators.

Walton's principles are also better able to accommodate viewpoints and shifts in narrative viewpoints of kinds that are common in works of fiction but seldom found in works of non-fiction. I argued in Section 2.5 that viewpoints that do not trouble us in works of fiction can do so in works of non-fiction. This is also true of shifts in narrative perspective—for example, between an omniscient point of view, a semi-omniscient point of view, the first-person point of view of one of the characters, and even that of the author herself. As E. M. Forster (1927: 79) notes, in novels such as *Bleak House* (1853) and *War and Peace* (1869), these shifts in perspective tend not to bother the reader, although they would render a work of non-fiction incoherent. However, Lewis's accounts entail, implausibly, that it is fictional in works narrated from an omniscient point of view that there is an omniscient narrator. They also raise uncomfortable questions concerning whether fictions with shifting narrative perspectives have multiple narrators each with a different narrative perspective or a single narrator who successively occupies many different narrative perspectives. Such questions do not arise on Walton's principles of indirect generation, because they are sensitive only to the contents ascribed from these differing narrative perspectives, not to the perspectives themselves.

Nevertheless, there are some benefits to taking what is fictional in a work to be determined by situations in which it is narrated. Audiences of certain kinds of fiction and non-fiction narratives can legitimately take the events narrated to have a pertinence that ordinary events do not have simply in virtue of their occurrence. Henry Fielding makes this point nicely in an authorial interjection in *Tom Jones*:

> Though we have properly enough entitled this our work, a history, and not a life, nor an apology for a life, as is more in fashion; yet we intend in it rather to pursue the method of those writers who profess to disclose the revolutions of countries, than to imitate the painful and voluminous historian, who, to preserve the regularity of his series, thinks himself obliged to fill up as much paper with the detail of months and years in which nothing remarkable happened, as he employs on those notable eras when the greatest scenes have been transacted on the human stage.
>
> Such histories as these do, in reality, very much resemble a newspaper, which consists in just the same number of words, whether there be any news in it or not . . .
>
> Now it is our purpose, in the ensuing pages, to pursue a contrary method. When any extraordinary scene presents itself (as we trust will often be the case), we shall spare no pains nor paper to open it at large to our readers; but if whole years should pass without producing anything worthy his notice, we shall not be afraid of a chasm in our history, but shall hasten on to matters of consequence, and leave such periods of time totally unobserved.
>
> (Fielding 1825: 49)

One who reads the work of those historians who 'profess to disclose the revolutions of countries' can legitimately take the events they recount to have extraordinary significance, simply because they have chosen to represent them. The method of narration employed by authors of works of fiction is generally of this kind, rather than that of the 'painful and voluminous' historian whom Fielding pillories. This explains why, as Forster (1927: 53) notes:

> Food in fiction is mainly social. It draws characters together, but they seldom require it physiologically, seldom enjoy it, and never digest it unless specially asked to do so. They hunger for each other, as we do in life, but our equally constant longing for breakfast and lunch does not get reflected.

Because Lewis's accounts take what is fictional in a work to be determined by situations involving the production of narratives, he can account for the fact that audiences ascribe particular significance to events when they are recounted in a work of fiction, on the assumption that what is fictional is determined by a counterfactual situation in which that work is told as known fact by a narrator who employs Fielding's preferred method of narration.

Consider an example given by Walton (1990: 162) himself:

> Recall the suicide of Mrs Verloc in her voyage to the Continent in Conrad's *Secret Agent*. The newspaper headline, 'Suicide of Lady Passenger from a cross-Channel Boat', informs the reader of her death. But how can we jump so irresponsibly to the conclusion that she was the victim? We have some additional circumstantial evidence, to be sure . . . But little if any of this additional evidence is needed to establish the fact that fictionally it was Mrs Verloc who jumped from the ferry. And even this evidence would, in a real case, stand in need of confirmation; there could easily have been another suicidal passenger crossing the Channel the same night.

Walton acknowledges that neither his reality nor his mutual belief principle licenses the inference that it is fictional that Mrs Verloc has committed suicide. Nevertheless, it is fictional in *The Secret Agent* (1907) that she does so. Lewis's accounts are better able to accommodate this fact because they take general features of narratives to play a role in explaining what is fictional in that work. On his accounts, audiences are licensed to assume that the events recounted are germane in ways that their mere occurrence would not guarantee. As

Matravers (2014: 88) notes, the technique of mentioning a detail and leaving audiences to infer its significance is a general technique of narrative, not one peculiar to fiction narratives.

However, neither of Lewis's accounts accommodates the significance audiences ascribe to the events recounted in all fiction narratives. For example, consider the following excerpt from the story 'A Continuity of Parks' by Julio Cortázar (1964):

He had begun to read the novel a few days before. He had put it down because of some urgent business conferences, opened it again on his way back to the estate by train; he permitted himself a slowly growing interest in the plot, in the characterization. That afternoon, after writing a letter giving his power of attorney and discussing a matter of joint ownership with the manager of his estate, he returned to the book in the tranquility of his study which looked out upon the park with its oaks. Sprawled on his favourite armchair, its back toward the door—even the possibility of an intrusion would have irritated him, had he thought of it—he let his left hand caress repeatedly the green velvet upholstery and set to reading the final chapters.... Word by word, licked up by the sordid dilemma of the hero and heroine, letting himself be absorbed to the point where the images settled down and took on colour and movement, he was witness to the final encounter in the mountain cabin . . . they sketched abominably the frame of that other body it was necessary to destroy. Nothing had been forgotten: alibis, unforeseen hazards, possible mistakes . . .

Not looking at one another now, rigidly fixed upon the task that awaited them, they separated at the cabin door. She was to follow the trail that led north. On the path leading in the opposite direction, he turned for a moment to watch her running, her hair loosened and flying. He ran in turn . . . The estate manager would not be there at this hour, and he was not there. The woman's words reached him over the thudding of blood in his ears: first a blue chamber, then a hall, then a carpeted stairway. At the top, two doors. No one in the first room, no one in the second. The door of the salon, and then, the knife in hand, the light from the great windows, the high back of an armchair covered in green velvet, the head of the man in the chair reading a novel.   (trans. García-Carpintero 2007: 203–4, from Cortázar 2001)

It is fictional in 'A Continuity of Parks' that the man in the green velvet armchair is about to be killed by a character in the novel he is reading.

Audiences draw this inference because of the similarities between the contents of the fictive utterances by which Cortázar produced the first part of the story, which recounts the circumstances in which the man sits down to read the novel, and the contents of the fictive utterances by which he produced the second part of the story, which recounts what is fictional in the novel the man reads. Both feature an estate manager and a man reading in an armchair covered in green velvet with its back towards a door. However, if Cortázar's story were recounted as known fact, it would not have the content that the man in the green velvet armchair is about to be killed by a character in the novel he is reading, even if its narrator pursued Fielding's favoured method of narration. Audiences can legitimately draw such an inference only about *fiction* narratives, and Lewis's accounts would be circular if they appealed to situations in which fictions were recounted as such.

Ultimately, neither Walton's nor Lewis's principles of generation are able to explain why Cortázar's story has the content it does. It would be hasty to assume that this shows both sets of principles to be incorrect. However, it does show that, at best, they are incomplete. What stands in need of explanation is why audiences can legitimately take the events narrated in works of fiction to have a relevance that far exceeds that which they can legitimately take the events narrated in non-fiction to have.

This is not all that 'A Continuity of Parks' shows. It shows that there must be *some* determinants of fictive content other than the rules that govern the contents of authors' fictive utterances. None of Cortázar's fictive utterances has the content that the man in the green velvet armchair is about to be killed by a character in the novel he is reading. To answer the question of what determines the totality of a work's fictive content, therefore, we need to identify what else, other than the contents of authors' fictive utterances, goes to make it up. We have not yet ruled out the possibility that principles of generation like those postulated by Lewis and Walton play some role. However, if they do, they cannot be the only other determinants of fictive content.

4.2 Silly Questions

Walton himself identifies one consideration that appears to favour replacing, rather than supplementing, such principles of generation. He notes that his principles of indirect generation give rise to various 'silly questions' (Walton 1990: 174–83). Consider the following lines, spoken by Othello:

> Had it pleas'd heaven
> To try me with affliction; had he rain'd
> All kinds of sores and shames on my bare head,
> Steep'd me in poverty to the very lips,
> Given to captivity me and my hopes,
> I should have found in some place of my soul
> A drop of patience: but, alas . . .
>
> (Act 2, scene 2, in Shakespeare 1958: 152–8)

If Othello uttered the words above, it would be true (both in reality and according to the mutual beliefs of Shakespeare's community) that he uttered superb verse. Walton (1990: 175) asks:

> How did Othello, a Moorish general and hardly an intellectual, manage to come up with such superb verse on the spur of the moment, and when immensely distraught? Apparently he is to be credited with an almost unbelievable natural literary flair.

This question is silly because it is not one audiences generally ask, or one to which *Othello* supplies an answer. This poses a problem for Walton's accounts of indirect generation, because they cannot explain the interpretative illegitimacy of this question. If either of those accounts is right, this should be a perfectly legitimate question for audiences to ask, since each entails that it is fictional in *Othello* that Othello utters superb verse on the spur of the moment when very distressed. Both of Lewis's accounts also have this consequence.

Many works of fiction raise silly questions: narrators in novels often recount in great detail events that occurred many years ago (why do they have such excellent memories?); characters in novels are often represented as speaking in complete, grammatical sentences (why are they so articulate?); and English novels set in countries in which English is not widely spoken often represent all their characters as speaking fluently in English (where did they learn English; why don't they speak the local language?). In all these cases, were things as they are represented as being, things would be true (either in reality, or according to the mutual beliefs of the author's community) that are not fictional in the works that give rise to these questions.

Walton canvasses a variety of different ways in which one might explain the illegitimacy of these questions in a manner consistent with his accounts of indirect generation. One is to allow that it is fictional in *Othello* that Othello speaks in verse, but to take this aspect of the play's fictive content to be unimportant or de-emphasized, and thus as lacking further implications for what is fictional in the play (Walton 1990: 182). However, the adequacy of this solution depends on the availability of a principled answer to the question of under what conditions aspects of fictive content are de-emphasized, and Walton provides no such answer.

Another option he considers is to block the operation of his principles of indirect generation whenever they result in contradictory things being fictional in a work (Walton 1990: 181). To use his example, it is fictional in William Luce's play *The Belle of Amherst* (1976) that Emily Dickinson is very shy and reclusive, although it is part of the play's directly generated content that she speaks constantly. Walton's principles of indirect generation therefore have the consequence that Emily Dickinson is not shy at all, since someone who talks as much as it is fictional in *The Belle of Amherst* that Emily Dickinson talks would not be shy, and would be not be so according to the mutual beliefs of Luce's society. As Walton acknowledges, this raises the problem of at which point the principles of indirect generation should be blocked: at precisely the point at which they would otherwise generate a contradiction, or at some point earlier? Without an independently motivated way of modifying either Lewis's or Walton's principles of generation so that they do not raise silly questions, the problem posed by such questions suggests that we should reject both Lewis's and Walton's principles of generation.

4.3 Authors' Intentions to Elicit Effects in their Audiences

Before concluding that we should reject such principles, however, it is important to identify the assumptions about directly generated fictive content that underlie both of the solutions Walton countenances. Both are premised on the assumption that *Othello* has the directly generated content that Othello speaks lines of blank verse and that *The Belle of Amherst* has the directly generated content that Emily Dickinson is loquacious. In this section, I will argue that it is neither fictional in *Othello* that Othello speaks lines of blank verse, nor fictional in *The Belle of Amherst* that Emily Dickinson is loquacious. This shows the problem of silly questions to be more tractable than it might at first appear.

Silly questions are not invariably silly. Sometimes, shrewd audiences will ask such questions in response to works of fiction, and the answers to them will reveal aspects of what is fictional in those works. It could be fictional in an English novel set in a country in which English is not widely spoken that the characters represented speak fluently in English because they are the children of English immigrants, or because they refuse to speak the local language for political reasons. Whether or not certain questions are silly therefore depends on the context at hand. In a different context, a fictive utterance of the same words as Shakespeare uttered *could* make it fictional that someone speaks in blank verse.

This suggests the possibility of explaining the conditions under which such questions are silly by appeal to context-sensitive rules of the kind identified in Section 3.5. There, I distinguished two ways in which the code model can accommodate the context-sensitivity of the contents of fictive utterances: by picking out the utterances whose contents they govern by features of the contexts in which they are produced, and by ascribing contents to them indexically, by appeal to features of those contexts. Consistent with the first of these two ways of accommodating context-sensitivity, Walton (1990: 183) notes:

> A decision to disallow anomalous fictional truths is especially plausible when it is evident that there are other reasons for the presence in the work of the features that appear to generate them—when, for instance, they are needed to make the fictional world accessible to the audience, or to enhance appreciators' games of make-believe... If there is another ready explanation for the artist's inclusion of a feature that appears to generate a given fictional truth, it may not seem that he meant especially to have it generated. And *this* may argue against recognizing that it is generated.

I agree with Walton that whether or not a given feature of a work of fiction is relevant to determining what is fictional in that work depends on whether or not there is some other reason for that feature's presence in the work. Often, authors make fictive utterances of particular representations, not solely because they want to communicate imaginings with certain contents, but also to secure certain effects in their audiences. For example, authors often represent characters in novels as speaking in complete, grammatical sentences in order to make their conversations intelligible to readers. English language novelists often represent characters in non-English speaking places as speaking fluent English so as to enable their English-speaking readers to understand what those characters say. Shakespeare plausibly used blank verse to represent Othello's speech in order to elicit an aesthetic response in his audience. This suggests that some of the content-determining rules of fiction identify the utterances whose contents they govern partly by the effects that their authors intend to elicit in their audiences by means of those utterances.

Different rules govern the contents of utterances such as Shakespeare's and Luce's than those that would govern the contents of some other fictive utterances of the same representations. Which rule governs a fictive utterance of a representation sometimes depends on the effects that utterance is intended to elicit in its audience. Rules that are sensitive to the intended effects of the utterances they govern have the following form:

If an author utters representation R with the intention of eliciting effect Y, imagine X.

This is not a closet form of intentionalism about the contents of fictive utterances. That is, it does not take the contents of the prescribed imaginative responses to utterances of representations of type Z to be determined, even partly, by the imaginative responses their authors intended to elicit by those utterances. The intentions to which the rules appeal are not intentions to elicit imaginings with particular contents. They pertain to the *manner* in which imaginings are communicated, not to the nature of the imaginings communicated. For example, they are intentions that imaginings (whatever their contents) be accessible to audiences, or that imaginings (whatever they are) be communicated in a way that will elicit an aesthetic response.

Although rules of this form give authors' intentions a role in determining the contents of their fictive utterances, it is not the case, according to these rules, that the fictive utterances they govern have the contents they do because their authors intended them to have those contents. Moreover, the intentions at issue help constrain the contents of fictive utterances only given the rules that ascribe this content-determining role to them. Without the rules, these intentions would be irrelevant to content determination.

Let us take the case of Luce's *The Belle of Amhurst* first. Many of the utterances by which Luce produced this work are plausibly governed by a rule that is roughly as follows:

If an author utters a representation of character c as making an utterance with content T with the intention to make c's thoughts accessible to her audience, imagine that c thinks T.

The rule is only *roughly* as described. As with the other rules I will identify in this section, the specification of this rule may need to be finessed in order to exclude additional intentions that might accompany the author's intention to make *c*'s thoughts accessible to her audience. These further intentions might make it appropriate to imagine, not just that *c* thinks T, but also that *c* makes an utterance with content T. For example, an author might intend to make a character's thoughts accessible to her audience *by* making the contents of that character's speech accessible to them. To accommodate this, the rule could be amended to require the relevant intention to comprise a sufficient explanation of the nature of the representation uttered. Alternatively, it could be supplemented by a further rule according to which, if an author utters the same representation with the intention to make the contents of *c*'s speech accessible to her audience, audiences are to imagine that *c* makes an utterance with content T. On this last strategy, if an author's fictive utterance is produced with both intentions, it is governed by two rules, each of which ascribes a different content to it. Consequently, the content-determining rules that govern the utterance jointly prescribe imagining both things in response to it. In what follows, I remain neutral regarding which approach is best.

It is important to recognize that the precise content T of *c*'s thoughts might be determined independently, by further content-determining rules of fiction. The rules of fiction can have an iterative structure. That is, the imagining X prescribed by one content-determining rule can be part of the specification of the type of representation Z to which another such rule appeals.

In many of the utterances by which Luce produced *The Belle of Amhurst*, he represents Emily Dickinson as making utterances with certain contents with the sole intention to make her thoughts accessible to his audience. Consequently, the rules that determine the contents of those utterances prescribe us to imagine that Emily Dickinson entertains certain thoughts, but not that she utters the words that Luce represents her as uttering. Similarly, if an author represents a character in a film as verbally representing her thoughts in a voiceover solely in order to inform her audience of the character's thoughts, it is not part of the content of her fictive utterance that the character speaks her thoughts aloud.

Similar rules govern the fictive utterances of authors who represent narrators in novels as recounting in great detail events that occurred many years ago solely in order to apprise audiences of the historical background to their stories. The rule that governs such utterances is something like the following:

If an author utters a representation of a narrator n as asserting that event e occurred, with the intention to make what, fictionally, has already happened accessible to her audience, imagine that e occurred.

This rule prescribes audiences to imagine that *e* occurred, but it does not prescribe them to imagine either that *n* makes utterances with the content that *e* occurred or that *n* remembers that *e* occurred. When authors produce utterances of such representations solely in order to make events that are fictionally in the past accessible to audiences, silly questions such as that of why narrators have such excellent memories simply do not arise.

To understand why it is not fictional in *Othello* that Othello speaks in blank verse, we need to appeal to rules that are more complex in form. In particular, we need rules that combine the two forms of context-sensitivity identified in Section 3.5. In other words, we need rules of the basic form:

If an author utters representation R with the intention of eliciting effect Y, imagine X, where X is the content that a non-fictive utterance of R would communicate if it were made in context C.

We can build on this basic form to provide a rough characterization of the rule that governs Shakespeare's fictive utterance of the passage quoted by elaborating the variables as follows:

R: a representation with the content that character *a* utters representation S with content T

Y: an aesthetic response

X: that *a* utters representation V with content T, where V is a representation of whichever type a person of the type that, fictionally, *a* is would utter in C.

C: the internal, fictional context.

Such a rule prescribes audiences to imagine that Othello utters words with the same meaning as those Shakespeare represents him as uttering, but does not prescribe them to imagine that Othello utters the very words that Shakespeare represents him as uttering. Rather, it prescribes them to imagine that Othello utters whatever words a Moorish prince living in Venice in the early modern era would use to convey that meaning.

A similar rule also governs fictive utterances that are intended to communicate the contents of characters' speech in a manner that is accessible to audiences. Consider the following excerpt from Jean Rhys's novel, *Good Morning Midnight* (1939):

> 'Le peintre!' he says. 'Il est fou, le peintre. . . . Did you like him?'
> 'Yes, I liked him very much.'
> He lays his gloves carefully down on the table.
> 'Will you have a coffee, madame?'
> 'No, I'll have a brandy, please.'
> He looks anxious, orders the brandy and a coffee for himself. God, this is awful!
> 'Le peintre,' he says, 'he's mad. I don't know why he has been so impolite, but it's just what he would do . . .'   (Rhys 2019: 84)

In this passage, the male character's speech appears to alternate between French and English, even within the same sentence. However, it is not part of the content of Rhys's fictive utterances of these sentences that it does so. The rule that governs Rhys's utterance prescribes audiences to imagine that the man is speaking French, with parts of his speech represented using the actual French phrases he uses, and others by means of their contents. Rhys represents the man's speech using a combination of French and English solely in order to convey that he is a Frenchman speaking French while rendering his speech intelligible to her English-speaking readers, many of whom are unable to read other than very basic French. The same rule governs a wide range of other fictive utterances, including those intended to render ungrammatical or inarticulate speech or speech in Middle English or in an unfamiliar vernacular intelligible to readers. In all these cases, the rule prescribes imagining that the characters in question utter words with the same contents as those by which authors represent their speech, but of whatever type would be uttered by people of the type that, fictionally, those characters are.

Walton (1990: 182) thinks there is some strain in denying that Shakespeare's fictive utterance has the content that Othello utters precisely the words Shakespeare represents him as uttering. I disagree. It is fictional in *Othello* that Othello is a Moorish prince living in Venice. Taking it to be fictional in *Othello* that Othello speaks exactly the English words Shakespeare represents him as speaking would therefore raise a host of further silly questions. Moreover, it is not fictional even in those of Shakespeare's plays set in England that characters utter precisely the words by which Shakespeare represents their speech. As the critic James Wood (2008: 25) writes:

who really thinks that it is Leopold Bloom, in the midst of his stream-of-consciousness, who notices 'the flabby gush of porter' as it is poured into a drain, or appreciates 'the buzzing prongs' of a fork in a restaurant—and in such fine words? These exquisite perceptions and beautifully precise phrases are Joyce's, and the reader has to make a treaty, whereby we accept that Bloom will sometimes sound like Bloom and sometimes sound more like Joyce.

This is as old as literature: Shakespeare's characters sound like themselves and always like Shakespeare, too. It is not really Cornwall who wonderfully calls Gloucester's eye a 'vile jelly' before he rips it out—though Cornwall speaks the words—but Shakespeare, who has provided the phrase.

In his comedy *As You Like It* (1623), Shakespeare represents Jaques as addressing to Orlando the words 'Nay then, God buy you, an you talk in blank verse' (4.1.29, in Shakespeare 1971: 64). By doing so, Shakespeare makes it fictional that Orlando actually speaks in the blank verse in which he is represented as speaking. This passage is funny precisely because, although Shakespeare generally uses blank verse to represent his characters' speech, only in this case does his fictive utterance have the content that a character does so. Here, the effect Shakespeare intends to elicit in his audience is laughter. It is essential to his securing this effect that Jaques utter words with the content that Orlando speaks in blank verse. Although the content of this fictive utterance differs in this respect from those of Shakespeare's other fictive utterances, its content is also governed by the same rule that governs the content of Rhys's fictive utterance. It is not part of the content of Shakespeare's fictive utterance that Jaques utters the very English words Shakespeare represents him as speaking, but rather that he utters French words with the same contents as the words by which Shakespeare represents his speech. *As You Like It* is set in France. Both Shakespeare's and Rhys's fictive utterances have indeterminate contents. They make it fictional in the works they help to produce that characters make utterances with certain contents, but not that they utter specific words with those contents.

The specific words an author uses to represent a character's speech can be essential to appreciating the work of fiction she produces even when it is not fictional that the character utters those specific words. Shakespeare might not have succeeded in eliciting in his audience the aesthetic response he sought if he had not used the very words he did to represent Othello's speech. Small changes to authors' fictive utterances may not affect the contents of those utterances but can adversely affect their ability to elicit their intended effects.

Moreover, in Section 4.5, I will argue that, even when the specific words an author uses to represent a character's speech do not make it fictional that the character utters those words, the specific words comprising an author's fictive utterance can still play a role in determining what's fictional in the work she produces, by helping to determine the interpretative fictive content of that work.

In order to conform to rules of the kinds described, and therefore in order to identify the contents of the fictive utterances they govern, audiences must identify authors' intentions to elicit aesthetic responses or to render the contents of characters' speech intelligible to audiences. These are not reflexive, communicative intentions. A communicative intention, recall, is a reflexive intention to elicit a certain response in one's audience, for them to recognize this intention, and for their recognition of this intention to function as a reason for them to respond in the manner intended. Audiences' recognition that an author intends to elicit an aesthetic response or that she intends them to comprehend the contents of her utterances does not function as a reason for responding aesthetically to her utterance or for comprehending that utterance. The intentions at issue are instead ordinary, non-communicative intentions in action. In Section 3.3, I argued that agents pursue such intentions by whichever methods they think are most likely to lead to the satisfaction of their broader goals, whether or not audiences are familiar with those methods. Audiences identify those intentions by drawing inferences to the best explanation of why authors produced the utterances they did on the basis of all the background knowledge that is available to them.

In Section 3.3, I denied that audiences have access to the background knowledge that would be required to identify authors' non-communicative intentions to elicit imaginings with certain contents in their audiences. This does not undermine the claim that audiences have access to the background knowledge required to work out that an author intends to elicit an aesthetic response in them or that she intends to render the contents of her fictive utterances intelligible to them. One crucial point of difference is that, while there are no rational constraints on which imaginings an author intends to elicit in her audience, there are rational constraints on how an author pursues the goal of eliciting an aesthetic response in her audience or of rendering the contents of her fictive utterances intelligible to her audience.

In that section, I agreed with Stock that which imaginings an author intends to elicit in her audience may be rationally constrained by her further goals but denied that audiences always have access to the background knowledge required to identify those goals. However, in contrast to the goals to which

Stock appeals (such as selling lots of copies or improving one's skill as a writer), the intentions at issue here are essentially audience-directed. They are intentions to elicit certain effects *in one's audience*. This guarantees that audiences have access to at least some background knowledge relevant to identifying those intentions.

There is a limited number of effects that authors could elicit in their audiences purely in virtue of their manner of communication. Authors plausibly intend to elicit only some of these effects in their audiences, because it is desirable to elicit only some such effects. While authors could communicate imaginings in a manner that audiences find soporific or irritating, under most circumstances they will not desire and therefore will not intend to do so. Moreover, the effects an author's fictive utterances in fact elicit in audiences often provide them with good evidence concerning the effects she intends to elicit in them. This is not to claim that authors intend to elicit every effect their fictive utterances provoke in their audiences, or that they always succeed in eliciting in their audiences the effects they intend to elicit. To identify the effects an author intends to elicit, audiences need to reason both about whether she is likely to have desired to elicit certain of the effects her utterances in fact provoke in them and about the effects her utterances would have provoked in them under different circumstances: had they been less tired, or more partial to blank verse, or had the author been a better poet.

My account of the rules that govern those fictive utterances that seemed to give rise to silly questions therefore meets the epistemological constraint identified in Section 3.2. In addition, it shows that those utterances do not give rise to such questions. This is because they do not have the contents that Walton took them to have. Shakespeare's fictive utterance of the lines from *Othello* does not have the content that Othello speaks lines of verse, and the fictive utterances by which Luce produced *The Belle of Amhurst* do not have the content that Emily Dickinson is loquacious. Silly questions are silly because they result from misidentifying the contents of fictive utterances. One who asks such questions takes certain contents to be fictional that are not in fact fictional.

4.4 Understanding Works of Fiction

In Section 4.1, I argued that fictive content cannot be limited to the contents of the fictive utterances by which authors produce works of fiction. This raises the question of what else helps to determine what is fictional in the resultant works. General principles of generation such as those to which Walton and Lewis appeal do not give rise to the silly questions they appeared to raise. Consequently, it remains possible that such principles have a role to play in determining what is fictional in a given work, although the case of Julio Cortázar's 'A Continuity of Parks' shows that they cannot be the only other determinants of fictive content. In this section, I will argue that such principles do not in fact play any role in determining fictive content.

Because it is not part of the content of the fictive utterances by which Shakespeare produced *Othello* that Othello speaks in blank verse, Walton's principles of indirect generation do not have the consequence that Othello spontaneously spouts superb verse when immensely distressed. Contrary to initial appearances, silly questions do not threaten to undermine such principles, and therefore pose no impediment to embracing them.

On the model we are considering, general principles such as those posited by Walton and Lewis generate further fictive content on the basis of the contents of authors' fictive utterances. If that model is correct, it would be inaccurate to equate the contrast between the two levels of fictive content with that between content that is directly generated, independently of any other fictive content, and content that is generated indirectly, on the basis of other fictive content. As I have argued, the contents of many fictive utterances are also generated indirectly, on the basis of the contents of other fictive utterances. This is true in particular of fictive utterances governed by rules that specify their contents indexically, by appeal to the internal fictive context in which they are produced. It is also true of fictive utterances such as those mentioned in Section 4.3, whose contents are governed by rules with an iterative structure, which specify utterances of the type they govern partly in terms of the contents that other content-determining rules of fiction assign to those utterances.

There is good reason to deny that further fictive content is generated by principles such as those proposed by Walton and Lewis. Those principles over-generate fictive content (Walton 1990: 148). They take a work's fictive content to incorporate facts about the world or what are mutually believed to be facts about the world that are intuitively irrelevant to the work. For example, the members of Jane Austen's community mutually believed that Australia is in the Southern Hemisphere. Thus, according to their mutual beliefs, were things as *Emma* (1815) represents them as being, Australia would be in the Southern Hemisphere. Consequently, both of Walton's principles and both of Lewis's accounts have the counter-intuitive consequence that it is fictional in *Emma* that Australia is in the Southern Hemisphere. If any of those principles were correct, the fictive content of *Emma* would overlap with that of *American Psycho* (1991) and of any other work in a naturalistic genre more than it diverges.

This consequence is counter-intuitive because audiences are unlikely to attribute to *Emma* the content assigned to it by such principles. Moreover, we do not take this to impugn their competence as audiences. The norms for the successful understanding of a work of fiction do not require audiences to ascribe such content to a work. Indeed, they proscribe it. As Friend (2017: 38) notes, someone who attempted to represent all the contents generated by such principles would fail altogether to understand it. This raises the question of what motivation there could be for taking works of fiction to have contents that far outstrip both those that audiences ascribe to them and those that audiences need to ascribe to them in order to understand them.

We should not be motivated to do so merely by talk of *truth* in fiction or of fictional *worlds*. This may suggest that what is fictional in a work is just what is true in the world of that work, where the world of a fiction is a world incompletely described by the fictive utterances involved in producing it. However, such talk is not to be taken seriously. Truth in fiction is not a kind of truth. That is another reason, apart from the fact that fictions can have non-propositional contents, to prefer talk of what is fictional in a work to talk of what is true in a fiction. Moreover, there are no such things as fictional worlds that contain truth-makers for fictive contents. At best, these are convenient ways of talking.

Some philosophers claim that we must take fictions to have apparently over-generated contents in order to account for certain other, important aspects of their content. Derek Matravers takes this to be true of both fiction and non-fiction narratives. He asks us to consider a non-fiction narrative of a wedding party in the Cotswolds:

> Is it really part of the content of that narrative that there is instability in the Middle East and that the Milky Way is vast? One reason for thinking it is is that the narrative could be supplemented in surprising ways. Someone could joke that the passage to the register being signed in the Cotswolds was as fraught with uncertainty as the passage to a treaty being signed in Jerusalem, or the best man could compare the size of the bridegroom's ego unfavourably with the size of the Milky Way. Such comments, which are eminently comprehensible, would make no sense if the uncertainty in the Middle East or the size of the Milky Way was not part of the wedding narrative.
>
> (Matravers 2014: 82)

Matravers's line of reasoning here seems to be that, because a person who figures *in the narrative* could make an utterance that would be comprehensible only if the Milky Way were vast, we should take it to be part of the content of the narrative that the Milky Way is vast. If Matravers is right, the same would be true of works of fiction. It would be odd for it to be fictional in a work that, by uttering the words 'his ego is as big as the Milky Way', the best man asserted that the bridegroom has a big ego, unless facts about the size of the Milky Way were also fictional in the work.

This line of reasoning is fallacious. I have already argued, in Section 3.5, that facts about the world can play a part in enabling us to understand the contents of authors' fictive utterances without themselves being part of fictive content. This is the case irrespective of whether or not it is fictional that the contents at issue are communicated by characters who figure in the narrative.

We saw this in the case of Chandler's utterance in *The High Window*. It is fictional that these words are uttered by Philip Marlowe, the novel's internal narrator. The rule that governs Chandler's utterance prescribes audiences to imagine the content that a non-fictive utterance of those words would communicate, if it were made by a person of the type who narrates the fiction, in the fictional context at issue. Audiences need to engage in complex counter-factual reasoning in order to identify what such a person would communicate by uttering those words in that context. However, this does not entail that the background knowledge to which they appeal in order to do so is itself part of fictive content.

A better motivation for endorsing principles of generation such as those proposed by Walton and Lewis is that audiences often do take it to be fictional that Dorothea Casaubon has blood in her veins, eats regular meals, and sleeps at night, although Eliot's fictive utterances do not have the content that she does so. There is empirical evidence to support this claim. For example, Deena Skolnick Weisberg and Joshua Goodstein (2009: 72) conducted a study in which they asked participants to read a series of stories and then asked, of a series of statements of fact, whether 'you believe these statements are true of the world described in the story you have just read'. Participants answered by choosing a rating on a four-point scale (definitely true, probably true, probably not true, definitely not true). Weisberg and Goodstein (2009: 75) took parti- cipants' responses to show that 'facts that hold true in reality generally also hold true in fiction, even in stories that are very different from reality'.

In response to works of fiction, audiences often engage in imaginings that fill in details left indeterminate by the contents of authors' fictive utterances. Often, the details they supply are consistent with Walton's and Lewis's principles of indirect generation. There is a widespread tendency to infer from this, as Weisberg and Goodstein do, that the factual details that audiences supply are fictional in the works in question. What justifies this inference? It cannot be that competent audiences invariably supply such details in imagination, for they do not. At best, Weisberg's and Goodstein's experiment shows that they do so when prompted. Nor, as I have argued, is it the case that we take audiences to have understood a fiction only if they fill in such details. It is an interesting psychological question why audiences tend to respond imaginatively to fictions in certain ways rather than others. However, that they do so does not alone establish that the contents of their imaginative responses are themselves fictional.

Friend endorses Walton's functionalist account of fictive content, according to which what is fictional in a work is what it prescribes audiences to imagine. She attempts to reconcile this with the fact that we do not take audiences to violate norms of understanding by failing to imagine everything that is fictional in a work by distinguishing different forms of obligation:

> I will say that a work *mandates* imagining that P if failure to imagine that P would mean falling below a minimum threshold for comprehension. A work *prescribes* imagining that P if we should imagine that P to have a full appreciation of the story. Finally, a work *invites* imagining that P on the following condition: if the question arises and we must choose between imagining that P and imagining that not-P, we are required to imagine the former. What is fictional in a work is what the work invites imagining.
>
> (Friend 2017: 30)

What about a work could require audiences to choose either imagining that P or imagining that not-P in situations in which the question of whether P or not-P just happens to arise? It is difficult to see why works of fiction would oblige audiences to imagine P in situations in which they do not themselves prompt audiences to question whether or not P. In such situations, it seems at least as reasonable for audiences to imagine neither P nor not-P.

Explanations of why works have the functions and impose the obligations they do generally appeal either to the intentions with which they were produced, or to the conventions or rules that govern them. Appeal to authors' intentions cannot help to explain why a work would oblige audiences to imagine P if the question should arise. Authors will not anticipate every question that could arise and will therefore lack intentions concerning how all such questions should be answered. Moreover, while an author could intend more generally that audiences engage in imaginings that are consistent with general principles of generation in response to any questions that happen to arise, it is implausible that authors invariably have such an intention.

Appeal to conventions or rules is of no more help here. If a rule governs works of fiction, one should be able to find evidence for its existence in the form of regularities in our responses to works of fiction that can be explained as resulting from conformity to that rule. However, audiences do not respond to works of fiction themselves by imaginatively filling in details left indeterminate by authors' fictive utterances in ways that exhibit the requisite regularity. Audiences' imaginative responses may supply details left indeterminate by authors' fictive utterances, but precisely which further details they supply will vary considerably. The only regularity is in their responses to external prompts in the form of questions about whether it is true of the world described in the story that P or that not-P. This suggests that, if there are rules that govern their imaginative responses, they govern responses to such questions, not to works of fiction themselves.

There is no justification for the claim that general principles of generation partly determine what is fictional in a work. Denying that they do so avoids the problem of over-generation and clarifies the norms for understanding a work of fiction. If they are correctly and completely to understand a work of fiction, audiences must identify the contents of the fictive utterances involved in its production.

4.5 Interpreting Works of Fiction

What is fictional in a work is not exhausted by the contents that audiences grasp when they successfully understand that work. As Cortázar's 'A Continuity of Parks' demonstrates, things can be fictional in works that are not part of the contents of their authors' fictive utterances. Understanding is not the only activity in which we engage in response to works of fiction. We also interpret them. The task of interpreting a work of fiction is that of explaining why it has the features it does. Whereas understanding is concerned with identifying the rule-governed contents of authors' fictive utterances, interpretation involves identifying the intentions with which it was produced. Merely understanding a work of fiction does not enable audiences to appreciate and evaluate it. In order to do so, they must grasp *why* its author made the fictive utterances she did. Knowing this puts them in a position to appreciate the role that a work's various features play in the realization of authors' intentions and to evaluate the effectiveness of the means authors employed in order to realize them.

The interpretation of a work of fiction can result in the identification of fictive contents that audiences do not grasp merely as a result of having understood it. There is another way for something to be fictional in a work than its comprising part of the contents of the fictive utterances involved in its production. Let us distinguish between the contents of fictive utterances and *interpretative fictive content*. A work has a certain interpretative fictive content if and only if:

1. its author intended to prompt her audience to imagine that content;
2. she intentionally produced utterances with certain features as an instrumental means of realizing that intention;
3. utterances with those features comprise a means of prompting an audience that lacks independent knowledge of the relevant intention to engage in the intended imagining; and
4. those utterances are not governed by content-determining rules of fiction that prescribe audiences to engage in the intended imagining.

It is fictional in *The Secret Agent* that Mrs Verloc committed suicide because Conrad intentionally made a fictive utterance with the content that a newspaper headline reports the death by suicide of a female passenger as a means of prompting his audience to imagine that Mrs Verloc committed suicide, and because producing a fictive utterance with that content is a means of prompting his readers to do so. Likewise, it is fictional in 'A Continuity of Parks' that the man in the armchair reading a novel is about to be killed by a character in the novel he is reading. Cortázar intentionally made a series of fictive utterances the contents of which bear certain resemblances to one another as a means of prompting his audience to imagine this to be the case, and producing such utterances is in fact a means of prompting his audience to do so. Moreover, it is not part of the contents of Conrad's fictive utterances that Mrs Verloc committed suicide, nor is it part of the contents of Cortázar's fictive utterances that the man in the armchair is about to be killed by a character in his novel.

The first of the four requirements listed makes my account a version of actual intentionalism about interpretative fictive content. However, it is a form of moderate, rather than extreme, actual intentionalism. It is necessary but not sufficient for a work of fiction to have a certain interpretative fictive content that it be intended to elicit imaginings with that content. For a work to have the interpretative fictive content that its author intends it to have, the additional three requirements must be met.

According to the second requirement, an author must have intentionally produced utterances with certain features in order to elicit the imaginings she intended to elicit. The utterances in question need not consist solely in fictive utterances. There is no reason in principle why an author should not intentionally exploit authorial interjections with certain features in order to prompt her audience to engage in imaginings that outstrip the contents of the fictive utterances involved in producing her work. For example, she might intentionally seek to prompt her audience to imagine that her characters' lives are unstable and unpredictable by means of frequent authorial interjections in which she deliberates about what fates to inflict on them.

Even when she seeks to elicit the imaginings at issue by producing fictive utterances with certain features, these features need not be limited to features of the fictive contents of her utterances. They may include formal or design features of her utterances. They may also include features of the contents of the representations she utters that are not part of the contents of her fictive utterances of those representations. In the 2016 BBC radio play *My Brilliant Friend*, based on Elena Ferrante's novel of the same name, the actors playing the characters speak in working-class regional British accents. It is not fictional in the radio play that the characters speak in those accents. Like the novel, the play is set in Naples and it is fictional that the characters are Italian. The content-determining rules that govern its contents prescribe audiences to imagine that the characters speak Italian words in a Neapolitan accent. Nevertheless, the accents in which the actors speak comprise an effective means of conveying interpretative fictive content concerning the characters' working-class backgrounds.

According to the third requirement, for an author's intention to prompt readers to engage in further imaginings to make the contents of those imaginings fictional in the work she produces, her utterances must actually serve as a means of prompting an audience without independent knowledge of her intentions to engage in those imaginings. Her intentions must be reflected in this way in her utterances. The fact that an author intended her utterances to serve as a means of prompting her audience to engage in certain imaginings entails that she *believes* that they can do so. However, it does not entail that they can actually do so. For example, an author may not have a sufficiently good grasp of the rules that govern the contents of her fictive utterances intentionally to exploit those rules to make fictive utterances with the contents she intends them to have. If her fictive utterances do not have the contents she intended them to have, this may prevent her from realizing her intention to use the contents of her utterances as an instrumental means of eliciting further imaginings in her audience.

It is consistent with the third requirement being met that an author's utterances comprise a less than optimally effective means of prompting her audience to engage in the imaginings she intends to elicit. They might serve as a means of prompting her audience to engage in the relevant imaginings only if a range of contingent constraints is met. For example, they might do so only if her audience is in possession of certain background information. It is consistent with all four conditions being met, and thus with a certain content being fictional, that an author's fictive utterances in fact fail to prompt her audience to imagine that content. Their failure to do so may negatively affect our evaluation of her work, especially if some other, more effective method of prompting them to do so was available to her. As I argued in Section 2.5, a feature of a work of fiction is a good feature in that work, considered as fiction, to the extent that it works, either alone or in conjunction with other features, readily and reliably to elicit the imagining its author intended it to elicit in the members of its intended audience. However, it is a bad feature in the work, considered as fiction, when it works, either alone or in conjunction with other features, to elicit that imagining in at least some of its audience, but not readily and reliably to do so in the members of its intended audience.

The fourth requirement serves merely to distinguish interpretative fictive content from the rule-governed contents of authors' fictive utterances. When competent authors who grasp the content-determining rules of a fiction institution intentionally exploit those rules to produce fictive utterances with the contents they intend them to have, the first three of the requirements are met. What distinguishes interpretative fictive content from the contents of fictive utterances, when the latter is intentionally produced, is just that content of the former kind is not determined by the rules of fiction institutions.

Although interpretation is concerned with identifying intentions while understanding is concerned with ascribing contents to utterances in accordance with the content-determining rules of fiction institutions, audiences' interpretations of works of fiction are often based on their understanding of them. This is because authors often exploit features of the contents of their fictive utterances as an instrumental means of getting their audiences to imagine interpretative fictive content. When this is the case, audiences' understanding of a work of fiction helps to guide their interpretation of it by apprising them of the means by which its author sought to realize her intention to prompt them to engage in further imaginings.

The intentions that audiences seek to identify when they interpret works of fiction are not reflexive, communicative intentions to elicit imaginings in an audience partly in virtue of their recognition of this intention. For the reasons elaborated in Sections 3.2 and 3.3, audiences lack the means of identifying such intentions. The intentions at issue are instead ordinary, non-communicative intentions to elicit imaginings, which authors pursue by whatever means they take to be the most likely to result in the realization of those intentions. To interpret a work, audiences must therefore draw inferences to the best explanation about which imaginings authors intend to elicit in them on the basis of all the relevant information available to them.

Which imaginings authors intend to elicit depends on their goals. Any information about authors' goals is therefore potentially relevant to enabling audiences to draw inferences about interpretative fictive content. Such information includes, but is not limited to: information about the generic and literary traditions of which the author is aware and which she might want her fiction to conform to or to challenge; issues of particular interest to her that she might aim to address in her fiction; issues prominent in the context in which she was working; the distinctive features of her narrative style; and her anticipated audience. For example, to work out that it is fictional in *The Secret Agent* that Mrs Verloc committed suicide, audiences might draw on their knowledge of Conrad's tendency to kill off the characters in his fictions.

They might also draw on their knowledge of features particular to fiction narratives, the relevance of which Walton and Lewis fail to explain. Knowledge of such features can be relevant to identifying interpretative fictive content for two reasons. First, the means authors employ to realize their intentions to prompt readers to engage in imaginings that outstrip the contents of their fictive utterances will often be influenced by the means by which other authors of fiction do so. Secondly, the significance audiences ascribe to a feature of a fiction narrative can be influenced by the significance that such features have in other fiction narratives. They might ascribe a certain significance to authors' fictive utterances precisely because, in other fictions they have encountered, the contents of authors' fictive utterances have significance beyond that which they would have in non-fiction narratives. Authors' ability to realize their intentions to prompt readers to engage in further imaginings by endowing their fictive utterances with such significance might depend on their audience's tendency to do so.

The contextual information that audiences must possess in order to identify interpretative fictive content need not be equivalent to the contextual information they must possess in order for authors' utterances to prompt them to imagine that content. One might be prompted to imagine a given content without recognizing that one is intended to do so. One must ascertain that the instrumental means authors employ to realize their intentions to prompt audiences to engage in further imaginings are in fact capable of doing so in order to identify a work's interpretative fictive content. However, this does not require one to be prompted to engage in such imaginings. One might lack the background knowledge one would require to be prompted to do so. One might instead work out that those means can prompt audiences to engage in the relevant imaginings by an alternative route, such as testimony by others that it prompted them to engage in those imaginings.

In Section 3.3, I argued that readers frequently lack the resources required to identify authors' non-communicative intentions to elicit imaginings. Indeed, it is a matter of luck whether or not audiences have access to the information required to enable them successfully to interpret works of fiction. The task of interpreting a work of fiction carries a real possibility of failure, because audiences may lack the contextual information required to explain why works of fiction have the features they do. I have rejected the claim that the contents of authors' fictive utterances are determined by their non-communicative intentions to elicit imaginings on the basis that audiences are often able to identify the contents of those utterances when they lack the resources required to identify such intentions. It is implausible that success-fully understanding a work of fiction involves identifying such intentions because audiences' ability to understand a fiction is not contingent on the availability of these resources.

However, audiences' ability successfully to interpret a fiction *is* contingent on the availability of these resources. This explains the tentative and defeasible nature of many interpretative hypotheses. For example, no decisive answer has been given to the question of whether it is fictional in Henry James's *The Turn of the Screw* (1898) that there are two ghosts or that the governess is delusional because nobody has discovered evidence that can establish conclusively whether James intended his audience to imagine the ghosts to be real, the governess to be delusional, or to imagine that *either* the ghosts are real or the governess is delusional, although James's fictive utterances are able to prompt his audience to engage in imaginings of all three kinds.

Interpretation involves identifying intentions rather than ascribing contents to works of fiction according to general principles of generation. Only the contents of imaginings that authors intend to elicit can legitimately be ascribed to a work of fiction as a consequence of its interpretation. On my account, although what is fictional in a work outstrips the contents of authors' fictive utterances, much less is fictional than Walton and Lewis claim. Stock (2017) also advocates a minimalist construal of fictive content. She claims that what is fictional in a work includes all and only the contents its author communicatively intends her readers to imagine. Nevertheless, there are significant differences between our accounts. While she denies that things can be fictional in a work that its author did not intend audiences to imagine, on my account, the contents of authors' fictive utterances are fictional in the work she produces whether or not she intended them to have those contents. Moreover, Stock is an *extreme actual intentionalist*: she holds that the fact that an author intended to elicit an imagining with a certain content by means of her fictive utterances *suffices* to make that content fictional in the work she produces. By contrast, on my account, insofar as authors' intentions determine what is fictional in the works they produce, they do so only when they are reflected in the features of their utterances.

My austere construal of fictive content raises the question of why audiences tend imaginatively to embellish works' fictive content with details left indeterminate by what is fictional in those works. I identified one reason why they do so in Section 3.5. In order to identify the content of an author's fictive utterance, audiences must sometimes engage in counterfactual reasoning about what would be the case if a non-fictive utterance of the same representation were made in a given context. To work out what the content of such an utterance would be, they may need to draw on their background knowledge to flesh out the context at issue with details that would not themselves be part of the content of that utterance. In addition, as Stock (2017: 61) claims, doing so can be a way of identifying the intentions that help determine what is fictional in a work. One way of prompting an audience to imagine a certain interpretative fictive content is to exploit counterfactuals of the kind to which Lewis's and Walton's principles of generation appeal. For example, one might produce fictive utterances such that, if their contents were recounted as known fact, things would be as one intends one's audience to imagine them to be.

It is important to emphasize, however, that this is just one of a wide variety of ways in which one might prompt one's audience to imagine something. In 'A Continuity of Parks', Cortázar conveys the interpretative fictive content that the man in the green velvet armchair is about to be killed by a character in the novel he is reading by using a completely different strategy. He intentionally produces a series of fictive utterances some of which resemble others in content (the estate manager, the green velvet upholstery) as a means of prompting his readers to imagine this. Counterfactual reasoning about what would be the case were things as Cortázar's fictive utterances represent them as being does not help audiences to identify his intentions. Moreover, one is not tempted, reading his story, to embellish it with details in a manner consistent with such reasoning.

It is an empirical psychological question exactly what methods authors can employ to convey interpretative fictive content. In Section 2.5, I argued that Tolstoy made it fictional in *Anna Karenina* that Anna's unhappiness had a certain source partly by his assertion that 'All happy families are alike; each unhappy family is unhappy in its own way'. This constitutes a thematic statement that focuses readers' attention on the infidelity that is the source of unhappiness in Anna's brother's marriage, and thereby on the contribution that Anna's infidelity makes to her own unhappiness. The strategy of prompting audiences to reason counterfactually about what would be the case were things as one's fictive utterances represent them as being has no special status among the range of possible methods of conveying interpretative fictive content. It may be contingently true that this is a method employed particularly commonly by authors, but things could have been otherwise. The method does not constitute a general principle of generation for interpretative fictive content.

We are now in a position better to interpret William Luce's play *The Belle of Amherst*. Walton thinks it is a silly question to ask why Emily Dickinson is represented as talking non-stop throughout the play, although, fictionally, she is shy and reclusive. On the contrary, I think this is an important interpretative question that can help us to appreciate Luce's play. In Section 4.3, I argued that the content-determining rules of fiction are such that, if an author represents a character as speaking solely in order to inform her audience of her thoughts or her experiences, it is not part of the content of her fictive utterances that the character is speaking. While some of Luce's fictive utterances of representations of Emily Dickinson speaking are governed by such a rule, not all of them are. Luce does not invariably represent Emily Dickinson as speaking just in order to make her thoughts accessible to the play's audience or to apprise them of her experiences. At various points in the play, he represents her as explicitly addressing an audience. At one point, for example, she responds to her audience's supposed request for her cake recipe by reciting it, and then repeating her recitation in case it had initially been too quick. It is fictional in *The Belle of Amherst* that, at least some of the time, Emily Dickinson talks to an audience.

This does not generate the contradictory fictive content that worried Walton. It is not fictional in *The Belle of Amherst* that Emily Dickinson is both shy and reclusive and extraordinarily outgoing because it is not fictional that she is extraordinarily outgoing. It is fictional that she addresses an audience only some of the time. This raises the question of why Luce made *any* fictive utterances with the content that Emily Dickinson addresses an audience, given that it is also fictional in *The Belle of Amherst* that she is shy and retiring. The reason is that this was the best means available of capturing Emily Dickinson's distinctive voice, expressed in her voluminous written correspondence with friends, many of whom her shy and retiring nature prevented her from actually meeting. A play in which it is fictional that Emily Dickinson composes, dictates, or reads her letters aloud would make poor theatre. By writing a play in which she verbally addresses an unseen and unobtrusive audience, Luce was able simultaneously to engage his own audience, and to convey Dickinson's distinctive conversational voice.

Conclusion

In this chapter, I have argued that a work's fictive content consists in the contents of the fictive utterances by which it was produced, together with the interpretative fictive content that its author intentionally conveys. Contrary to Walton's and Lewis's accounts of generation, I have argued that there are no general principles that determine interpretative fictive content on the basis of the contents of authors' fictive utterances. The instrumental means that authors employ successfully to prompt audiences to engage in the imaginings they intend to elicit can vary markedly from case to case.

My account of fictive content is much more austere than most rival conceptions, and better reflects actual interpretative practice. Audiences must often appeal to contextual information in order to identify both the contents of authors' fictive utterances and the interpretative fictive content of the works they produce, but such information is not itself part of fictive content. Indeed, while this contextual information sometimes consists in facts about the world of the kind that Walton and Lewis take to be among the indirectly generated contents of works of fiction, it can also consist in facts about artistic traditions and particular artists' oeuvres that, if included in the contents of works of fiction, would render them incoherent. It would distort the content of *The Secret Agent*, for example, to take it to be fictional that Conrad had a tendency to kill off the characters in his novels.

I am an anti-intentionalist about the contents of fictive utterances. That is, I deny that fictive utterances ever have the contents they do because their authors intend them to elicit imaginings with those contents. However, I am a moderate actual intentionalist about interpretative fictive content. The fact that an author intended her fictive utterances to prompt her audience to engage in imaginings whose contents outstrip those of her fictive utterances can make those contents fictional in the work she produces. However, it can do so only on two conditions. First, her utterances must actually have the features by means of which she intended them to elicit those imaginings. Secondly, fictive utterances with those features must comprise a means of prompting an audience to engage in the imaginings in question.

5

Fictional Entities

Introduction

Let us now turn to the second distinctive feature of the coordination problems posed by the communication of imaginings. Recall that communication, as we are construing it, is a process involving two agents, in which the first agent modifies the physical environment of the second and, as a result, the second agent constructs a mental representation similar to one possessed by the first. To communicate a specific thought to an audience, therefore, one must modify that audience's environment so as to elicit in them a specific thought, such that we would legitimately judge it to identify (in the ontologically neutral sense identified in Section 1.1) the same entity or entities as one's own. In Section 2.2, I argued that solutions to the coordination problems posed by the communication of specific beliefs could be adequate to the vast majority of our communicative projects even if they did not solve the problem posed by the communication of specific beliefs that lack referents. By contrast, solutions to the coordination problems posed by the communication of specific imaginings would not be adequate to the majority of our communicative projects if they did not solve the problem posed by the communication of specific imaginings that lack referents.

The account of fictive utterances as declarations that I provided in Chapter 2 suggests an explanation of how fiction institutions solve this problem. Declarations are distinctive among speech acts in being able to create new entities simply in virtue of their successful performance. For example, an act of marrying creates a marriage, and an act of filing an article of incorporation brings a corporation into existence. Declarations like these create new social entities because they are governed by institutional rules according to which the production of utterances with certain features is sufficient for the creation of such entities. I will argue in this chapter that, in addition to making their contents fictional, certain kinds of fictive utterances also create fictional entities. They do so because they meet the conditions sufficient for the creation of fictional entities determined by the reference-fixing rules of fiction institutions.

Fiction: A Philosophical Analysis. Catharine Abell, Oxford University Press (2020). © Catharine Abell.
DOI: 10.1093/oso/9780198831525.001.0001

Effectively, therefore, these rules solve the coordination problems posed by the communication of imaginings that lack referents by supplying referents for those imaginings. The specific imaginings they enable us to communicate do not lack referents, but would lack them were it not for those reference-fixing rules. These rules enable Jane Austen to create the fictional entity Emma Woodhouse by her fictive utterance of the opening sentence of *Emma*:

> Emma Woodhouse, handsome, clever, and rich, with a comfortable home and happy disposition, seemed to unite some of the best blessings of existence; and had lived nearly twenty-one years in the world with very little to distress or vex her.   (Austen 1882: 1)

By creating Emma Woodhouse, Austen's fictive utterance enables her audience to engage in an imagining with the content that Emma is handsome, clever, and rich. More generally, an author who entertains the specific imagining that x is P, when there is no entity, x, to which her imagining refers, can make a fictive utterance that serves to create a fictional entity e and to prompt her audience to imagine that e is P. Once she has created e, the author can engage in thoughts that refer to e and ascribe further properties to e. She can then communicate these thoughts to her audience by means of further fictive utterances that prescribe her audience to imagine that e has the properties in question. When she does this, her audience's imaginings co-identify with her own because they refer to the same entity (in Section 6.3, I will address the issue of the basis on which we judge the author's imagining that x is P to co-identify with the imagining that e is P).

While the claim that authors create fictional entities by certain of their fictive utterances explains how they are able to communicate imaginings that would otherwise lack referents, it raises further philosophical problems. These problems arise because there are two different perspectives we can take on the content of a work of fiction. We can take an *internal* perspective on a work, and engage imaginatively with its content, focusing on what is represented. Alternatively, we can take an *external* perspective on it, from which we construe it as an authorial construct, and focus on its manner of representation (cf. Lamarque and Olsen 1994: 144). Each perspective involves a different kind of thought and talk about fiction. The internal perspective involves internal thought and talk about works of fiction, in which audiences engage imaginatively with their contents, and ascribe to Emma Woodhouse such properties as *being a young woman of considerable intelligence*. By contrast, the external perspective involves external thought and talk about fictions, in which audiences construe works of fiction as authorial constructs. From this perspective, they ascribe to Emma Woodhouse such properties as *being the fictional entity created by Jane Austen's fictive utterance of the opening lines of Emma* and *being an engaging character.*

While the two sets of properties can overlap, the properties we ascribe to characters in fiction when we think and talk about them from an internal perspective generally differ from those we ascribe to them when we do so from an external perspective. In what follows, I will talk of fictional entities as *exhibiting* certain properties from an internal perspective and others from an external perspective. The properties they exhibit from each perspective are those that it is correct to ascribe to them from each perspective. This raises the problem of which properties they actually possess. The properties they exhibit from an internal perspective are often incompatible with those they exhibit from an external perspective. A single entity cannot be both a woman and created by a fictive utterance. Consequently, fictional entities cannot possess all the properties they exhibit.

A further problem concerns the identity conditions for fictional entities. From a perspective internal to Jean Rhys's novel *Wide Sargasso Sea* (1966), the fictional entity Antoinette Cosway is identical to Bertha Mason of Charlotte Brontë's *Jane Eyre* (1847). However, from an external perspective, the two fictional entities are distinct: for example, one was created by Charlotte Brontë, while the other was created by Jean Rhys. The properties we ascribe to fictional entities from each perspective also suggest different ways of individuating them. Sometimes, we distinguish between fictional entities from an internal perspective, but do not do so from an external perspective. For example, an author might make a fictive utterance with the content that a given character has three very bossy brothers, but never mention them again. Considered from an internal perspective, there are three distinct brothers. Considered from an external perspective, however, there is no property that any brother exhibits that the three brothers do not, on the basis of which one could distinguish one brother from the others. This raises the problem of how many fictional entities the author creates by her fictive utterance. In addition to explaining which properties fictional entities actually possess, any adequate realist account must explain what the identity conditions for fictional entities are, and how they are individuated.

In this chapter, I will develop a realist account that meets these challenges. I will begin, in Section 5.1, by explaining how the regulative rules of institutions enable the creation of social entities. In Section 5.2, I will draw on this account of the creation of social entities to identify the existence conditions for fictional entities. I will argue that there are two distinct ways in which authors can create fictional entities, one of which results in fictional entities that are constituted by other things, and one of which does not. When there is something that constitutes a fictional entity, the properties of that thing help to determine the contents of fictive utterances that refer to the fictional entity in question.

In Section 5.3, I will distinguish the metaphysical grounds for facts about the existence of fictional entities, which are determined by the rules of fiction institutions, from the anchors that put those rules in place. The existence of fictional entities depends metaphysically on both the grounds and the anchors for facts about their existence. I will argue that there is nothing metaphysically objectionable about either the grounds or the anchors for facts about the existence of fictional entities.

In Section 5.4, I will give an account of the nature of fictional entities. I will argue that the properties they actually possess are those they exhibit from an external perspective. It is merely fictional that they possess the properties they exhibit from an internal perspective. In Section 5.5, I describe the identity and individuation conditions for fictional entities. Because the properties fictional entities possess are those they exhibit from an external perspective, I argue that their identity and individuation conditions are also determined entirely from this perspective. Finally, in Section 5.6, I compare my account of fictional entities with Amie Thomasson's account of fictional entities as abstract artefacts and argue that, despite obvious similarities, there are fundamental metaphysical differences between our accounts.

5.1 Existence and Constitution Conditions for Social Entities

On the account I will defend, fictional entities, like marriages and corporations, are social entities created by declarations governed by the rules of institutions. To identify the conditions that must be met for a fictional entity to exist, and to determine what kinds of things fictional entities are, therefore, we first need to know how institutional rules enable agents to create social entities.

Social entities have normative attributes. They can confer rights or impose obligations. For example, £10 notes entitle those who possess them to exchange them for goods and services, and laws mandate conformity. Sometimes they can also limit obligations, as in the case of Limited Liability Corporations (LLCs), which limit their members' personal liability for the company's debts or other liabilities. Following Guala, I have construed insti-tutions as consisting in systems of regulative rules with the conditional form 'if X, then do Z.' Such rules capture the normative import of something's being X by prescribing certain responses to situations in which these X conditions are met. However, because they make no mention of social entities, they do not make it clear either how institutional rules enable the creation of social entities or what role such entities play in securing the prescribed responses.

Frank Hindriks argues that social entities have their normative attributes in virtue of status rules that specify that they have those attributes (Hindriks 2009). For example, money is to be used as a means of exchange because there is a status rule 'money is to be used as a means of exchange', which assigns that status to it. Likewise, Limited Liability Companies (LLCs) preclude their owners from being held personally liable for the company's debts or liabilities in many circumstances because there is a status rule 'LLCs proscribe holding their members personally liable for [certain] actions'. Status rules help regulate agents' actions by instructing them how to respond to social entities of the relevant type.

Hindriks argues that we can construe some regulative institutional rules as conjoining conditions sufficient for the existence of social entities of a given type with a status rule specifying their normative attributes. For example, we can understand the regulative rule 'if something is a piece of paper with specific physical features and a certain history of production, use it a means of exchange' as conjoining conditions sufficient for the existence of money with the status rule specifying the normative attributes of money:

If something is a piece of paper with specific physical features and a certain history of production, it is money, and money is to be used as a means of exchange.

However, Hindriks argues that participants in the institution of money do not need to represent this conjunction of rules in order for there to be such a thing as money and for it to serve as means of exchange. Instead, he argues, they need only represent the regulative rule:

If a piece of paper has specific physical features and a certain history of production, use it as a means of exchange.

It is important that participants in institutions mentally represent these regulative rules. If they did not do so, such rules could not serve as external correlation devices that help them to coordinate on equilibrium solutions to coordination problems. Regulative rules function as external correlation devices because they actually influence participants' behaviour and do not merely describe it. For such rules to play this causal role, participants must mentally represent those rules either tacitly or explicitly. Nevertheless, all kinds of institutional statuses, such as that of being money, can exist without our mentally representing them as existing. Moreover, they can exist without participants having the concepts that would be required to represent them as existing, so long as they represent regulative rules that capture their existence conditions and normative attributes (Hindriks 2009: 270).

It is important to recognize two different ways in which a regulative rule of a social institution could capture the existence conditions and normative attributes of social entities of a given kind. As it has been elaborated, the rule that captures the existence conditions and normative attributes of money has the form:

If X, X is Y, and Y has normative status Z.

Rules with this form implicitly assume that the conditions sufficient for the existence of an entity of type Y also suffice for Y to be constituted by an entity of type X. If X (a piece of paper with certain physical properties and a certain history of production), is Y (money), it is sufficient for something to constitute money that it meets conditions X. It is also sufficient for money to exist that something meets conditions X. However, as Brian Epstein argues, the conditions sufficient for the existence of a social entity of a given kind may come apart from the conditions sufficient for its being constituted by an entity of a given kind. He gives the example of the US Supreme Court. He argues that, while the conditions sufficient for the Supreme Court to be constituted by a certain set of people include the conditions sufficient for the Supreme Court to exist, the converse is not the case. The existence of the Supreme Court may instead be contingent on the occurrence of a certain event, such as the commissioning of its first member. In this case, the rule that specifies conditions sufficient for the existence of the Supreme Court states that, if someone has received a commission as the first Supreme Court justice at *t* or earlier, the Supreme Court exists at *t* (Epstein 2015: 160). Rules such as these, which specify conditions sufficient for the existence of an entity without specifying conditions sufficient for its being constituted by some entity or entities, have the form *if X, Y exists*.

The fact that the existence conditions for social entities of a given type can come apart from their constitution conditions shows that social entities can exist even when there is nothing that constitutes them. Supposing the conditions sufficient for the existence of the Supreme Court to be as just described, the Supreme Court can exist even when it has no members. If, for example, all its members resigned *en masse*, the Supreme Court would continue to exist during the intervening period before new members were appointed. Facts about the existence of natural objects, such as rocks, are more tightly tied to facts about their constitution. A rock does not have all its parts essentially. If someone chips a piece off a rock, it still exists, although its constitution changes. However, the rock cannot exist without there being something that constitutes it. By contrast, there are few constraints on how the rules that determine the conditions sufficient for the existence of the Supreme Court, and for all social objects, specify those conditions (Epstein 2015: 168). The absence of restrictions on their specification explains the flexibility and power of the social world.

We therefore need to recognize an alternative form that the regulative rules that capture the existence conditions and normative attributes of social entities of a given kind can take:

If X, Y exists, and Y has normative status Z.

The elaborated version of the regulative rule that captures the existence conditions and normative attributes of LLCs has this form. This rule holds something like the following: 'If an article of incorporation has been filed, giving a certain name and listing certain people as members, an LLC exists, and that LLC proscribes holding the people listed personally liable for the actions they subsequently perform in that name.' The filing of that article does not constitute the LLC. Nevertheless, an LLC can exist and can have the normative attribute of limiting the personal liability of its owners as a consequence of agents' actions being regulated by the rule 'If an article of incorporation has been filed, giving a certain name and listing certain people as members, do not hold those people personally liable for the consequences of the actions they subsequently perform in that name'.

5.2 Existence and Constitution Conditions for Fictional Entities

I have claimed that fiction institutions enable the communication of specific imaginings that would otherwise lack referents by supplying referents for those imaginings. They do so because they enable the creation of fictional entities, and fictional entities are to be taken to fix the reference of fictive utterances of specific terms. Regulative rules that enable the creation of fictional entities specify conditions sufficient for the creation of a fictional entity, and assign this normative attribute to the entity thereby created.

To identify the conditions that are sufficient for the existence of a fictional entity and therefore to identify the regulative rules that enable their creation, we need to introduce two technical notions: that of a *specific representation*, and that of *speaker-reference*. The notion of a specific representation is akin to that of a specific term, but generalized to include representations that are not linguistic or not purely linguistic. Specific representations are those whose role is to refer to a particular entity or entities. They may be singular, such as 'my mother', or plural, such as 'my parents'. Specific representations contrast with general representations, which have the role of picking out whichever entities happen to possess certain represented attributes, such as 'the largest pebble on the beach'. A representation can have the role of referring to a particular entity or entities, and thus qualify as a specific representation, even if there is nothing to which it refers (Crane 2013: 140). For example, 'the King of France' is a specific representation, even though it fails to refer.

Speaker-reference is something that speakers do by their utterances, and requires more than merely an intention to refer. As Kent Bach (2006) argues, it is a four-place relation between a speaker, an expression, an audience, and a referent: speakers use expressions to refer audiences to specific things. For present purposes, we can understand it as a four-place relation between an utterer (remaining neutral about whether her utterance is verbal or not), a representation, an audience, and a referent. Although speaker-reference involves an intention to use a certain representation to refer an audience to a specific thing or things, having such an intention does not suffice for speaker-reference. For speaker-reference to occur, an additional, epistemic constraint must be met. In particular, one's audience must identify the specific thing(s) the speaker's utterance is about *as* the specific thing(s) the speaker intends her utterance to be about (Bach 2006: 524). This requires putting the audience in a position to have specific thoughts about the thing or things in question by means of non-descriptive, *de re* modes of presentation that connect the audience to the relevant thing(s) via a chain of representations (Bach 2006: 522).

A chain of representations consists in a series of representations that are causally connected to one another such that each successive representation in the chain is produced with the intention that it refer to the same thing as the previous representation in the chain. Each representation in a chain inherits its referent from earlier representations in the chain. Bach (2006: 528) argues that we can have specific thoughts about things we are perceiving, have perceived, or have been informed of and remember. Although he claims that chains of representation must be grounded in perceptions of the specific thing(s) at issue, I will assume that, in the case of non-perceptible things, the chains can be grounded instead by perceptions of some perceptible manifestation of a non-perceptible thing, such as a perception of (some trace of) the act by which it was created, and that perception of such an act or a trace is sufficient to enable audiences to have specific thoughts about the thing in question.

In what follows, I will not assume that, to refer to an entity by a non-fictive utterance, speakers must invariably speaker-refer to that entity by their utterance. I will assume instead that a non-fictive utterance refers to an entity if it was produced with an intention to share the referent of previous utterances in a chain of representations that ultimately terminates in a perception of the entity in question or, in the case of non-perceptible entities, in a perception of some perceptible manifestation of that entity. However, to guarantee that audiences are able to follow them, the reference-fixing rules of fiction must appeal to speaker-reference rather than to any weaker notion of reference that does not incorporate an epistemological constraint. If an author intends to use a certain representation to refer an audience to a specific thing, but her utterance of that representation does not put her audience in a position to have specific thoughts about that thing, then her audience will not be able to follow any rule that takes the reference of her utterance to depend on what she intends to refer them to.

It is sufficient for the existence of a fictional entity that an author makes a fictive utterance in which she uses a specific representation without speaker-referring to anything by doing so. If we conjoin this existence condition to the status rule that describes the normative attributes of fictional entities, we get the following regulative rule:

If an author produces a fictive utterance of a specific representation R without using R to speaker-refer to an existing entity, fictional entity f exists, and f is to be taken to fix the reference of R.

Participants in fiction institutions do not need to represent this conjunction of rules in order for there to be such things as fictional entities and for them to fix the reference of fictive utterances of such specific terms. Instead, they need only represent the regulative rule:

If an author produces a fictive utterance of a specific representation R without speaker-referring to an existing entity, take the reference of R to have been fixed.

In her fictive utterance of the opening sentence of *Emma*, Austen uses the specific term 'Emma Woodhouse'. Because there is no existing entity to which she speaker-refers by doing so, her utterance meets conditions sufficient for the existence of a fictional entity, and therefore serves to create such an entity. Once Emma Woodhouse has been created, Austen can speaker-refer to Emma by her subsequent fictive utterances. Likewise, her audience can refer to Emma Woodhouse by engaging in either internal or external talk in which they utter further representations with the intention to refer to the same entity as Austen's initial, creative fictive utterance, or with the intention to refer to the same entity as utterances that form part of a chain of communication that can ultimately be traced back either to Austen's initial, creative fictive utterance, or to some trace of that initial, creative fictive utterance. Such traces include reproductions of that initial utterance in copies of *Emma*. Consider, for example, Austen's subsequent fictive utterance of the following sentence:

> The real evils, indeed, of Emma's situation were the power of having rather too much her own way, and a disposition to think a little too well of herself: these were the disadvantages which threatened alloy to her many enjoyments.   (Austen 1882: 1–2)

By her fictive utterance of this sentence, Austen speaker-refers to Emma, the fictional entity created by her initial fictive utterance. By doing so, she succeeds in communicating certain imaginings about Emma to her audience. The nature of the imaginings about Emma that she communicates is determined by the content-determining rules of fiction that govern her utterance of that sentence.

The reference-fixing rules of fiction institutions govern only fictive utterances. Whether or not an utterance is a fictive utterance is determined independently, by the content-determining rules of fiction. To be a fictive utterance, an utterance must be governed by a content-determining rule of a fiction institution. This requires, among other things, that there be a practice of fiction to which audiences' responses to the series of utterances of which it is a part are intended to conform. The reference-fixing rules take which utterances are fictive for granted, and determine the reference of just those utterances.

By contrast, the content-determining rules of fiction institutions take the reference of fictive utterances for granted, and determine their contents, given what they refer to. The reference-fixing rule I have just identified entails that many fictive utterances refer to fictional entities. In Section 3.5, I argued that the contents of some fictive utterances are governed by rules with the following form:

If an author utters representation R, imagine X, where X is the content that a non-fictive utterance of R would communicate if it were made in context C.

Let us suppose, merely for the purpose of illustration, that Austen's fictive utterance of the sentence just reproduced is governed by such a rule. It would distort the content of her fictive utterance if this rule took the content of her fictive utterance of that sentence to be determined by the content that a non-fictive utterance of that sentence *that referred to a fictional entity* would communicate. However, this is not how the reference-fixing rules and the content-determining rules of fiction institutions interact. Rather, the content-determining rules take the referents of authors' fictive utterances to be the things that, *fictionally*, those referents are. Because Austen's initial fictive utterance ascribes to Emma the properties of being handsome, clever, and rich, the rule that governs the content of her subsequent utterance takes its referent to be a specific thing with these properties. Which properties her initial fictive utterance ascribes to Emma is itself determined by content-determining rules of fiction. Nevertheless, there is no circularity here. Independently of the rule that governs the content of the utterance by which Austen creates Emma Woodhouse, there are no properties that, fictionally, Emma possesses. The rule therefore determines its content merely on the basis that there is *something* to which Austen's utterance refers. As Austen ascribes more and more properties to Emma by her subsequent fictive utterances, the fictional nature of the entity to which her utterances refer becomes more and more determinate.

There is not just one reference-fixing rule that specifies conditions sufficient for the existence of a fictional entity. To see this, consider those fictive utterances by which Henry James produced *The Portrait of a Lady* (1881) in which he refers to the fictional entity Isabel Archer. These include his fictive utterance of the following sentence:

On the third floor there was a sort of arched passage, connecting the two sides of the house, which Isabel and her sisters used in their childhood to call

the tunnel and which, though it was short and well lighted, always seemed to
the girl to be strange and lonely, especially on winter afternoons.

(H. James 1883: 23)

Contrast this with those fictive utterances by which David Lodge produced his
novel *Author, Author* (2004) in which he refers to Isabel Archer. These include
the following:

> *The Portrait of a Lady* she pronounced a masterpiece—more ambitious and
> therefore greater than *Daisy Miller*—and Isabel Archer was a triumph of
> insight into a particular type of imaginative, idealising girl doomed to be
> unhappy.   (Lodge 2004: 71)

Author, Author is a work of fiction about the novelist Henry James. By his
fictive utterance of this sentence, Lodge speaker-refers to Isabel Archer, the
fictional entity created by Henry James in producing his novel *The Portrait of
a Lady*. Intuitively, however, the two fictive utterances do not share a referent.
The referent of Henry James's fictive utterance is fictionally a woman, while
the referent of David Lodge's fictive utterance is fictionally a fictional entity.

The problem here is not merely that the properties it is fictional that each
possesses differ. An author could write a work of fiction about the Isabel
Archer of *The Portrait of a Lady* in which it is fictional that Isabel does and says
things that it is not fictional in *The Portrait of a Lady* that she does and says. In
order to do so, there is likely to have to be some overlap in the properties it is
fictional in each work that Isabel Archer possesses. The epistemic constraint on
speaker-reference can be met partly because of the descriptive information
the speaker associates with the specific representation she uses. If I talk about
'my brother Guy', you may be able to identify my brother, rather than
anyone else named Guy, as the individual I am referring you to partly
because I describe the bearer of that name as my brother. Similarly, when
an author makes a fictive utterance of a specific representation, she may
succeed in speaker-referring to an existing fictional entity partly because she
associates that representation with descriptive information on the basis of
which her audience is able to identify that entity as the entity to which she
intends to refer them. Consequently, as Thomasson (1999: 68) notes, it
seems implausible that Sherlock Holmes could appear in a work of fiction
as a rock, a dog, or a town. It is very unlikely that, if an author were to give
the name 'Sherlock Holmes' to something that, in the work she produces, is
fictionally a rock, dog, or town, her audience would be able to identify the

fictional entity created by Conan Doyle as the entity she intends to talk about. In order for them to do so, she would have to represent the entity she names 'Sherlock Holmes' as possessing at least some of the properties that it is fictional in existing works about Sherlock Holmes that Sherlock Holmes possesses.

The problem is instead that the descriptive information on which David Lodge relies in order to speaker-refer to Isabel Archer is fundamentally different from that on which an author who wrote a new novel about the Isabel Archer of *The Portrait of a Lady* would need to rely. Such an author would have to rely only on descriptive information concerning properties that it is *fictional* in James's novel that Isabel Archer possesses. However, Lodge secures speaker-reference to Isabel Archer by relying on descriptive information about properties that Isabel Archer exhibits from an external, rather than an internal, perspective. Lodge's fictive utterance is not about the same fictional entity as James's because it meets the following conditions sufficient for the existence of a fictional entity:

If an author produces a fictive utterance of a specific representation R by which she speaker-refers to an existing entity e, but does not speaker-refer to any fictional entity, considered from a perspective internal to a work of fiction, fictional entity f exists.

Lodge succeeds in speaker-referring to Isabel Archer partly by relying on descriptive information concerning properties Isabel Archer exhibits only from an external perspective. It is fictional in *Portrait of a Lady* that Isabel Archer is an imaginative, idealizing girl doomed to be unhappy, while it is fictional in *Author, Author* that Isabel Archer is a fictional entity whose representation in *Portrait of a Lady* is informed by James's insights into such girls. The Isabel Archer of *Author, Author* is a different fictional entity from the Isabel Archer of *Portrait of a Lady*.

The same existence condition enables authors to create fictional entities by speaker-referring to things other than fictional entities. For example, in chapter III of book one of *War and Peace*, Tolstoy writes:

It was an anecdote, then current, to the effect that the Duc d'Enghien had gone secretly to Paris to visit Mademoiselle Georges; that at her house he came upon Bonaparte, who also enjoyed the famous actress's favours, and that in his presence Napoleon happened to fall into one of the fainting fits to which he was subject, and was thus at the duc's mercy.   (Tolstoy 2010: 14)

Tolstoy's fictive utterance of this sentence is the first time, in *War and Peace*, that he speaker-refers to Paris, to Mademoiselle Georges, or to Napoleon. He speaker-refers, respectively, to a real city, a real woman (the actress Marguerite Georges), and a real man by his utterances of the specific representations 'Paris', 'Mademoiselle Georges', and 'Bonaparte'. However, there are no fictional entities to which his fictive utterances of any of these representations refer. Consequently, his fictive utterances of those representations create the fictional entities the Paris of *War and Peace*, the Mademoiselle Georges of *War and Peace*, and the Bonaparte of *War and Peace*.

Considered in isolation, the conditions sufficient for the existence of the Isabel Archer of *Author, Author* and the Bonaparte of *War and Peace* do not explain how the former is related to the Isabel Archer of *Portrait of a Lady* or the latter to the man Napoleon Bonaparte. The Isabel Archer of *The Portrait of a Lady constitutes* the Isabel Archer of *Author, Author* and the man Napoleon Bonaparte *constitutes* the Bonaparte of *War and Peace*. The existence conditions identified earlier are not only sufficient for fictional entity *f* to exist, but are also sufficient for *e* to constitute *f*. That is:

If an author produces a fictive utterance of a specific representation R by which she speaker-refers to an existing entity e, but does not speaker-refer to any fictional entity, considered from a perspective internal to a work of fiction, fictional entity f *exists and* e *constitutes* f.

Constitution is distinct from identity. Unlike identity, it is an asymmetrical relation. It does not follow from the fact that a lump of clay constitutes a statue that the statue constitutes the lump of clay. Similarly, it does not follow from the fact that entity *e* constitutes fictional entity *f* that *f* constitutes *e*. Moreover, distinct fictional entities can be constituted by the same thing. Napoleon the man constitutes the Bonaparte of *War and Peace*. He also constitutes the Bonaparte of Stendhal's *The Charterhouse of Parma* (1839), a different fictional entity. Constitution is also distinct from *fictional* identity. It is fictional in Jean Rhys's novel *Wide Sargasso Sea* that Antoinette Cosway is identical to Bertha Mason, the character in Charlotte Brontë's *Jane Eyre*. However, this does not suffice for Bertha Mason to constitute Antoinette Cosway, because Rhys speaker-refers to Bertha Mason considered from a perspective internal to *Jane Eyre*. That is, she relies on properties it is fictional in *Jane Eyre* that Bertha Mason possesses to speaker-refer to Bertha Mason by her fictive utterances. Furthermore, it is not necessary for something to constitute a fictional entity that it be fictional that it is identical to that fictional entity, since the fiction in which it constitutes that fictional entity need not refer separately to the fictional entity and the entity that constitutes it in order to posit an identity between them.

Many fictional entities are not constituted by anything. There is nothing that constitutes fictional entities such as Emma Woodhouse or Dorothea Casaubon. However, when they are constituted, fictional entities have distinctive normative attributes. Epstein (2015: 148) notes that, when some object *a* constitutes social object *b*, facts about *b* depend on facts about *a*. For example, facts about the mass of the Supreme Court depend on facts about the mass of the group of people that constitutes the Supreme Court. Likewise, facts about fictional entities depend on facts about the things that constitute them. In particular, facts about the properties it is fictional that a fictional entity possesses depend on facts about the entity that constitutes it. When fictional entity *f* is constituted by entity *e*, its normative attributes are determined by the following status rule:

Fictional entity f, *constituted by* e, *is to be taken to fix the reference of R and, fictionally, to fix R's reference to* e.

Participants in the institution of fiction need only represent the regulative rule that links the conditions sufficient for *f* to exist and to be constituted by *e* directly with the normative consequences of these conditions being met. That is, they represent the rule:

If an author produces a fictive utterance of a specific representation R by which she speaker-refers to an existing entity e, *but does not speaker-refer to any fictional entity, considered from a perspective internal to a work of fiction, the referent of R is to be taken to be fixed and, fictionally, to be fixed to* e.

I have argued that the content-determining rules take the referents of authors' fictive utterances to be the things that, *fictionally*, those referents are. Because Napoleon the man constitutes the Bonaparte of *War and Peace*, those of Tolstoy's fictive utterances that refer to the Bonaparte of *War and Peace* fictionally refer to the man. Consequently, facts about Napoleon the man help determine the contents of Tolstoy's subsequent utterances, in accordance with the content-determining rules of fiction. This means that, although Tolstoy might make different things fictional of the Bonaparte of

War and Peace than are true of Napoleon the man, he can also rely on facts about how Napoleon the man is to determine how, fictionally, the Bonaparte of *War and Peace* is. For example, he may rely on facts about the man's military activities to help determine facts about the military activities in which it is fictional in *War and Peace* that the Bonaparte of *War and Peace* engages. For example, consider Tolstoy's subsequent fictive utterance of the following sentence:

> 'From what I have heard,' said Pierre, blushing and breaking into the conversation, 'almost all the aristocracy has already gone over to Bonaparte's side'.   (Tolstoy 2010: 20)

This utterance makes it fictional in *War and Peace* that the side the Bonaparte of *War and Peace* occupies is the side occupied by the man Napoleon in the Napoleonic Wars. Similarly, in 'The Executor' (1983), Muriel Spark writes:

> I wished with all my heart that I was a strong woman, as I had always felt I was, strong and sensible. I stood in the hall by the telephone, shaking. 'O God, everlasting and almighty,' I prayed, 'make me strong, and guide and lead me as to how Mrs Thatcher would conduct herself in circumstances of this nature'.   (Spark 2001: 181)

Spark's utterance both creates a fictional entity Mrs Thatcher and makes it the case that the late Prime Minister Margaret Thatcher constitutes that entity. As a consequence, the content-determining rules that govern Spark's fictive utterance take its referent to be the late Prime Minister. Her utterance therefore makes it fictional that the mode of conduct the narrator wishes to emulate is that in which Margaret Thatcher would engage in the relevant circumstances.

It is a consequence of these existence conditions for fictional entities that a fictive utterance of 'people from Moscow wear warm hats' creates the fictional entity Moscow if it is not used to speaker-refer to an existing fictional entity Moscow from a perspective internal to some work of fiction. However, a fictive utterance of 'Muscovites wear warm hats' does not create a fictional entity, because it does not involve the fictive utterance of a specific representation. This does not entail, however, that the two fictive utterances have different truth conditions. Because the city Moscow constitutes the fictional entity created by the first fictive utterance, the referent of 'Moscow' is, fictionally, fixed to the city. Consequently, the content-determining rules of fiction assign to that fictive utterance the content that people from that city wear warm hats. Although one creates a fictional entity while the other does not, the two fictive utterances have identical truth conditions.

It may seem strange to claim that authors create fictional entities by referring to existing entities by their utterances. Even those who accept that authors can create fictional entities often deny that they can do so in this manner (e.g. Thomasson 2003b: 148). However, recognizing that fictional entities can be created in this way and can be constituted by entities of various kinds is important, for three reasons. First, it enables us to accommodate the fact that the Isabel Archer of *Author, Author* is a distinct fictional entity from the Isabel Archer of *Portrait of a Lady*. If authors could not create fictional entities by referring to existing entities by their utterances, but simply referred to the entities in question, we would be forced to construe these two fictional entities as one and the same. However, the relation between the fictional entities is quite different from that which would hold between Isabel Archer as described in *The Portrait of a Lady* and Isabel Archer as described in subsequent novels about the very same entity, were there any such novels. While David Lodge can rely on facts about the properties the Isabel Archer of *The Portrait of a Lady* exhibits from an external perspective to help to determine the contents of his fictive utterances about the Isabel Archer of *Author, Author*, the author of a subsequent novel about the Isabel Archer of *The Portrait of a Lady* could instead rely only on facts about the properties it is *fictional* in *The Portrait of a Lady* that Isabel Archer exhibits to help determine the contents of her fictive utterances.

Secondly, it enables us to provide a unified account of the kinds of entities to which authors refer by their fictive utterances. Whenever an author makes a fictive utterance of a specific representation, there is some fictional entity to which she thereby refers. Third, it explains the difference between the properties of Napoleon the man and those of the Bonaparte of *War and Peace*. At least some of the properties that the Bonaparte of *War and Peace* exhibits from an internal perspective depend on those of Napoleon the man in virtue of the fact that the latter constitutes the former. However, considered from an external perspective, the Bonaparte of *War and Peace* exhibits properties that differ from and are independent of those of Napoleon the man, such as that of *being the product of extensive research*.

5.3 The Grounds and Anchors for Facts about Fictional Entities

The existence conditions for fictional entities show that their existence is metaphysically dependent on the production of fictive utterances of specific representations that are not used to speaker-refer to existing entities, or are used to speaker-refer to existing entities without speaker-referring to any fictional entity from an internal perspective. To see on what else the existence of fictional entities depends metaphysically, it helps to distinguish the question of what the existence conditions for fictional entities are from the question of what makes it the case that they have those existence conditions. Following Epstein (2015), we can construe the first question as asking what *grounds* facts about the existence of fictional entities, and the second question as asking what *anchors* those grounds for the existence of fictional entities. The *anchors* for facts about social entities are what put the rules that determine their grounds in place. The existence of fictional entities depends metaphysically not just on what grounds their existence, but also on what anchors the grounds for their existence specified by the reference-fixing rules already identified. If there were no rules specifying conditions sufficient for the existence of fictional entities, there would be no such things as fictional entities.

Epstein construes anchoring and grounding as fundamentally different types of metaphysical dependence relation. He also denies that the anchors for the rules that describe the existence conditions for social entities are among the grounds for facts about the existence of such entities. Both claims are contentious. For example, Katherine Hawley (2017) denies that we need to take anchoring and grounding to be distinct types of dependence relation and, consequently, takes the anchors to be among the grounds for facts about the existence of social entities. We do not need to decide these issues here. What is important for present purposes is the nature of the things on which the existence of fictional entities is metaphysically dependent, not the nature of the metaphysical dependence relations at issue.

I argued in Section 2.2 that the rules of fiction institutions are external correlation devices that enable participants to coordinate on equilibrium solutions to the problem of communicating imaginings. Because institutions solve coordination problems, and because coordination requires agents to be able to predict one another's behaviour, institutions facilitate inductive infer-ences. Guala (2016b: 145–6) argues, on this basis, that the rules of institutions are anchored by the fact that they perform these predictive and coordinating functions. However, the reason the rules of fiction institutions are able to perform these functions is that they are conventions. It is, therefore, more appropriate to construe the anchors that put the rules in place as the common interest participants in fiction institutions have in communicating imaginings and the (actual or merely potential) common beliefs they have about one another that give them reason to adopt the salient strategies provided by the rules of fiction institutions. Such a construal is consistent with my discussion of Lewis's account of convention in Section 3.4.

Neither the anchors that put in place the rules that specify the grounds for facts about the existence of fictional entities nor the grounds themselves involve anything metaphysically mysterious. Nobody should find the existence of fictional entities metaphysically problematic if they accept that authors can produce fictive utterances in which they use specific representations without speaker-referring to anything; that authors can produce fictive utterances in which they use specific representations to speaker-refer to entities without speaker-referring to any fictional entity, considered from an internal perspective; that participants in fiction institutions have tacit knowledge of the reference-fixing rules described in Section 5.2; and that they do because they share a common interest in communicating imaginings and common beliefs about one another that give them reason to follow those rules.

One might wonder under what conditions, once they have been created, fictional entities continue to exist. Thomasson (1999: 36) argues that, once created, the continued existence of a fictional entity depends on the continued existence of either some copy of a literary work about that entity or a memory of such a copy, and on the continued existence of some person or persons capable of understanding the work. I disagree. Fiction institutions *could* incorporate rules describing conditions under which fictional entities cease to exist, just as the institution of marriage incorporates rules describing conditions under which marriages are dissolved and annulled. Such rules *could* specify the grounds for the destruction of a fictional entity to be just those Thomasson describes. But why would fiction institutions incorporate rules specifying such grounds? Certainly, if no copy of any work about a fictional entity or memory of that entity remains, we will not know of its existence. This is a purely epistemological fact. Rules describing conditions sufficient for the destruction of fictional entities would not serve any purpose relevant to the communication of imaginings that the epistemological facts alone do not serve. The superfluity of such rules suggests that fiction institutions do not anchor grounds that specify conditions sufficient for the destruction of fictional entities.

Once met, the conditions sufficient for the existence of a fictional entity continue to be met. The only way in which a fictional entity could cease to exist, therefore, is if the anchors that put in place the grounds for the existence of fictional entities ceased to hold. This would occur, for example, if people ceased to share a common interest in communicating imaginings, or if they ceased to have common beliefs about one another that give them rational grounds for adopting the salient equilibrium strategies provided by the rules of fiction institutions.

5.4 The Nature of Fictional Entities

On the account I have provided, fictional entities are social objects. Some social objects, such as the Supreme Court, qualify as material objects because, although they can exist without there being anything that constitutes them, when they are constituted, they are materially constituted (Epstein 2015: 181). By contrast, fictional entities are abstracta. When they are constituted, fictional entities need not be materially constituted. They can instead be constituted by other fictional entities that are not themselves constituted by anything, or by abstracta of some other type. Fictional entities qualify as abstracta because, like marriages and laws, they lack spatial location. However, like the former, they have temporal properties, such as *having been created at time* t. They do so because their existence is contingent on authors performing fictive utterances with the features just described. Consequently, they come into existence at the time such utterances are made.

The characteristic properties of fictional entities are functional. They have normative attributes that enable them to determine the reference of the fictive utterances of specific representations by which they are created. By determining the reference of such utterances, they enable us to refer to them from both an internal and an external perspective. Fictional entities are able to perform these functions even though, as abstracta, they are not causally efficacious. They fix the reference of the fictive utterances by which they are created because the actions of participants in fiction institutions are guided by regulative rules that capture their normative attributes. They enable us to refer to them from both an internal and an external perspective because we are able to establish chains of communication by uttering representations with the intention to refer to the same thing as previous utterances in the chain. Utterances refer to a given fictional entity when they are part of a chain of communication that can ultimately be traced back to a perception of either the utterance by which that entity was created, or some trace of that act.

The properties that authors ascribe to fictional entities by their fictive utterances and that we ascribe to them when we think and talk about them from an internal perspective are frequently properties that, as abstracta, they cannot possess. For example, when we think about Emma Woodhouse from an internal perspective, we ascribe to Emma such properties as *being a young woman of considerable intelligence*. While it may be fictional in a work that a fictional entity possesses such a property, no fictional entity can in fact do so. Fictional entities do not really possess the properties they exhibit from an internal perspective. It is merely fictional that they do so. Nevertheless, the properties it is fictional that they possess help to determine certain of the properties they in fact possess. In addition to their functional properties, fictional entities possess those properties they exhibit from an external perspective, and those properties depend on those properties it is fictional that they possess. For example, Emma Woodhouse actually possesses the property of *being fictionally a young woman of considerable intelligence*. In addition, fictional entities can also possess such properties as *being the product of extensive research, having been created by author* a *in writing work* w, and *being a vehicle for its author's reflections about* x.

Although fictional entities usually do not possess the properties they exhibit from an internal perspective, we can accommodate the apparent truth of statements made in internal discourse about fiction so long as we understand such discourse as involving implicit appeal to a fiction operator, *it is fictional . . .* and thus as reporting on properties that it is *fictional* that fictional entities possess. It is fictional in *Emma* that Emma Woodhouse is a young woman of considerable intelligence, although Emma is in fact no such thing. Its being fictional in *Emma* that Emma possesses such properties entails its being true that the fictive utterances by which Austen produced *Emma* have the content that Emma is handsome, clever, and rich.

This raises a problem. Fictive utterances cannot themselves be understood as implicitly prefixed by a fiction operator. The contents of fictive utterances *determine* what is fictional in the works they help to produce. Fiction operators do not feature as part of the contents of fictive utterances. Austen's fictive utterance has the content that Emma Woodhouse is handsome, clever, and rich, not that it is fictional in *Emma* that Emma Woodhouse is handsome, clever, and rich. Authors' fictive utterances therefore frequently ascribe to fictional entities properties that, as abstract objects, they cannot actually possess.

As Thomasson (2003c: 212) notes, the reference to Emma Woodhouse in the passage quoted is pure *de re* reference, so the content of Austen's utterance is not that something is both an abstractum and handsome, clever, and rich. However, she worries that it remains the case that the things referred to *de re* are not the sorts of things that can have the properties ascribed to them. This leads her to remain noncommittal regarding whether authors refer to fictional entities by their fictive utterances, or whether those utterances ascribe content *de dicto*, claiming, for example, not that Sherlock Holmes was a detective, but only that there once was a man such that he was named 'Holmes' and was a detective, and so on.

This does not, however, require us to deny that authors refer to fictional entities by their fictive utterances. The fact that fictional entities frequently cannot possess the properties authors ascribe to them by their fictive utterances should trouble us only if there were something defective about such utterances as a consequence. It would be a problem, for example, if fictive utterances purported to report on independent matters of fact. However, they do not do so. They do not even *pretend* to purport to report on independent matters of fact. They are declarations. Their function is to make their contents fictional. This is compatible with them referring *de re* to things and ascribing to them properties they cannot actually possess. The only other reason one might legitimately worry that fictive utterances ascribe to fictional entities properties they cannot possess would be if there were some principle of generation that enabled one legitimately to infer, from the fact that Austen made a fictive utterance that functioned to make it fictional in *Emma* that Emma Woodhouse is handsome, clever, and rich, that it is also fictional in *Emma* that the abstractum Austen created by her utterance of the opening lines of *Emma* is handsome, clever, and rich. However, as I argued in Section 4.4, there are no general principles for the generation of fictive content.

5.5 Identity and Individuation Conditions for Fictional Entities

We have already touched on the issue of when a fictional entity that appears in one work of fiction is the same fictional entity as appears in another. An account of the identity and individuation conditions for fictional entities will tell us both under what circumstances they are the same fictional entity and when a given work of fiction features two distinct fictional entities, rather than a single such entity. These conditions follow straightforwardly from the existence conditions for fictional entities, together with facts about speaker-reference. The utterances of specific representations by which authors create fictional entities fix the reference of those utterances to the fictional entities thereby created. Once they have performed these initial, creative fictive utterances, authors are then able to speaker-refer back to the entities those utterances create by their subsequent fictive utterances. Audiences are also able to refer to them by utterances made in both internal and external talk about fiction, and both authors and audiences are able to think about those entities. They can do this so long as their utterances or thoughts belong to a chain of representations originating with either a perception of the original creative fictive utterance, or a perception of a trace of such an utterance. Fictional entity a and fictional entity b are identical if and only if references to a and to b can be traced back, via a chain of representations, to perceptions of the same act or perceptions of traces of the same act of creating a fictional entity. When the representations in the chain are fictive utterances, the references at issue must be acts of speaker-reference, and must meet the epistemic constraints on speaker-reference.

Once a perception of a creative fictive utterance or a trace of such an utterance is reached, the chain of representations established by acts of speaker-reference to fictional entities terminates and cannot be traced back any further. Consequently, although the fictive utterance whereby David Lodge created the Isabel Archer of *Author, Author* itself speaker-refers to the Isabel Archer of *Portrait of a Lady*, these are two distinct fictional entities, since Lodge's subsequent speaker-references to Isabel Archer in *Author, Author* can be traced back to a perception of (a trace of) this creative act, whereas James's speaker-references to Isabel Archer in *Portrait of a Lady* can be traced back to a perception of (a trace of) a creative fictive utterance performed by James.

The Lord Peter Wimsey of Jill Paton Walsh's novel *The Attenbury Emeralds* is the same fictional entity as the Lord Peter Wimsey of Dorothy L. Sayers's novels, because Paton Walsh's speaker-references to Lord Peter Wimsey in *The Attenbury Emeralds* can be traced back via a chain of representations to the fictive utterance in *Whose Body?* by which Sayers created Lord Peter Wimsey. Lord Peter Wimsey is a single fictional entity created by Sayers and developed by her and subsequently by Paton Walsh over a series of works of fiction.

The fictional entity Superman is identical to the fictional entity Clark Kent. The first fictive utterances involved in producing 'Superman', which appeared in *Action Comics No. 1*, portray Clark Kent's amazing strength. They are followed by a fictive utterance of the following representation:

Early, Clark decided that he must turn his titanic strength into channels that would benefit mankind. And so was created . . . Superman!

(Siegel and Shuster 1938)

Action Comics No. 1 introduces Superman, not by a distinct creative fictive utterance, but as an identity assumed by Kent. It is fictional in *Action Comics No. 1* that Superman is an identity assumed by Clark Kent.

Nevertheless, it does not suffice for the identity of fictional entity *a* and fictional entity *b* that it is fictional in some work that one is identical to the other. Being fictionally identical and being identical are distinct properties that can, but need not, be co-instantiated. The fictional entity Antoinette Cosway of Jean Rhys's novel *Wide Sargasso Sea* is not identical to Bertha Mason of Charlotte Brontë's *Jane Eyre*, although it is fictional in *Wide Sargasso Sea* that they are identical, because Rhys's speaker-references to Antoinette Cosway in *Wide Sargasso Sea* can be traced back to a creative fictive utterance of her own, rather than to one performed by Brontë.

The same holds for fictional entities that originate in the same work of fiction. It is sometimes claimed, as if it were obvious, that the fictional entities Jekyll and Hyde of Robert Louis Stevenson's story *The Strange Case of Dr Jekyll and Mr Hyde* (1886) are identical. This is not so. Jekyll and Hyde are distinct fictional entities because they are introduced by distinct creative fictive utterances. Stevenson's speaker-references to Mr Hyde can be traced back to the following creative fictive utterance:

All at once, I saw two figures: one a little man who was stumping along eastward at a good walk, and the other a girl of maybe eight or ten who was running as hard as she was able down a cross street. Well, sir, the two ran into one another naturally enough at the corner; and then came the horrible part of the thing; for the man trampled calmly over the child's body and left her screaming on the ground. It sounds nothing to hear, but it was hellish to see. It wasn't like a man; it was like some damned Juggernaut.

(Stevenson 2014: 6)

His speaker-references to Dr Jekyll can be traced back to a different such utterance:

There he opened his safe, took from the most private part of it a document endorsed on the envelope as Dr Jekyll's Will and sat down with a clouded brow to study its contents.   (Stevenson 2014: 9)

Stevenson's fictive utterance of the specific representation 'Dr Jekyll's Will' creates both the fictional entity Dr Jekyll's Will and the fictional entity Dr Jekyll, since the term 'Dr Jekyll's Will' inherits its specificity from the specificity of 'Dr Jekyll'.

Anthony Everett (2013: 206) suggests that an adequate realist account of fictional entities should construe Jekyll and Hyde as identical because it is fictional in Stevenson's story that Jekyll is the same person as Hyde. However, while it is fictional in Stevenson's story that Jekyll and Hyde are the same person, it is also fictional in the story that they are distinct *personalities*:

> My two natures had memory in common, but all other faculties were most unequally shared between them. Jekyll (who was composite) now with the most sensitive apprehensions, now with a greedy gusto, projected and shared in the pleasures and adventures of Hyde; but Hyde was indifferent to Jekyll, or but remembered him as the mountain bandit remembers the cavern in which he conceals himself from pursuit. Jekyll had more than a father's interest; Hyde had more than a son's indifference. To cast in my lot with Jekyll, was to die to those appetites which I had long secretly indulged and had of late begun to pamper. To cast it in with Hyde, was to die to a thousand interests and aspirations, and to become, at a blow and forever, despised and friendless.   (Stevenson 2014: 70–1)

There is no good reason to think that the identity conditions for fictional entities should mirror those for people, even when it is fictional that those entities are people. The tendency to refer to many fictional entities as 'fictional characters' may unhelpfully encourage the thought that they do, since it suggests that the kind of entity at issue is a fictional *person*.

Our judgements regarding the identity of fictional entities are highly context sensitive (cf. Everett 2005; Friend 2014). Sometimes, we are concerned not with actual identity, but with fictional identity. One concerned with what is fictional in *Wide Sargasso Sea* may claim that Antoinette Cosway is identical to Bertha Mason, while one concerned with what is fictional in *Jane Eyre* would deny this. Sometimes, what we are concerned with is not whether *a* and *b* are identical, but whether *a* is *modelled on b*. One fictional entity is modelled on another if and only if, *fictionally*, it has certain properties because, *fictionally*, the other has just those properties. Anoinette Cosway is modelled on Bertha Mason. Jean Rhys makes it fictional in *Wide Sargasso Sea* that Antoinette Cosway has properties such as being of Creole heritage, being brought up in Jamaica and, later, going to live in England, and being referred to by the name

'Bertha' precisely because it is fictional in *Jane Eyre* that Bertha Mason has those properties.

Similarly, the Bruno Antony of Alfred Hitchcock's film *Strangers on a Train* is closely modelled on the Charles Anthony Bruno of Patricia Highsmith's novel of the same name. The two fictional entities are not identical, because there is no chain of representations linking Hitchcock's speaker-references to Bruno Antony back to the fictive utterance by which Highsmith created Charles Anthony Bruno. Nevertheless, they bear a close qualitative similarity to one another. This similarity is a result of the fact that Hitchock made it fictional in the film that Bruno Antony had certain properties *because* Highsmith made it fictional in her novel that Charles Anthony Bruno had those properties.

Everett claims that a realist about fictional entities should take their individuation conditions to mirror the ways they are individuated in the fictions in which they appear. Because it is fictional in Hardy's *Tess of the d'Urbervilles* (1891) that Tess is arrested at Stonehenge by sixteen policemen, he claims, a realist about fictional entities is committed to Hardy having created sixteen fictional policemen, even though he does not distinguish between them (Everett 2013: 191). If this is correct, realists about fictional entities will be committed, unacceptably, to the existence of fictional entities that are genuinely indeterminate in number, since it can be fictional in a work that there is a number of entities without it being fictional in that work that there is any particular number of them. It might, for example, have been fictional in *Tess of the d'Urbervilles* merely that *several* policemen arrest Tess.

However, my realist account does not have the unacceptable consequence that there is genuine ontic indeterminacy, because the way fictional entities are individuated is not determined by how it is fictional that they are individuated. The individuation conditions for fictional entities, like their identity conditions, follow straightforwardly from their existence conditions. The number of entities a fictive utterance creates is determined by the number of different specific terms it contains, each of which meets the conditions for creating a fictional entity. One such specific term results in one fictional entity, irrespective of whether that term is singular or plural.

In *Tess of the d'Urbervilles*, Hardy introduces the sixteen policemen as follows:

> At the same time something seemed to move on the verge of the dip eastward—a mere dot. It was the head of a man approaching them from the hollow beyond the Sun-stone. Clare wished they had gone onward, but in

the circumstances decided to remain quiet. The figure came straight towards the circle of pillars in which they were.

He heard something behind him, the brush of feet. Turning, he saw over the prostrate columns another figure; then before he was aware, another was at hand on the right, under a trilithon, and another on the left. The dawn shone full on the front of the man westward, and Clare could discern from this that he was tall, and walked as if trained. They all closed in with evident purpose. Her story then was true! Springing to his feet, he looked around for a weapon, loose stone, means of escape, anything. By this time the nearest man was upon him.

'It is no use, sir,' he said. 'There are sixteen of us on the Plain, and the whole country is reared.'   (Hardy 2016: 315)

By his fictive utterances, Hardy creates the fictional entity that is fictionally approaching from the hollow beyond the Sun-stone. He then creates the fictional entity that, fictionally, walked as if trained, and the fictional entity that, fictionally, is nearest. Finally, he creates the fictional entity, the sixteen on the Plain. It is fictional in *Tess of the d'Urbervilles* that each of the three former fictional entities is part of the latter fictional entity. In reality, however, the four fictional entities are distinct.

5.6 Fictional Entities are not Pleonastic

My account of fictional entities bears many similarities to Thomasson's realist account (1999, 2001, 2003a,b,c). Like her, I take fictional entities to be contingent, abstract artefacts akin to other abstract, cultural creations. Like her, I claim that fictional entities actually possess the properties they exhibit from an external perspective, whereas it is merely fictional that they possess the properties they exhibit from an internal perspective. I have already noted several respects in which my account of fictional entities differs from hers. In this section, I will argue that there are also more fundamental differences between our accounts.

Thomasson takes fictional utterances to be, not declarations, but acts of pretending to refer and to assert. This raises the question of how merely pretending to refer to something can bring a fictional entity into existence, as she thinks it can do. Her answer relies on a deflationary metaphysics of fictional entities according to which:

> The truth of 'Jane Austen wrote a work of fiction pretending to refer to and describe a young woman named "Emma Woodhouse" (not referring back to an extant individual…)' is, *in virtue of the concepts involved, logically sufficient* to ensure that we can make reference to 'the fictional character Emma Woodhouse'.   (Thomasson 2003b: 148; emphasis added)

Logical sufficiency of the kind at issue holds partly in virtue of relations among concepts, not merely in virtue of purely syntactic rules of logic. Thomasson takes it to be a conceptual truth that, if someone writes a work of fiction pretending to refer to an entity by a certain name, when there is in fact nothing thereby referred to, she creates a fictional entity. This is a fact about our linguistic concept of a fictional entity, she holds, not a substantive metaphysical discovery about the word. With Stephen Schiffer (1996), she takes fictional entities to be *pleonastic*: mere shadows of pretending uses of names, whose natures are determined entirely by the practices that recognize them in our ontology.

Thomasson adopts this view of the nature of fictional entities because she takes us collectively to accept the conditions sufficient for the existence of fictional entities. It is a conceptual truth that, if someone writes a work of fiction pretending to refer to an entity without referring back to an existing entity, there is a fictional entity, because this is the content of an existence condition for fictional entities that we collectively accept, and it is only because we do so that there are such things as fictional entities. Because fictional entities exist only because we collectively accept conditions sufficient for their existence, she claims, we cannot be wrong in thinking that, if these conditions are met, there is a fictional entity (Thomasson 2003a: 589–90). We have privileged epistemic access to the conditions sufficient for the existence of fictional entities.

Thomasson's account has some counter-intuitive consequences. The conditions that she takes to be logically sufficient for the existence of a fictional entity defer to the world, and we can be mistaken about how the world is. It is, therefore, possible that the acts by which Thomasson takes authors to produce fictional entities are not in fact acts of pretend reference (if I am right, they are declarations, not acts of pretend reference, but this is not essential to my present point). Supposing that they are not acts of pretend reference, if we collectively accept existence conditions that make it a conceptual truth that fictional entities are produced by acts of pretend reference, it would turn out that there are no fictional entities after all. This is implausible. In such a situation, there are fictional entities, although we are wrong about their existence conditions.

On the account I have offered, the conditions sufficient for the existence of fictional entities have the form 'if x is W, Y exists'. However, my account does not require us to represent a rule of this form in order for fictional entities to exist as a consequence of those conditions being met. The only rules participants in fiction institutions need to represent are regulative rules of the form 'if X, then do Z', and these rules make no explicit mention of fictional entities. It is true that this requires them mentally to represent conditions that suffice for the existence of fictional entities, even though they do not need mentally to represent those conditions as being sufficient for the existence of fictional entities. However, it does not require them *explicitly* mentally to represent those conditions. As I argued in Section 2.1, regulative rules of the form 'if X, then do Z' can still serve as external correlation devices that influence the behaviour of participants in fiction institutions in ways that enable them to coordinate on equilibrium solutions to coordination problems of communicating imaginings when they represent those rules only tacitly. Agents with tacit knowledge of the reference-fixing rules of fiction institutions do not need to possess the concepts that a theorist would use to specify those rules. Consequently, the fact that participants in fiction institutions tacitly mentally represent the reference-fixing rules identified here does not give them privileged epistemic access to the existence conditions or nature of fictional entities.

Pace Thomasson, if we were mistaken about the nature of the acts to which we systematically respond by behaving in ways that suffice for the performance of the functions characteristic of fictional entities, we would not be mistaken about the existence of fictional entities. Our practices of engaging in certain imaginings in response to certain kinds of acts determine the existence conditions for fictional entities, not our beliefs about either the nature of the acts in question or fictional entities themselves. Determining the nature of fictional entities is a matter not of conceptual analysis, but of substantive metaphysical enquiry into the grounds for their existence, taking our practices as a guide.

Conclusion

In this chapter, I have argued that the rules of fiction institutions enable authors to create fictional entities by making fictive utterances with certain features. When they create fictional entities by speaker-referring to existing entities without speaker-referring to any fictional entity from a perspective internal to some work of fiction, the entities to which they speaker-refer *constitute* the fictional entities they thereby create.

On the account I have provided, fictional entities are abstracta. This does not make them metaphysically mysterious entities that we should reject from our ontologies. The grounds for facts about the existence of fictional entities are limited to facts about what, if anything, authors speaker-refer to by their fictive utterances. These grounds are in turn anchored by the (actual or potential) common beliefs and common interest in communicating imaginings of participants in fiction institutions. Anyone who accepts the existence of such common beliefs and common interests and who accepts that authors can fail to speaker-refer to anything (or to speaker-refer any existing fictional entity from a perspective internal to some work of fiction) by their fictive utterances of specific representations should, therefore, accept the existence of fictional entities.

The characteristic properties of fictional entities are functional. They help to solve coordination problems of communicating imaginings because they have the normative attribute of fixing the reference of fictive utterances. If there were nothing that performed this function, there would be no fictional entities, no matter what participants in the institution of fiction believed about the conditions sufficient for their existence. In addition to these functional properties, fictional entities possess the other properties they exhibit from an external perspective, such as having been created by author a at time t. They do not possess those properties they exhibit from an internal perspective. It is merely fictional that they do so.

The individuation and identity conditions for fictional entities are likewise determined from an external perspective. The number of fictional entities an author creates is determined by how many creative fictive utterances of specific terms she makes. One such utterance creates one fictional entity no matter how many entities it is fictional that the fictional entity thereby created comprises. Likewise, whether or not fictional entity a is the same fictional entity as b depends on whether or not there are chains of representation linking representations of a and representations of b back to the same creative fictive utterance, rather than on whether it is fictional that a and b are identical.

6

External Thought and Talk about Fiction

Introduction

My aim in this chapter is twofold. First, I want to draw out the ontological implications of the fact that we engage in both internal and external thought and talk about fictional entities. Secondly, I want to explain the role that external thought and talk can play in enabling fiction institutions to provide correlated equilibrium solutions to coordination problems of communicating imaginings.

While I have presented my realist account of fictional entities and argued that it has various advantages over Thomasson's realist account, I have not yet provided any reasons for preferring it to its anti-realist rivals. *Prima facie*, there might seem to be good reason to prefer anti-realism about fictional entities to the realist account I offered in the previous chapter. My realist account proposes to explain judgements of co-identification as based on co-reference. However, it cannot explain the basis for all our judgements of co-identification. I argued that an author who entertains the specific imagining that *x* is P, when there is no entity, *x*, to which her imagining refers, can make a fictive utterance that creates a fictional entity *e* and prompts her audience to imagine that *e* is P. Once she has created *e*, the author can make further fictive utterances with the content that *e* has the properties in question. Such utterances prompt her audience to engage in imaginings that refer to *e* and thus co-identify with her own imaginings. This does not explain on what basis we would judge the author's initial imagining that *x* is P to co-identify with her audience's imagining that *e* is P. It is clear, however, that we often do judge such imaginings to co-identify. For example, we judge that the imagining that a specific, non-existent woman named 'Emma Woodhouse' is handsome, clever, and rich, which prompted Austen to write the opening lines of *Emma*, was itself about Emma Woodhouse. If, as I claim, Emma did not exist before Austen began writing, how do we account for the apparent fact that her preceding thoughts were about Emma?

In order to accommodate such judgements of co-identification, I must allow some judgements of co-identification to have their basis in relations other than

Fiction: A Philosophical Analysis. Catharine Abell, Oxford University Press (2020). © Catharine Abell.
DOI: 10.1093/oso/9780198831525.001.0001

co-reference. Moreover, whatever the relation to which I appeal to explain such judgements, it will be one to which anti-realists can also appeal, since it cannot require there to be fictional entities to which authors refer before they make their initial, creative fictive utterances. At this point, it would be sensible to question whether fictional entities are required to explain co-identification at all. Given that some judgements of co-identification have their basis in some relation other than co-reference, one would get a simpler and more unified theory by holding all such judgements to be based on that relation.

However, things are not so simple as this line of questioning supposes. I will argue that, although an account of co-identification in terms other than co-reference is required to explain why we judge the imaginings in which authors engage before they create fictional entities to identify the fictional entities they subsequently create, no anti-realist account is able to accommodate *all* instances of co-identification. In particular, no such account is able to accommodate all cases of the co-identification of fictional entities by internal and external thought or talk. This, I will argue, provides decisive a reason to prefer my realist account.

My second aim, of explaining the role of external thought and talk about fiction in helping to solve coordination problems of communicating imaginings, is important because it might be hard to see how external thought and talk can help to solve such problems. On the face of it, fiction institutions would be just as good at enabling their participants to coordinate on equilibrium solutions to such problems if their participants never thought or talked about fiction from an external perspective and only ever thought and talked about fiction from an internal perspective that reflected imaginative engagement with the contents of works of fiction. If external thought and talk about fiction play no role in solving coordination problems of communicating imaginings, however, the fact that participants in fiction institutions routinely engage in such thought and talk looks very puzzling. I will argue that external thought and talk are in fact very important to enabling fiction institutions to perform their distinctive function. I will argue that external thought and talk play a variety of roles in enabling participants in fiction institutions to coordinate on equilibrium solutions to coordination problems of communicating imaginings. In particular, they play a critical role in enabling audiences to interpret works of fiction; they enhance the stability of those equilibrium solutions; and they enable audiences to coordinate, on the fly, on equilibrium solutions to novel coordination problems of communicating imaginings.

In Section 6.1, I will briefly outline the main form of anti-realism about fictional entities, the *pretence theory*, and explain how it proposes to accommodate the fact that talk involving fictional names appears to be meaningful, and that some such talk also appears to be true. While the pretence theory provides an explanation of this fact, it cannot, on its own, explain our judgements of co-identification. In Section 6.2, I will outline the available anti-realist accounts of the basis for our judgements of co-identification and will argue that none can accommodate all judgements of co-identification by internal and external thought or talk about fiction. I will argue that fictional entities play an ineliminable role in explaining our judgements of co-identification, and that we therefore need to admit them into our ontologies. In Section 6.3, I will argue that this does not also require us to admit mythical entities and failed scientific posits such as Vulcan into our ontologies. We can engage in analogues of internal and external thought or talk about mythical entities and failed scientific posits, and we can judge internal and external thought and talk to co-identify such entities. However, I will argue that this is compatible with their non-existence, because judgements of the co-identification of such entities from the internal and external perspectives rely solely on systematic relations between the properties that those entities exhibit from each perspective, whereas the co-identification of fictional entities does not.

In the remaining sections, I will turn to the role of external thought and talk about fiction in enabling the communication of imaginings. In Section 6.4, I will argue that they play a crucial role in enabling audiences to draw the inferences about authors' intentions required to identify interpretative fictive content. In Section 6.5, I will argue that external thought and talk help participants in fiction institutions to coordinate on equilibrium solutions to problems of communicating imaginings in three distinct ways. First, external talk helps to improve the stability of the rules of fiction institutions by making participants aware of one another's preferences about the means by which imaginings with certain contents are communicated. Secondly, external thought and talk in which participants engage in artistic evaluation and debate can improve the stability of those rules by helping to bring their preferences into alignment when they diverge. Finally, I will argue that external thought in which participants in fiction institutions judge the artistic merits of different imaginative responses to utterances with certain features can enable them to coordinate on ad hoc solutions to novel problems of communicating imaginings by making certain such responses salient.

6.1 Anti-Realism about Fictional Entities

Anti-realism about fictional entities has three main putative advantages in comparison with realism. First, it is thought to be better able to explain the fact that negative existential statements such as 'Emma Woodhouse does not exist' often strike us as true. Secondly, it is supposed to be ontologically more parsimonious because it does not posit fictional entities. Finally, it may be thought to have greater unifying potential than realism because it can plausibly be extended to provide a solution to the more general problem of how we are able to think and talk about things that do not exist. Realists claim that our ability to think and talk about fictional entities is not an instance of this more general problem. Nevertheless, anti-realists can claim that it is bad methodological practice to single out fictional entities for realist treatment without good independent reason for doing so, when a solution to the more general problem is likely to render them otiose (Friend 2007: 154). I will address the first of these supposed advantages in this section, the second in Section 6.2, and the third in Section 6.3.

The most prominent form of anti-realism about fictional entities is that espoused by pretence theorists (Walton 1990; Friend 2007; Everett 2013). Although it is not necessary to endorse a direct reference theory of names in order to be a pretence theorist, pretence theorists are generally motivated by a desire to reconcile anti-realism about fictional entities with direct reference theories of proper names, which hold that the semantic contribution a name makes to a sentence containing it is simply its referent, rather than any descriptive sense (Marcus 1961; Kripke 1980). If this is correct, no utterance containing an empty name can be meaningful, because it cannot express a complete proposition. Pretence theorists aim to reconcile the facts that utterances containing fictional names appear to be meaningful and that some, moreover, appear to be true with the claim that fictional names are empty names. They claim that, when we engage in talk involving fictional names, we are engaged in the pretence that there are entities to which those names refer. Although our talk is not really meaningful and therefore cannot be true, they claim, it can be both meaningful and true *according to the pretence in which we engage*. The pretence theory can also explain the apparent meaningfulness and truth of thoughts that identify fictional entities. Recall that I am using the notion of identification to talk about object-directedness without implying any ontological commitment. According to the pretence theory, although such thoughts are not meaningful and so cannot be true, thoughts that identify fictional entities are meaningful and can be true according to the pretences in which we engage when we have such thoughts.

On such an account, thought and talk that identify fictional entities exemplify or allude to games of pretence according to which they refer and can express true propositions. Our thoughts and utterances will appear to be true, pretence theorists claim, if they either exemplify or allude to games of pretence according to which they are true. When they do so, they pragmatically convey the true proposition that to make such an utterance is an appropriate move in a game of pretence of the kind at issue (Walton 1990: 399).

The apparent truth values of thoughts and utterances that identify fictional entities are not subjective, pretence theorists claim, because works of fiction authorize audiences to engage in certain games of pretence, but not others. Pretence theorists are not committed to any particular explanation of what determines which games of pretence a given work authorizes. Such an explanation may appeal to authors' intentions, or to common practice, tradition, or convention (Walton 1990: 52). Internal thought and talk about a fiction exemplify or allude to games of pretence of kinds authorized by that work. By contrast, external thought and talk about a fiction exemplify or allude to distinct, *unofficial* games of pretence that can be thought of as modifications to authorized games (Walton 1990: 411). These include, for example, games according to which there are such things as fictional entities, and according to which authors can create them in the process of producing works of fiction.

Pretence theorists propose to explain the apparent truth of negative existential statements such as 'Emma Woodhouse does not exist' by construing them as constituting a disavowal of the game of pretence according to which there is a woman named Emma Woodhouse, and thus as serving pragmatically to convey the truth that one who attempted to refer in the manner associated with that game would not succeed in referring to anything (Walton 1990: 425). This may seem to be a better explanation of the apparent truth of such statements than is available to realists about fictional entities, who seem committed to taking such utterances to be false. However, there are ways in which realists can accommodate the apparent truth of negative existential statements. For example, Thomasson (2007: 48) argues:

> If N is a proper name that has been used in predicative statements with the intention to refer to some individual of category C, then 'N does not exist' is true if and only if the history of those uses does not lead back to a grounding in which the application conditions associated with C are met.

On this proposal, if 'Emma Woodhouse' is being used with the intention to refer to a woman, utterances of 'Emma Woodhouse does not exist' are true, because the history of such uses of the name leads back to a grounding in which the name is used to create a fictional entity, rather than to name a woman. By contrast, if it is being used with the intention to refer to a fictional entity, such utterances are false, because the history of relevant uses leads back to a grounding in which the existence conditions for fictional entities *are* met. The explanatory advantage, therefore, does not lie entirely with the pretence theorist, who must find a way of accommodating the apparent falsity of utterances of 'Emma Woodhouse does not exist' made with the intention to refer to a fictional entity.

Negative existential statements, therefore, do not give pretence theorists a decisive advantage over realist accounts. More generally, while any ontology of fictional entities must accommodate our intuitions concerning the truth values of thoughts and utterances involving fictional names, these intuitions are highly context-sensitive. Advocates of any ontological position are, therefore, likely to have to develop supplementary arguments in order to accommodate them. Consequently, it would be a mistake to let this requirement alone dictate one's choice of theory.

6.2 Identifying Fictional Entities

Considerations of parsimony also fail to provide pretence theorists with an advantage over the realist account that I developed in the previous chapter. Arguably, what is really at stake when people contrast different theories in terms of parsimony is the relative complexity of what those theories demand of the world, the idea being that more complexity is less likely than less complexity, if all else is equal. On my account, the existence of fictional entities requires the grounding conditions for facts about the existence of fictional entities to be met and the anchors that establish those grounds to be in place. That is, it requires authors to utter specific representations that fail to speaker-refer to anything (or fail to speaker-refer to any existing fictional entity from a perspective internal to some work of fiction), and requires participants in fiction institutions to have a common interest in communicating imaginings and (actual or potential) common beliefs about one another. Anti-realists have no particular reason to deny that these requirements are met. If they are met, however, the existence of fictional entities follows automatically.

Their existence demands no further complexity of the world. Given the existence of the anchors and the grounds, fictional entities are an ontological free lunch. They impose no further ontological cost.

Pretence theorists need *something* to determine which games of pretence a fiction authorizes. Just as I require rules that determine the contents of fictive utterances and the reference of specific terms used in such utterances, and anchors that put those rules in place, they require something that determines the conditions under which certain games of pretence are appropriate. Pretence theorists say vanishingly little about what those conditions are. Depending on whether they appeal to intentions, common practice, tradition, or conventions, those conditions may end up being very similar to the common interests and common beliefs that anchor the grounds for facts about the existence of fictional entities. However, my account can explain the meaningfulness and truth conditions of *all* forms of thought and talk about fictional entities given only the anchors and grounds for facts about the existence of fictional entities given in the previous chapter. By contrast, pretence theorists require distinct games of pretence, each with their own appropriateness conditions, for each form of thought and talk that identifies fictional entities. Every further, unofficial game of pretence requires further appropriateness conditions. The pretence theory therefore demands *more* complexity of the world than my own account, by demanding further appropriateness conditions for each additional game of pretence.

Even in the unlikely event that the pretence theory *did* turn out to require less complexity of the world than my realist account, this would not give us reason to prefer it to my account. One can legitimately prefer one theory to another on grounds of parsimony only if it posits fewer entities *and* can explain everything that the rival theory can explain. Ontological parsimony is not a theoretical virtue if it is achieved at the expense of explanatory power. As it stands, the pretence theory claims only that thoughts and utterances that identify fictional entities are made within the scope of a pretence according to which there are entities to which they refer. It offers no explanation of *which* fictional entities we legitimately judge such thoughts and utterances to identify. Even those who deny that there are such things as fictional entities must give some account of the conditions under which we judge a given thought or utterance to identify Emma Woodhouse, rather than Dorothea Casaubon. My realist account explains our judgements of co-identification as based on co-reference. If it is to have the same explanatory power as my account, therefore, the pretence theory needs to be supplemented with an account of the basis on which we judge different thoughts and utterances that identify fictional entities to identify the same fictional entities. My aim in the remainder of this section is to show that, no matter how we supplement it, the pretence theory has less explanatory power than the realist account outlined in the previous chapter. It cannot accommodate every case in which we judge internal thought and talk about fiction to identify the same fictional entities as external thought and talk about fiction.

In Section 5.5, I argued that a thought or utterance identifies a given fictional entity if it forms part of a chain of representations, each intended to refer to the same thing as previous representations in the chain, that can be traced back to a perception of the act of creating that entity or to a perception of some trace of that act. Two distinct thoughts or utterances identify the same fictional entity if and only if there is a chain of representations linking each back to a perception of the same act or to perceptions of traces of the same act of creating a fictional entity. For a realist account like mine, explaining co-identification is easy: co-reference is both necessary and sufficient for co-identification.

It is much harder for anti-realists to explain what it is for distinct thoughts or utterances to identify the same fictional entity, since they must do so without positing fictional entities. Moreover, it is not enough for an anti-realist account to explain under what circumstances distinct fictive utterances co-identify, distinct internal thoughts or utterances co-identify, and distinct external thoughts or utterances co-identify, although it must do this. It must also explain under what circumstances thoughts and utterances of distinct kinds co-identify. No anti-realist account of identification meets this criterion.

Everett proposes one such account. He claims that uses of fictional names, complex demonstratives, descriptions, possessives, and mental representations that allude to or exemplify games of pretence according to which they refer give rise to chains of representation in which successive representations inherit their apparent reference from the apparent reference of previous representations in the chain. While none of the representations in such a chain in fact refers, he argues, we treat each as if it were about the same thing as previous representations in the chain (Everett 2013: 93).

He argues that we legitimately judge distinct mental representations or token uses of a specific term to identify the same fictional entity if there is a chain of representations linking each back to fictive utterances that refer to the same thing within the scope of the pretence associated with the fiction they help to produce (Everett 2013: 96). If the fictive utterances to which each leads back occur in different fictions, whether or not we take them to identify the same fictional entity will depend on which fiction is salient to us and whether, within the scope of the pretence associated with that fiction, they refer to the same thing. Thus, if *Wide Sargasso Sea* is salient to us, we will treat apparent references to Antoinette Cosway as identifying the same fictional entity as apparent references to Bertha Mason, although, if *Jane Eyre* is salient to us, we will not. Fictive utterances of different names or specific terms co-identify, according to Everett, so long as they do so within the scope of the pretence associated with the relevant fiction.

This account is problematic, because, as I argued in Section 5.5, whether or not it is fictional that Jekyll and Hyde are identical depends on whether one is concerned with their fictional identity *qua* human beings or *qua* personalities. More importantly for present purposes, this account is unilluminating without an account of the circumstances under which distinct fictive utterances co-identify within the scope of the pretence associated with a fiction, and Everett provides no such account. Manuel García-Carpintero (2018) calls this the 'cart-before-the-horse' problem. He claims that all realist accounts that ana-lyse co-identification as co-reference also face this problem. He is wrong about this. Realists face this problem only if they deny that authors refer to fictional entities by their fictive utterances (for example, because they take fictive utterances to involve only *pretend* reference). I am immune to this problem because I take authors to speaker-refer to fictional entities by their fictive utterances.

García-Carpintero's own account of the basis for our judgements of co-identification cannot explain our judgements of co-identification by external and internal thoughts or utterances. He argues that speech acts take place against a background of presuppositions that include descriptive information that helps to fix the referents of specific representations. Audiences inherit these reference-fixing presuppositions through 'quasi-anaphoric links' consti-tuted by intentions to use referential devices in the way that they are used by the interlocutors on whom they rely (García-Carpintero 2018). In the case of fictions, García-Carpintero argues, these presuppositions originate with their authors, and are merely pretended. He argues that x's thoughts or utterances identify the same fictional entity as y's thoughts or utterances if they identify the same entity according to the pretended reference-fixing presuppositions they have inherited from the author of the relevant fiction. In other words, if the pretended presuppositions of both x's and y's thoughts or utterances were true, x's thoughts or utterances would pick out the same entity as y's.

The problem with García-Carpintero's account is that the reference-fixing presuppositions we make from the internal perspective are very different from those we make from the external perspective. External thoughts and utterances that identify Emma Woodhouse presuppose that what is referred to is a fictional entity, whereas internal thoughts and utterances that identify Emma Woodhouse presuppose that what is referred to is a woman. If the presuppositions of both were true, each would invariably pick out different entities.

While Everett's and García-Carpintero's accounts of the basis for our judgements of co-identification presuppose the pretence theory, this is not true of all anti-realist accounts of co-identification. For example, Mark Sainsbury (2015) proposes an account that has implications for the co-identification of fictional names, when those names are taken to be empty. On the account he offers, there are two conditions that are jointly sufficient for an utterance of a fictional name to identify the same fictional entity as some previous utterance of a fictional name. First, it must be made with the intention to use the same name as that previous utterance. It is consistent with this intention being realized that the same name is spelled or pronounced differently by different speakers. What is crucial for sameness of name is just that it be a copy, even an imperfect copy, of some previous use of a name (Sainsbury 2015: 207). Secondly, both utterances of that name must be made with the intention to identify the same thing as other people involved in the same name-using practice identify by their use of that name.

Sainsbury's account does not answer the question of what fiction entity people involved in a given name-using practice identify by their use of a given fictional name. However, it does suggest conditions sufficient for external thoughts and utterances to co-identify with internal thoughts and utterances. One use of a fictional name, whether in thought (inner speech) or utterance, co-identifies with another if one is intended to comprise a use of the same name as the other, and both are intended to identify the thing that is conventionally identified by uses of that name, irrespective of the perspective from which those utterances are made. This account can accommodate some cases in which we judge internal thought and talk about fiction to identify the same fictional entities as external thought and talk about fiction. However, it clearly cannot accommodate all such cases because Sainsbury's account applies only to uses of fictional names, not to uses of other specific terms to identify fictional entities. We judge utterances of the specific term 'the fictional entity created by Jane Austen by her fictive utterance of the opening sentence of *Emma*' to co-identify with 'Emma Woodhouse', even though neither utterance is intended to comprise a use of the same name as the other.

Tim Crane proposes another anti-realist account of co-identification that does not presuppose the pretence theory. He claims that specific thoughts involve 'mental files' containing bodies of information that the thinker is disposed to treat in a way that enables them to make sense of that information only as being true of just one thing (in the case of singular thoughts) or only as being true of more than one thing, but not of each of those things individually (in the case of plural specific thoughts) (Crane 2013: 159). On this view, Austen can have thoughts about a specific handsome, clever, and rich woman without that woman existing. When she does so, her thought involves a mental file representing a woman and containing the information that the woman is named Emma and is handsome, clever, and rich, which plays a cognitive role such that Austen can make sense of that information being true of only one thing. Crane (2013: 164) argues that two thoughts about non-existent objects may correctly be judged to co-identify when they involve mental files that contain similar information. In such cases, our judgements of co-identification are grounded in qualitative similarity, rather than numerical identity.

Crane does not address exactly what degree of similarity the information in my mental file must bear to that in another thinker's mental file for our thoughts to co-identify, but it will have to be fairly high to accommodate the fact that thoughts can identify distinct fictional entities (such as Tweedledum and Tweedledee) despite involving mental files containing very similar information. However, two thinkers can have thoughts that identify the same fictional entity although they involve mental files containing very different information. For example, someone who reads *Emma* and thinks about the novel only from an internal perspective will associate with the name 'Emma Woodhouse' a mental file containing the information that she is handsome, clever, and rich, although disposed to think too well of herself, while someone who does not read *Emma*, but reads only critical studies of it, might instead associate with the name 'Emma Woodhouse' a mental file containing the information that Emma is one of Austen's heroines, develops in surprising ways over the course of *Emma*, and is *represented* in *Emma* as handsome, clever, and rich. Appeal to similarity cannot capture both the fact that some internal thoughts identify Tweedledum while others identify Tweedledee, and the fact that internal thoughts and external thoughts about Emma Woodhouse co-identify. Crane's account cannot explain on what basis we judge thought and talk from an internal perspective to co-identify with thought and talk from an external perspective. At best, qualitative similarity can explain judgements of the co-identification of thoughts and utterances from the same perspective.

Like Crane's, Friend's account (2014) of the basis for our judgements of co-identification is independent of the pretence theory. It also appeals to mental files containing information that agents are disposed to treat as if it were true of one specific thing or plurality of things. It is also unable to explain our judgements of co-identification by external and internal thoughts or utterances. Like Everett, Sainsbury, and García-Carpintero and unlike Crane, Friend proposes an account of the co-identification of non-existent entities that is designed to reflect the determinants of co-reference. Her account deliberately mirrors Gareth Evans's hybrid causal/descriptivist account of reference (1973), according to which the referent of a name is whichever entity is the dominant source of the information we associate with that name.

Friend argues that, just as we have mental files containing information that we associate with existing entities, we have mental files containing information that we associate with fictional names, even though there is nothing they name. The transmission of information from these files through communication results in chains or networks of mental files, the information in which is derived from previous mental files in the chain or network. Networks of mental files associated with existing entities can presumably be traced back to perceptions of the entities in question. By contrast, she argues that networks of files associated with fictional names can be traced back to mental files freely created by agents who stand in the producer relation to the fictional names associated with those files. Someone stands in the producer relation to a name if she has the capacity legitimately to introduce new information into the chain or network associated with that name. For example, Flaubert stands in the producer relation to the name 'Emma Bovary'. Friend (2014: 325) claims that Flaubert's distinct fictive utterances of 'Emma' in the course of producing *Emma Bovary* (1856) co-identify so long as the same freely created mental file guides each use of that name. Audiences' uses of fictional names co-identify so long as the information in the mental files they associate with those names is dominantly derived from the same mental file of a producer. Uses of distinct fictional names can co-identify, she argues, because information derived from the same mental file can be transmitted by the use of different names. Likewise, Friend could allow uses of fictional names to co-identify with uses of other specific terms so long as the information in the mental files associated with each is dominantly derived from the same mental file of a producer.

Friend allows that producers' mental files can contain information concerning properties associated with fictional names from an external as well as an internal perspective. For example, she claims that the file Shakespeare associated with the name 'Hamlet' would have included the information that Hamlet is a fictional entity of his own invention (Friend 2014: 329). However, it is possible for someone's thoughts and talk to identify a fictional entity, although the information in their mental file includes information predominantly not derived from the relevant producer's mental file. Consider the mental file that a person will associate with the name 'Emma Woodhouse' if she has read only critical studies of *Emma* and not the novel itself, and consequently thinks about it from a purely external perspective. Her file is likely to include information that is not in the mental file Austen associated with the name. This might be because, for example, it reflects an evaluative perspective that Austen did not adopt (that Emma is an insightful, well-crafted, engaging, derivative, or implausible character. Such a person's thoughts and utterances can identify Emma, even if the information in her mental file is predominantly not derived from the mental file that Austen associated with the name 'Emma Woodhouse'.

The obvious response is that, although the information in such a person's mental file does not replicate that in Austen's mental file, it nevertheless depends on it and—Friend will hope to argue—therefore qualifies as having been derived from it. The information that Emma is a well-crafted character does not depend solely on the information in the mental file that Austen associated with the name 'Emma Woodhouse' because whether or not a character is well crafted depends not only on which properties it is fictional that the character possesses, but also on Austen's manner of representation: that is, on *how* her fictive utterances make it fictional that the character possesses those properties. Nevertheless, let us assume, for the sake of argument, that whether or not a character is well crafted depends predominantly on the information in the mental file of its author. Emma Woodhouse would not be a well-crafted or an engaging character if Austen's freely created mental file had not included the information it did. However, it is not sufficient for information to be derived from a producer's mental file that it have been caused, however indirectly, by it. Minimally, the nature of the information at issue must bear some further relation to the nature of the information in the producer's mental file. The crucial question is how they must be related.

In addressing this question, it is important to distinguish between different kinds of properties we associate with fictional names from an external perspective. We must distinguish between properties such as *being engaging* or *being derivative*, on the one hand, and, on the other, properties such as *being fictionally handsome, clever, and rich* and *being fictionally a young woman of considerable intelligence*. Which properties we associate with a fictional name from an internal perspective has necessary implications regarding which properties of the latter type it is rational to associate with that name from an external perspective. For example, if, from an internal perspective, one associates with a given fictional name the property *is a young woman of considerable intelligence*, it is rational to associate with that name from an external perspective the property *is fictionally a young woman of considerable intelligence*. Moreover, it is *invariably* rational to do so. There are no circumstances under which it is not.

We can use these necessary rational relations to help specify conditions sufficient for the information in the mental file that an audience member associates with a fictional name *n* from an external perspective to be derived from the information in the mental file that a producer associates with a fictional name *m* from an internal perspective. The former is derived from the latter if the former consists in the information that *n* is fictionally F and the latter consist in the information that *m* is F and the audience member's mental file contains the information that *n* is fictionally F *because* the producer's mental file contains the information that *m* is F.

However, it is possible for the thoughts and utterances of someone who thinks about *Emma* from a purely external perspective to identify Emma, even if the information in her mental file is not predominantly of a kind that meets these conditions. This is because the information in her mental file could consist largely in the information that Emma has such properties as being engaging and well crafted. Intuitively, such information does depend at least partly on the information that Austen associates with the name 'Emma Woodhouse' from an internal perspective and can therefore legitimately be characterized as having been at least partly derived from the information in Austen's mental file. However, it is not possible to capture these dependence relations without presupposing that the audience member's and Austen's thoughts or utterances co-identify. From an external perspective, one can associate with a fictional name properties such as *being well-crafted* or *being engaging*, because, from an internal perspective, one associates with that name any of a wide variety of different properties. There are no properties that it is necessary for a character to exhibit from an internal perspective in order for it to exhibit such properties from an external perspective. Consequently, there are no necessary rational relations between the properties one associates with a fictional name from an internal perspective and the properties one associates with that name from an external perspective in terms of which one can characterize what it is for the information one associates with that name from an external perspective to have been derived from the information one associates with that name from an internal perspective.

The relation of information derivation was supposed to help the anti-realist to explain the conditions under which distinct uses of a fictional name co-identify. However, anti-realists cannot characterize these information derivation relations independently of the notion of co-identification. Friend needs some way of elucidating this relation in terms of dependence. We can characterize one such dependence relation as follows:

P1:   It is fictional in *Emma* that Emma Woodhouse possesses the properties of being a young woman of considerable intelligence and being apt to think too highly of herself.

P2:   To be an engaging character is fictionally to possess properties that audiences find interesting.

P3:   Audiences find the properties of being a young woman of considerable intelligence and being apt to think too highly of one's self interesting. Therefore,

C: Emma Woodhouse is an engaging character.

To address my objection to Friend's account, anti-realists need a person's thoughts and utterances to identify Emma *because* her mental file includes the information that Emma is an engaging character. However, it is only because the use of 'Emma Woodhouse' in the conclusion of the argument above co-identifies with the use of 'Emma Woodhouse' in the first premise that the argument is valid. Claiming that the information that Emma is engaging depends on the information that Emma is a young woman of considerable intelligence apt to think too highly of herself therefore does not help to address my objection, because the notion of dependence being appealed to presupposes co-identification.

   Anti-realists who, like Sainsbury, take intentions to use the same name and to defer to a name using practice to suffice for co-identification can explain the fact that the two uses of 'Emma Woodhouse' co-identify, and can therefore make sense of the claim that the information that Emma is engaging depends on the information that Emma is a young woman of considerable intelligence apt to think too highly of herself. However, they cannot do so in all cases. We can replace 'Emma Woodhouse' in the conclusion of the argument above with 'the fictional entity created by Jane Austen by her fictive utterance of the opening sentence of *Emma*'. On my account, we can preserve the argument's validity by adding, as a fourth premise, that Emma Woodhouse is identical to the fictional entity created by Jane Austen by her fictive utterance of the opening sentence of *Emma*. We can do so because the first premise and the conclusion refer to the same fictional entity. However, Sainsbury's account does not license the introduction of such a premise and therefore cannot explain the validity of the revised argument.

The inability to characterize such dependence relations independently of the notion of co-identification causes further problems for pretence theorists. We often think and talk about fiction in a way that mixes internal and external perspectives, rather than adopting a perspective that is exclusively internal or exclusively external. Such mixed discourse about fiction is often used to talk about dependence relations between the properties fictional entities exhibit from an external perspective and those they exhibit from an internal perspective. For example, E. M. Forster (1927: 160) writes of Henry James's characters:

> the characters, beside being few in number, are constructed on very stingy lines. They are incapable of fun, of rapid motion, of carnality, and of nine-tenths of heroism. Their clothes will not take off, the diseases that ravage them are anonymous, like the sources of their income, their servants are noiseless or resemble themselves, no social explanation of the world we know is possible for them, for there are no stupid people in their world, no barriers of language, and no poor. Even their sensations are limited. They can land in Europe and look at works of art and at each other, but that is all.

Forster shifts here between talking about James's characters from an external perspective (the stinginess of their construction) and from an internal perspective (their clothes and sensations). Moreover, he does so in order to comment on the way in which the properties they exhibit from an external perspective depend on those they exhibit from an internal perspective. James's characters are stingily constructed, Forster argues, partly because they have limited sensations.

Pretence theorists take the internal and external perspectives to involve distinct games of pretence. As I noted in the previous section, they take it to be true according to the *official* game of pretence prescribed by *Emma* that Emma has properties such as being a young woman of considerable intelligence, but true only according to an *unofficial* game of pretence that Emma has properties such as being an engaging character. These different properties can be ascribed to Emma only within the scope of distinct games. Accordingly, Friend (2007: 152–3) claims that the pretence theorist can construe mixed discourse as involving a shift between different games of pretence.

This alone cannot accommodate the fact that the properties Emma exhibits from an external perspective *depend* on those Emma exhibits from an internal perspective. To capture these dependence relations, pretence theorists must hold that what it is appropriate to imagine in an unofficial game of pretence depends on what it is appropriate to imagine in an official game of pretence. That is, they must hold that the principles of generation that determine what it is appropriate to imagine when one engages in unofficial games depend on the principles of generation that determine what it is appropriate to imagine when one engages in official games. Moreover, if they are to *determine* what it is appropriate to imagine in a given game of pretence, the principles of generation must be independent of the imaginings appropriate in that game of pretence. However, pretence theorists claim that it is only within the scope of a game of pretence that there is such a thing as Emma Woodhouse. Moreover, it is only within the scope of unofficial games of pretence that thoughts or utterances that ascribe to Emma properties such as being an engaging character identify the same entity as Austen's fictive utterances. Because one must take co-identification for granted in order to capture the relevant dependence relations, pretence theorists cannot specify the principles of generation at issue without presupposing what it is appropriate to imagine in unofficial games of pretence, and this is the very thing those principles are supposed to explain. Consequently, the pretence theorist is precluded not merely from appealing to such dependence relations to explain co-identification, but from giving an account of how unofficial games of pretence are related to official games of pretence that can enable them to make sense of mixed discourse of the kind in which Forster engages.

The account of fictional entities that I developed in the previous chapter takes internal and external thoughts or utterances to identify the same fictional entity if and only if they refer to the same fictional entity. This enables it to accommodate the various circumstances under which distinct thoughts and utterances identify the same fictional entities. By contrast, none of the five anti-realist accounts considered here can accommodate all cases of co-identification. Moreover, my account can accommodate the fact that the properties fictional entities exhibit from an external perspective depend on those they exhibit from an internal perspective while pretence theories cannot. My realist account, therefore, has greater explanatory power than its antirealist rivals.

6.3 The Co-Identification of Thought and Talk about Non-Existents

We are now in a position to address the problem for my realist account of fictional entities identified in the introduction to this chapter. Insofar as it construes our judgements of co-identification as underlain by co-reference, my account cannot explain our judgement that the imagining that a specific, non-existent woman named 'Emma Woodhouse' is handsome, clever, and rich that prompted Austen to write the opening lines of *Emma* was itself about Emma Woodhouse. Emma Woodhouse did not exist until Austen wrote those opening lines.

In the previous section, we discussed three anti-realist accounts of co-identification that do not presuppose the truth of the pretence theory: Sainsbury's, Crane's and Friend's. I have rejected Sainsbury's account because it cannot explain the co-identification of specific thoughts and utterances that are not uses of the same fictional name. However, both Crane's and Friend's accounts offer plausible explanations of the conditions under which we judge specific thoughts and utterances of specific representations that are made *from the same perspective* to co-identify, even though neither is adequate as an account of how internal thoughts and utterances can co-identify with external thoughts and utterances. Because Austen's initial specific imaginings about a woman who is handsome, clever, and rich are from the same perspective as the imaginings in which her fictive utterance of the opening lines of *Emma* prompts audiences to engage, we can therefore explain our judgement that they co-identify in the manner suggested by either Crane or Friend. That is, we can construe Austen's initial imaginings as co-identifying with her audiences' imaginings either because each involves a mental file containing qualitatively similar information, or because her audiences' imaginings involve mental files containing information that is dominantly derived from the information in the mental file implicated in her initial imaginings. Both explanations are consistent with the fact that there is a fictional entity to which her audiences' imaginings refer and nothing to which her own imagining refers.

Unlike some realists about fictional entities (e.g. Salmon 1998), I think that thought and talk about mistaken theoretical posits, such as Vulcan, and about mythical entities, such as Hermes, involve thinking and talking about things that do not exist. There are such things as fictional entities because the common interests and common beliefs of participants in the institution of fiction anchor grounds for the existence of fictional entities, and these grounds require only the production of utterances with certain features. By contrast, the attitudes, behaviours, and practices of participants in scientific institutions do not anchor grounds for the existence of postulated planets, just as those of participants in religious institutions do not anchor grounds for the existence of mythical gods. Their attitudes concern *actual* planets and *actual* gods. Le Verrier wrongly thought that Vulcan was an actual planet, and the Greeks wrongly thought that Hermes was an actual god. There is not, nor ever was, any such planet or any such god.

This raises the question of how we are to explain our judgements that certain thoughts and utterances identify Vulcan, while other thoughts and utterances identify Hermes. One can adopt analogues of both an internal and an external perspective on Vulcan or on Hermes, and thus engage in analogues of both internal and external thought or talk about them. When one considers them from an internal perspective, one takes things to be as Le Verrier thought they were or as the ancient Greeks did. By contrast, when one considers them from an external perspective, one is concerned with how things really are. Considered from an internal perspective, Vulcan is a planet and Hermes is a god, while, considered from an external perspective, Vulcan is a postulated planet and Hermes is a mythical god. One might worry that, if a realist account is needed to explain how internal and external thought or talk can identify the same fictional entity, it will also be required to explain how internal and external thought can identify the same mythical entity or failed scientific posit.

This is not so. The properties we ascribe to failed scientific posits and to mythical entities from an external perspective are much more limited than those we ascribe to fictional entities from an external perspective. While we ascribe to them such properties such as *being a postulated planet, being a mythical god*, and *being supposed to be the son of Zeus*, we rarely, if ever, ascribe to them such properties as *being engaging* or *being original*. Insofar as the properties we ascribe to failed scientific posits and mythical entities from an external perspective are limited to properties that bear necessary rational relations to the properties we ascribe to them from an internal perspective, we can explain the co-identification of internal and external thought or talk about such entities in the manner Friend proposes. If Friend's account of what underlies our judgements of the co-identification of specific terms that lack referents is correct, even when the mental file an agent associates with the name 'Vulcan' includes only information concerning properties such as *being a postulated planet* not included in the mental file Le Verrier associated with that name, we can legitimately judge their thoughts and utterances to be about the same non-existent entity as Le Verrier's. We can do so because we can make sense of the claim that the information in the agent's mental file was derived from that in Le Verrier's mental file without presupposing that the agent's thoughts and utterances identify the same non-existent entity as Le Verrier's.

It is beyond the scope of the present discussion to determine whether or not Friend's account is correct. The important point for present purposes is that it is open to me to explain our judgements regarding when both internal and external thought and talk identify Vulcan in the manner Friend suggests, even though, as I have argued, her account cannot explain the circumstances under which we judge internal and external thought and talk to be about the same fictional entity. When we think about fictional entities from an external perspective, we can think of them predominantly as possessing properties whose relations to those they exhibit from an internal perspective cannot be characterized independently of the notion of co-identification. Our capacity to think and talk about fictional entities predominantly as possessing such properties gives us good reason to accept them into our ontology, even when that ontology is too parsimonious to embrace mythical entities and failed scientific posits. There is good reason to single out fictional entities for realist treatment.

6.4 The Interpretative Role of External Thought and Talk

This raises the question of *why* participants in fiction institutions engage in external thought and talk in which they ascribe such properties to fictional entities, whereas participants in scientific institutions do not ascribe such properties to postulated planets, and participants in religious institutions do not ascribe such properties to mythical gods. I will argue that participants in fiction institutions engage in certain forms of external thought and talk about both works of fiction and fictional entities because doing so can help fiction institutions to provide equilibrium solutions to coordination problems of communicating imaginings. My aim, in the remaining two sections of this chapter, is to explain how external thought and talk about fiction can help fiction institutions to perform this function.

There is a wide variety of different forms of external thought and talk about fiction. This includes such thoughts as 'Emma Woodhouse is a fictional character', as well as formalist critical discourse, more general literary-critical discourse, and socio-political critical discourse such as queer studies or post-colonial readings of *Emma*. Not every form of external thought or talk plays a role in enabling fiction institutions to perform the function of communicating imaginings. Nevertheless, I will argue that certain forms of external thought and talk play an important such role.

In this section, I will argue that thought and talk about the properties works of fiction would exhibit from an external perspective if they had particular interpretative fictive contents play an important role in enabling us success-fully to interpret works of fiction. Such talk involves, but does not consist solely in, external talk about fiction. Like Forster's discussion of Henry James's characters, it mixes the internal and the external perspectives in order to identify dependencies between the properties fictional entities exhibit from each.

In Section 4.5, I argued that a work has a certain interpretative fictive content if and only if:

1. its author intended to prompt her audience to imagine that content;
2. she intentionally produced utterances with certain features as an instrumental means of realising that intention;
3. utterances with those features comprise a means of prompting an audience that lacks independent knowledge of the relevant intention to engage in the intended imagining; and
4. those utterances are not governed by content-determining rules of fiction that prescribe audiences to engage in the intended imagining.

I argued that audiences identify interpretative fictive content by drawing inferences to the best explanation about authors' ordinary, non-communicative intentions to elicit imaginings by their fictive utterances. In making such inferences, they can draw on any information that is available to them. This will include information about the contents of authors' fictive utterances, but such information alone will not be sufficient to enable audiences to identify interpretative fictive content. To do so, audiences need to identify the goals that led authors to produce their works of fiction, since these impose constraints on which further imaginings it is rational for them to intend to elicit by their fictive utterances.

Very often, an author intends to prompt her audience to engage in imaginings that outstrip the contents of her fictive utterances because her goal is to produce a work of fiction that exhibits certain properties from an external perspective. From an external perspective, works of fiction exhibit both non-evaluative properties, such as belonging to a certain genre or literary tradition and featuring fictional entities that are modelled on real-life individuals, and evaluative properties, such as having a well-structured plot, being strikingly original, and featuring engaging characters. An author's goal may simply be to produce a work that belongs to a certain genre or literary tradition, or whose characters are modelled on certain real-life people. Alternatively, it may be to produce a work that exhibits certain evaluative properties.

Audiences can work out that authors had such further goals by a variety of different means. For example, they might know that an author's goal was to produce a work that is strikingly original because she declared this to have been her goal in a radio interview. However, to use their knowledge of her goal in order to identify the further imaginings in which she intends them to engage and thus to identify the work's interpretative fictive content, they must work out which of the further imaginings her fictive utterances comprise a means of prompting would result in the realization of this goal. This requires them to engage in counterfactual reasoning about the properties a work would exhibit from an external perspective if it had certain interpretative fictive contents. This, in turn, requires them to iden-tify dependence relations between the properties the work exhibits or would exhibit from an external perspective and those it exhibits or would exhibit from an internal perspective. This involves thinking about works of fiction from both an external and an internal perspective. Mixed thought and talk about fiction therefore play an essential role in enabling audiences to identify interpretative fictive content in those cases in which authors convey that content in order to produce works that exhibit certain properties from an external perspective.

For example, Forster argues that Henry James's goal in writing *The Ambassadors* (1903) was to write a novel with the pattern of an hourglass. It exhibits this pattern, he claims, because the two characters Strether and Chad change places over the course of the novel. Strether is sent to Paris to bring Chad, on whom the city is thought to be having a corrupting influence, back to America. However, when he arrives, Chad seems liberated and enlightened, with appealing friends including a woman named Mme de Vionnet. Strether shifts allegiance and prevents Chad from returning to America. He then discovers, however, that Chad is not fundamentally changed by his experience in the city but is engaged in a commonplace temporary liaison with Mme de Vionnet. Forster (1927: 159) writes:

So Strether loses them too. As he says: 'I have lost everything—it is my only logic.' It is not that they have gone back. It is that he has gone on. The Paris they revealed to him—he could reveal it to them now, if they had eyes to see it, for it is something finer than they could ever notice for themselves, and his imagination has more spiritual value than their youth. The pattern of the hour-glass is complete; he and Chad have changed places...James knew exactly what he wanted, he pursued the narrow path of aesthetic duty, and success to the full extent of his possibilities has crowned him. The pattern has woven itself with modulation and reservations Anatole France will never attain. Woven itself wonderfully.

Forster is able to construe James as having achieved the goal of producing a work that exhibits an hourglass pattern precisely because he interprets *The Ambassadors* as having the interpretative fictive content that it is ultimately Strether who is spiritually enlarged by his experiences in Paris. The work's exhibiting an hourglass pattern from an external perspective depends on its prompting audiences who engage with it from an internal perspective to imagine that Strether and Chad have changed places. Forster's hypothesis regarding James's goal enables him to draw inferences about James's intentions regarding the work's content and therefore to interpret it.

In Section 2.5, I argued that we evaluate works as good or bad *qua* fiction. However, we also evaluate them artistically. Some philosophers distinguish between *artistic* and *aesthetic* evaluations of works, where the former are evaluations of works considered as art that, they claim, need not be aesthetic evaluations. Other philosophers deny that the two forms of evaluation are really distinct. In what follows I will describe all evaluations of works of fiction, considered as works of art, as artistic, and will remain neutral regarding whether such evaluations are, properly understood, always aesthetic evaluations. External thought and talk are essential to the artistic evaluation of works of fiction, because the properties of being artistically good and being artistically bad can be ascribed to them only from an external perspective. Furthermore, determining whether they are good or bad artistically involves reasoning about whether or not they have evaluative properties such as having a well-structured plot and featuring engaging characters.

The concept of fiction is descriptive, rather than evaluative. That is, categorizing a work as fiction, unlike categorizing it as literature, does not entail any particular artistic evaluation of it, whether good or bad. As I argued in Section 2.5, good works of fiction are simply those that use the rules of fiction institutions effectively to communicate imaginings. They can, therefore, be good *qua* fiction, without being artistically good.

Although it does not play a role in determining how good works are *qua* fiction, artistic evaluation is nevertheless important to interpretation, because authors often produce works of fiction with artistic goals. Forster (1927: 150) is clear, for example, that James's goal of producing a work with a certain pattern is artistic (or, as he claims, aesthetic):

> But whereas the story appeals to our curiosity and the plot to our intelligence, the pattern appeals to our aesthetic sense.

Authors can have the goal of producing works that are artistically good, or that have certain positive evaluative properties, such as exhibiting an hourglass pattern, and these goals can determine which further imaginings they intend their fictive utterances to prompt audiences to engage in. Audiences therefore need to consider the evaluative significance of various interpretative hypotheses if appeal to such goals is to help them to identify interpretative fictive content.

6.5 The Role of External Thought and Talk in Coordination

The content-determining rules of fiction institutions determine the way in which works of fiction communicate imaginings by establishing relations between utterances with certain features and imaginings with certain contents that do not obtain independently of the rules themselves. We can prefer imaginings with contents of a certain kind to be communicated by utterances with features of one kind rather than another. Consequently, we can prefer the rules of a fiction institution to take one form rather than another. These preferences may simply be the result of habit or tradition. That is, we might prefer certain imaginings to be communicated by utterances with particular features because that is how such imaginings have always been communicated to us in the past, and it would cost us extra cognitive effort to engage in those imaginings in response to utterances with different features. Alternatively, they can result from our judgements regarding which relations between utterances with certain features and imaginings with certain contents are artistically the best.

Whatever their basis, to communicate these preferences to one another, participants cannot merely follow the rules that prescribe particular imaginative responses to fictive utterances with certain features, as they do when they engage with works of fiction from an internal perspective, but must engage in external talk about fiction that enables them to discuss their manner of representation. We find such discourse in discussions of the comparative merits of different fiction techniques, whether by professional critics, casual readers, or members of book or film clubs. For example, one reader might express a preference for the contents of characters' thoughts to be communicated by utterances in the first person. By contrast, another might express a preference for their thoughts to be communicated using free indirect discourse.

In this section, I will argue that there are three ways in which external thought and talk in which we identify and express our preferences regarding how imaginings are communicated can improve how effectively fiction institutions solve coordination problems of communicating imaginings. First, such external talk can improve the stability of the rules of fiction institutions by making participants in fiction institutions aware of the preferences of other participants. Secondly, external talk in which participants engage in debate about the artistic merits of different ways of communicating certain types of imaginings can improve the stability of the rules of fiction institutions by helping to bring about a coincidence in participants' preferences. Finally, external thought about the artistic merits of various ways of responding imaginatively to utterances with certain features can enable participants to coordinate, on the fly, on equilibrium solutions to novel coordination problems of communicating imaginings.

In Section 2.1, I argued that the rules of institutions are arbitrary in the sense that there is always some other equilibrium solution to the coordination problems they solve than those that the rules provide. It is, therefore, always possible for the rules of an institution to have been different. An equilibrium is simply a pattern of behaviour that persists because individuals have no incentive to deviate from that pattern if others do not. Agents will lack any incentive to deviate from that pattern of behaviour so long as it satisfies their preferences better than, or at least as well as, any other pattern of behaviour they can achieve by acting unilaterally, and they think that other agents will conform to that pattern of behaviour. An equilibrium is *stable* to the extent that it persists. The stability of an equilibrium is affected by changing circumstances, including changes to agents' beliefs about how other agents will behave. When agents think, whether wrongly or rightly, that other agents might also deviate from an equilibrium, this gives them an incentive to deviate from it too, especially if there is some other pattern of behaviour that better satisfies their preferences.

There is no guarantee that the rules of an institution represent whichever equilibrium best satisfies agents' preferences. The numerical values assigned to the various possible strategies in the payoff matrix for a coordination game represent how well the outcomes satisfy agents' subjective preferences, with higher numbers representing outcomes that satisfy agents' interests better than outcomes represented by lower numbers. There are institutions whose rules represent equilibria that satisfy agents' preferences better than the available out-of-equilibrium outcomes, but do not satisfy them as well as some alternative equilibrium strategy. Figure 4 represents the payoff matrix for a

	C	P
C	2,2	0,0
P	0,0	1,1

Figure 4. Equilibria that do not satisfy agents' preferences equally

game in which there are two equilibrium strategies, (CC) and (PP), but one (CC) clearly satisfies both agents' preferences better than the other.

Consider, for example, a game in which two housemates must each shop for food to prepare together. Suppose that one works near a greengrocer's and the other works near a dry goods store, so they must coordinate the shopping they do on their way home if they are to have the ingredients required to prepare a tasty and balanced meal. Neither will be able to eat a tasty and balanced meal if each shops for food for a different kind of meal (CP) and (PC). They can either each shop for ingredients to make pasta (PP) or they can each shop for ingredients to make Thai curry (CC). Although a situation in which each shops for ingredients for Thai curry satisfies the preferences of both agents best, they may nevertheless end up in a situation in which they both shop for ingredients for pasta because neither believes that the other agent will do her part in shopping for ingredients for Thai curry. Each might mistakenly believe, for example, that the other housemate prefers to eat pasta than to eat Thai curry.

A similar situation can arise with equilibrium solutions to coordination problems of communicating imaginings. Participants in a fiction institution could all prefer one equilibrium solution to a coordination problem of communicating imaginings with certain contents, but end up adopting a rule that provides an equilibrium solution that satisfies their preferences less well because each wrongly thinks that the other participants prefer that solution and will therefore continue to conform to that pattern of behaviour. Let us simplify and suppose that there are just two participants who need to coordinate their behaviour, an author and an audience of one. Let us further suppose that both prefer the contents of characters' thoughts to be communicated using free indirect discourse. If the author wrongly thinks her audience prefers them to be communicated by utterances in the first person, she may represent characters' thoughts using utterances in the first person because she believes that her audience will respond to such utterances by taking them to represent the contents of characters' thoughts, but will not respond to free indirect discourse in this way. Likewise, if the audience wrongly thinks the author prefers the contents of characters' thoughts to be represented by utterances in the first person, she may respond to such utterances by taking them to represent the contents of characters' thoughts, since she believes that the author would use such utterances, but not free indirect discourse, to convey the contents of characters' thoughts.

When the individual participants in a fiction institution are not aware of the preferences of its other participants, they can end up in situations analogous to that of shopping for pasta instead of Thai curry, in which they adopt content-determining rules that fail to satisfy their preferences as well as alternative rules would do. Such rules are less stable than rules that better satisfy their preferences, because participants have more incentive to deviate from the pattern of behaviour prescribed by those rules if they think it possible that other participants might also do so.

External talk in which participants in fiction institutions discuss their preferences regarding the kinds of utterances by which certain types of imaginings are communicated plays an important role in enabling them to coordinate on stable content-determining rules, because it enables them to make their preferences regarding the nature of its rules clear, disabusing one another of mistaken beliefs they may hold about the nature of one another's preferences and likely behaviour. There are two ways in which this improves the stability of the equilibrium solutions to problems of communicating imaginings provided by the rules of fiction institutions. First, when such talk makes it clear that a certain rule satisfies participants' preferences better than any proposed alternative, this knowledge undermines any incentive participants might otherwise have had to deviate from that rule, thereby improving its stability. Secondly, when it makes it clear that some existing rule does *not* satisfy participants' preferences as well as a proposed alternative, it makes participants aware that the alternative better satisfies their preferences, and provides the impetus for all participants to change their behaviour so as to coordinate on a different equilibrium solution that satisfies their preferences better. The resultant equilibrium will be more stable than that represented by the previous rule, because participants will have less incentive to deviate from it, even if they think it possible that others will do so.

External talk in which participants in fiction institutions express their preferences regarding the kinds of utterances by which imaginings with certain types of contents are communicated will not help them to coordinate on stable content-determining rules if their preferences do not coincide. Consider a situation in which some participants prefer imaginings of type Z to be communicated by utterances of type X, while others prefer them to be

	If X, imagine Z	If Y, imagine Z
If X, imagine Z	2,1	0,0
If Y, imagine Z	0,0	1,2

Figure 5. Diverging preferences

communicated by utterances of type Y. In cases like this, there is no single equilibrium strategy that best satisfies all participants' preferences. Again, let us suppose that there are just two participants who need to coordinate their behaviour. Figure 5 represents the solutions available to them. Neither of the two equilibrium solutions to this coordination game is very stable, since, whichever is adopted, one participant is likely to deviate from it if she thinks it possible that the other agent will also do so.

The solution to a coordination problem of communicating imaginings with a certain content provided by a rule of a fiction institution is no worse *qua* solution to that problem for being artistically inferior to an alternative such solution. Nevertheless, artistic judgements have an important feature in virtue of which they can play a role in enabling participants to coordinate on stable solutions to such coordination problems in cases in which their preferences diverge. They have a *normative force* that preferences determined by habit or tradition lack. That is, if an agent judges that a particular kind of utterance constitutes an artistically better means of communicating imaginings with certain contents than utterances of alternative kinds, then her judgement entails that imaginings with those contents *should*, artistically, be communicated by utterances of the kind in question.

Participants in fiction institutions often have artistic grounds for preferring one kind of utterance to another as a means of communicating imaginings with certain types of contents. For example, David Lodge notes that free indirect discourse enables authors to omit intrusive authorial tags such as 'she thought' and 'he asked himself', and that, although it allows authors to keep to the vocabulary that is appropriate to the character whose thoughts they are reporting, it also enables them to improve on a character's mode of speech by using their own words to report that character's thoughts (Lodge 1992: 43–5). These are artistic reasons to prefer utterances in free indirect discourse as a means of communicating characters' thoughts to utterances that communicate characters' thoughts from either a straightforward third-person or first-person point of view.

As Guala (2016a: 80) notes, norms can alter the payoffs of coordination games by imposing additional costs for noncompliance with those norms.

A participant's artistic judgement can alter her preferences by imposing an additional cost, c, for pursuing a strategy other than that which her artistic judgement prescribes. This cost will take the form of an internalized, self-inflicted punishment such as feeling displeasure at failing to respond in the way she judges that, artistically, she ought to respond. This cost must be deducted from the payoffs for pursuing any strategy other than that which she judges to be artistically superior.

Let us suppose that the initial preferences of the two participants in our coordination game are determined by non-normative factors. They are then prompted to evaluate the two equilibrium solutions to their coordination problem artistically. Both judge it to be artistically better to use utterances of type X to communicate imaginings with contents of type Z than to use utterances of type Y to do so. This affects the coordination game illustrated in Figure 5 in the manner represented in Figure 6.

The normative force of agents' artistic judgements will determine how great the value of c is. If it greater than one, it will undermine the initial preference of Agent 2 for imaginings with contents of type Z to be communicated by utterances of type Y, leading her to prefer them instead to be communicated by utterances of type X. By bringing their preferences into alignment in this way, participants' artistic judgements can make it easier for them to develop a rule that solves a particular coordination problem of communicating imaginings. They can also improve the stability of the resultant rule.

However, their artistic judgements can play this role only if they *coincide*. If one agent believed one equilibrium strategy to be artistically superior while the other believed the alternative strategy to be artistically superior, their artistic judgements would impose costs that exacerbate the divergence in their preferences, making any equilibrium solution they adopt less stable, rather than more stable.

Whether or not there are objective facts concerning which strategies agents ought artistically to pursue, differences in artistic judgement occur. Nevertheless, unlike preferences due to the increased cognitive cost of changing a habitual pattern of behaviour, artistic judgements are responsive to reasons. New considerations can provide an agent with reasons to change her

	If X, imagine Z	If Y, imagine Z
If X, imagine Z	2,1	0,0
If Y, imagine Z	0,0	$1-c, 2-c$

Figure 6. Diverging preferences modified by artistic judgements

artistic judgement concerning the kinds of utterances by which imaginings of a certain type should be communicated. External talk about fiction in which participants debate the comparative artistic merits of different means of communicating certain types of imaginings can help to bring their artistic judgements into alignment by providing reasons to which the artistic judgements of all are responsive. Insofar as it can do this, such talk can help participants to coordinate on solutions to coordination problems of communicating imaginings that are stable, because they have little incentive to deviate from them and know that other participants also lack such an incentive.

Artistic judgements can improve the stability of equilibrium solutions to coordination problems of communicating imaginings even when artistic debate does not enable participants to resolve the differences in their artistic judgements. Participants in fiction institutions sometimes normatively privilege the artistic judgements of literary and cultural critics, holding that others should make the same artistic judgements as they do. The normative status of such judgements is expressed in sanctions against those whose preferences are not consistent with critics' artistic judgements. These sanctions are not self-imposed punishments such as feelings of displeasure, but socially imposed costs, such as being judged to be unsophisticated, philistine, or intellectually inferior. Whatever individual participants' own artistic judgements and their effects on their preferences, such external social costs may, if big enough, override the internal costs of non-compliance with their own artistic judgements and thereby help to bring about a coincidence of participants' preferences. External talk about fiction in which expert judgements concerning the comparative artistic merits of different means of communicating imaginings of certain types are expressed and the social costs of non-compliance with those judgements made clear can therefore play a role in helping participants in fiction institutions to coordinate on stable content-determining rules.

The artistic judgements of participants in fiction institutions can also help them to coordinate with one another in order to develop rules that provide solutions to novel coordination problems of communicating imaginings to which there are no existing solutions. In Section 3.4, I argued that the content-determining rules of fiction institutions are external correlation devices that enable participants to coordinate on equilibrium solutions to coordination problems of communicating imaginings that would not otherwise have been available to them. Consequently, I argued, they are arbitrary in the strong sense that the nature of the connection they establish between authors' fictive utterances and audiences' imaginings is irrelevant to their providing equilibrium solutions to those problems. There are, therefore, no rational grounds for preferring one such rule to another as a solution to a problem of communicating imaginings of a certain type. The rules of fiction emerge because participants at first succeed in coordinating their behaviour through good luck, or by adopting whichever strategy seems the most salient, without having any particular reason to do so, other than that it is salient. I argued that a given strategy could be salient because arbitrary human psychological mechanisms make it stand out more than other strategies, or because it is a strategy that agents have adopted in the past.

However, there need not always be any human psychological mechanism that makes a particular solution to a novel problem of communicating imaginings particularly salient. Moreover, the novelty of such problems means that no strategies are salient in virtue of having been used to solve them in the past.

Nevertheless, participants need not rely on sheer good luck to enable them to coordinate on a rule that solves such problems. Particular ways of responding imaginatively to utterances with certain features may be salient to audiences, because they judge them to be artistically the best ways of responding to them. Consequently, authors may be able to coordinate with their audiences on a solution to a novel problem of communicating imaginings with a certain content by producing utterances to which they judge that the most artistically meritorious response is to engage in imaginings with that content. For example, suppose that a filmmaker wants to represent certain events as having been remembered by one of her characters. She may judge that the most artistically meritorious way of responding imaginatively to sepia-toned film is to imagine the events it represents as having been remembered, because such a response captures the association between memories and old photographs. Consequently, she may represent the events at issue using sepia-toned film. If her audiences' artistic judgements coincide with her own, they may respond to her utterance by imagining the events represented to have been remembered, because their artistic judgement makes such a response salient to them. Insofar as authors' and audiences' artistic judgements coincide, external thought and talk in which each judges the artistic merits of different ways of responding imaginatively to utterances of a certain type can, therefore, help them to coordinate on equilibrium solutions to novel coordination problems.

Neither authors nor audiences need always make judgements about the artistic merits of particular ways of responding imaginatively to utterances of a certain type. It is a contingent matter whether or not their artistic judgements make a particular pattern of behaviour salient to participants in a fiction institution. Nevertheless, it is possible for fiction institutions to give artistic judgements a central role in enabling their participants to develop such rules. They can do so by incorporating the following, conditional rule:

If an author utters representation R in context C, and an imagining with a certain content is the most artistically meritorious response to utterances of R in C, imagine that content if there is no existing content-determining rule regulating responses to utterances of R in C.

If it is to be governed by this rule, an utterance must be a prospective fictive utterance. As I discussed in Section 2.3, this requires audiences' responses to the series of utterances of which it is a part to be intended to conform to an institutional practice of fiction. This rule regulates the development of rules that provide solutions to novel coordination problems of communicating imaginings by using participants' artistic judgements as external correlation devices. Authors can exploit this rule to communicate imaginings with certain contents in the absence of existing solutions to the coordination problem of communicating imaginings with those contents. They can do so by producing those utterances to which they think audiences will judge that the most artistically meritorious response is to engage in imaginings with those contents. In this way, a rule can emerge that prescribes that imaginative response to utterances of R in C. This rule then enables authors to make fictive utterances with those contents.

This rule does not provide an infallible means of coordinating on equilibrium solutions to novel coordination problems of communicating imaginings. For such a rule to facilitate coordination, participants' artistic judgements must coincide. This will not always be the case. Judgements regarding which way of responding imaginatively to a particular type of utterance is most artistically meritorious are implicitly comparative. There is no guarantee that all participants will appeal to the same comparison class of alternative imaginative responses in forming such judgements. Even if they do, their artistic judgements may differ. Nevertheless, as I noted above, their artistic judgements are responsive to reasons, consideration of which can help to bring their judgements into alignment. Because participants' artistic judgements do sometimes coincide, especially when justified by reasons that support one such judgement over another, the rule increases the probability that they will succeed in coordinating on an equilibrium solution to a novel problem of communicating imaginings.

Institutions of fiction need not incorporate any rule regulating the way in which their participants coordinate on equilibrium solutions to novel coordination problems. They may simply rely on particular solutions to such problems being salient to their participants, whatever the cause of that salience. Nevertheless, the fact that artistic merit is a possible source of the salience of an equilibrium solution to a problem of communicating imaginings highlights the responsibility that participants in fiction institutions have, whether as authors or as audiences, to think about the reasons for which it could be better artistically to respond imaginatively in one way to utterances with certain features than another.

Conclusion

In this chapter, I have addressed two issues about external thought and talk about fiction. The first concerns the ontological implications of such thought and talk. I have argued that the ways in which we think and talk about fictional entities from an external perspective give us reason to accept their existence. Anti-realists are unable to provide a satisfactory explanation of the basis on which we judge external thought and talk to identify the same fictional entity as internal thought and talk. They cannot do so, because we associate different properties with fictional entities from an external perspective than we do from an internal perspective, and some of the properties we associate with a fictional entity from an external perspective depend on those we associate with it from an internal perspective in ways that cannot be captured independently of the claim that we associate each set of properties *with the same fictional entity*. The same line of reasoning does not compel us to admit the existence of mythical entities or failed scientific posits, however. When the properties we ascribe to such entities from an external perspective are related to those we ascribe to them from an internal perspective, they are related in ways that we can capture independently of the claim that our internal and external property ascriptions co-identify.

The second issue I have addressed is the role of external thought and talk in enabling fiction institutions to perform the function of enabling their participants to communicate imaginings. Because external thought and talk do not involve imaginative engagement with works of fiction, they might not appear to play any role in enabling fiction institutions to perform this function. However, I have identified various ways in which they help them to do so. First, mixed thought and talk in which audiences consider the ways in which the properties works of fiction exhibit from an external perspective depend on the contents with which audiences engage imaginatively from an internal perspective are important to the communication of interpretative fictive content. They play an important role in enabling audiences to draw the inferences about authors' intentions required to identify such content.

Secondly, external thought and talk improve the stability of the equilibrium solutions that the rules of fiction institutions provide to coordination problems of communicating imaginings. They do this by enabling participants in those institutions to communicate their preferences regarding the way in which imaginings with certain contents are communicated. They also do this by enabling them to engage in debate about the artistic merits of different ways of communicating imaginings, which has the potential to bring their preferences into alignment when they diverge. Finally, external thought in which participants assess the artistic merits of various possible ways of responding imaginatively to utterances with certain features can help to make particular solutions to novel coordination problems of communicating imaginings salient to them, and can therefore help them to coordinate on solutions to those problems.

Conclusion

In this book, I have explored the implications of taking seriously the claim that fiction is an institution. Drawing on Guala's account of institutions as systems of regulative rules that provide equilibrium solutions to coordination problems, I have argued that fiction institutions consist in systems of regulative rules that provide equilibrium solutions to coordination problems of communicating imaginings.

This construal of fiction institutions has enabled me to develop a coherent set of solutions to a range of philosophical problems concerning fiction. First, it has allowed me to provide an account of the nature of works of fiction that accommodates the fact that they need not be created solely by fictive utterances, but can be produced partly by ordinary assertions, while avoiding the implication that a work's fictionality is a matter of degree. On the account I have provided, a work is fiction so long as there is an institutional practice of fiction to which audiences' responses to the whole series of utterances by which it was produced are intended to conform, and at least one utterance in that series is governed by a content-determining rule that regulates that practice. Because only fictive utterances are governed by the content-determining rules of fiction institutions, this requires every work of fiction to include at least one fictive utterance. However, whether or not a work is fiction is an all-or-nothing affair, because audiences' responses to the whole series of utterances by which it was produced either were intended to conform to an institutional practice of fiction, or were not intended to do so. On this account, works of fiction are not distinctive in prescribing imaginative responses. They are distinctive only in the source of their prescriptions to imagine. Works of fiction alone prescribe imaginative responses in virtue of being produced by series of utterances that are intended to conform to an institutional practice.

Secondly, it has enabled me to explain why a work's being fiction rather than non-fiction affects how we evaluate it. A feature that strikes us as a good feature in a work of fiction may strike us as a bad or indifferent feature in a work of non-fiction, and *vice versa*. Fiction institutions perform the function of enabling the communication of imaginings. This function plays an

Fiction: A Philosophical Analysis. Catharine Abell, Oxford University Press (2020). © Catharine Abell.
DOI: 10.1093/oso/9780198831525.001.0001

important role in determining how we evaluate works considered as fiction. I have argued that a feature of a work is a good feature in a work considered as fiction when it comprises an effective means of communicating imaginings. This requires that feature to enable audiences readily and reliably to identify either the contents of fictive utterances or the work's interpretative fictive content.

Thirdly, this account of the nature of fictive utterances explains why, although their contents do not generally accurately reflect the way things are and their authors do not generally believe them to do so, they are neither insincere nor deceptive. It follows from my claim that fictive utterances are governed by the rules of fiction institutions that they are a type of *declaration*. Declarations are illocutionary acts that are distinctive in effecting changes to the existence and status of their objects simply in virtue of their successful performance. Fictive utterances can both create fictional entities and make certain things fictional of those entities. They are not insincere, because declarations bring about new matters of fact, rather than reporting on independent matters of fact. They do not purport to represent the beliefs of those who perform them. They are not deceptive, because the mere performance of a fictive utterance suffices to make it the case that, fictionally, things are as that fictive utterance represents them as being.

This account of the nature of fictive utterances has enabled me to solve a fourth philosophical problem: that of whether there are such things as fictional entities and, if there are, what sorts of things they are. The regulative rules of institutions enable us to create social entities with certain normative attributes by performing declarations that meet conditions sufficient for the existence of those entities. I have argued that the rules of fiction institutions enable authors to create fictional entities that have the normative attribute of fixing the reference of fictive utterances of specific terms by uttering specific terms without using them to speaker-refer to any existing fictional entity from an internal perspective. On this account, there is nothing metaphysically mysterious about either the grounds or the anchors for facts about the existence of fictional entities. Anyone who accepts that we have a common interest in communicating imaginings, that we have common beliefs that enable us to develop conventional means of doing so, and who accepts that authors produce utterances of the kind that I have described should accept their existence. Doing so enables us to explain our ability to engage in thought and talk from both an internal and an external perspective that we judge to be about the same fictional entities, although the properties we ascribe to them from each perspective can differ dramatically.

Those who deny the existence of fictional entities are unable to accommodate this fact.

My account of fictive utterances as declarations has also enabled me to solve a fifth, epistemological problem: that of how audiences identify the contents of fictive utterances. Many fictive utterances have context-sensitive contents. That is, different fictive utterances of the same representation can differ in their contents according to the contexts in which they are made. It is often claimed that the context-sensitive contents of fictive utterances are determined by authors' intentions to elicit imaginings in their audiences. That is, different fictive utterances of the same representation have different contents because they are intended to elicit different imaginings in their audiences. This account assumes that audiences can draw on their background knowledge to identify the intentions with which fictive utterances are made. However, there are no rational constraints on how the imaginings authors intend to elicit are related to the way the world is. Consequently, it is not clear what role audiences' background knowledge could play in enabling them to draw inferences about the imaginings authors communicatively intend to elicit. On this account, it is mysterious how audiences succeed in identifying the contents of fictive utterances.

The contents of declarations are determined by institutional rules. I have argued that those rules determine the contents of fictive utterances by establishing purely conventional relations between utterances with certain features and imaginings with certain contents. Those relations nevertheless incorporate two potential sources of context-sensitivity. First, some of those rules pick out the utterances whose contents they govern partly by appeal to features of the contexts in which they are produced. Secondly, some of those rules characterize the contents they assign to the utterances they govern indexically. In particular, they assign to fictive utterances of certain representations the contents that non-fictive utterances of those representations would have, were they made in contexts that resemble in particular respects those in which the fictive utterances themselves are made.

The rules that govern the contents of fictive utterances therefore incorporate two roles for audiences' background knowledge in enabling them to identify the contents of those utterances, one corresponding to each source of context sensitivity. This has enabled me to solve a sixth philosophical problem about fiction: that of the role of background knowledge in enabling audiences to identify the contents of works of fiction. It is often claimed that audiences' background knowledge plays a role in enabling them to do so because those contents are determined partly by general principles of generation. Roughly characterized, these principles specify that what is fictional in a work is as much like things are in reality or like we believe them to be in reality as is compatible with the contents of the fictive utterances by which it was produced.

Taking the contents of works of fiction to be determined partly by such principles has the consequence that the contents of works of fiction invariably vastly outstrip the contents that audiences assign to them. This consequence is unpalatable, because we do not take audiences' failure to assign such contents to works of fiction as evidence of their failure properly to understand those works. Such principles of generation are therefore incompatible with our norms of understanding. By contrast, my account construes background knowledge as playing a role that is consistent with those norms. Audiences must draw on their background knowledge to identify the imaginings with which the rules of fiction institutions prescribe them to respond to fictive utterances with certain features. Nevertheless, that background knowledge is not itself part of the contents of those fictive utterances. Understanding a work of fiction requires no more than grasping the contents of the fictive utterances by which it was produced.

Nevertheless, on the account I have proposed, the contents of works of fiction are not limited to the contents of the fictive utterances by which they were produced. In addition, works of fiction have interpretative fictive content, determined by authors' ordinary, non-communicative intentions to elicit imaginings in their audiences. The imagination's lack of direction of fit means that the assumption that authors are rational cannot alone explain how audiences are able to draw on their background knowledge to identify interpretative fictive content, because there are no imaginings that it would be irrational for authors to intend to elicit. However, authors have various goals that make it rational for them to seek to elicit certain imaginings rather than others in their audiences. Identifying those goals can therefore help audiences to identify the imaginings that authors intend to elicit and thus to identify interpretative fictive content.

To identify those goals, audiences draw inferences to the best explanation on the basis of all the background knowledge that is available to them. This includes their knowledge of the contents of authors' fictive utterances, together with any other background knowledge they have. Nevertheless, because authors need not share their goals with their audiences, they will pursue them in whatever way they think most likely to result in their achievement, irrespective of whether audiences have access to the background knowledge required to identify their behaviour as a means of pursuing those goals.

Interpretation therefore carries a real possibility of failure. Audiences who grasp the regulative rules of fiction institutions and are therefore able to understand works of fiction may nevertheless lack the resources required to interpret them.

This account of interpretation helps to solve two further philosophical problems. First of all, it helps to explain the role of external thought and talk about fiction in enabling the communication of imaginings. Although external thought and talk do not themselves involve imaginative engagement with works of fiction, they are necessary to identifying dependence relations between the properties that works of fiction exhibit from an external perspective and those they exhibit from an internal perspective. Because authors often have the goal of producing works of fiction that exhibit certain properties from an external perspective, identifying these dependence relations is essential to the interpretation of works of fiction. External thought and talk also play a more general role in enabling fiction institutions to perform the function of enabling the communication of imaginings, by improving the stability of their regulative rules and enabling participants to coordinate on ad hoc solutions to novel coordination problems of communicating imaginings.

Secondly, this account of interpretation helps to illuminate the role of authors' intentions in determining the contents of works of fiction. My account provides a much more nuanced picture of this role than existing contributions to the debate about the role of authors' intentions in determining the contents of their works. I have distinguished two different levels of fictive content and accorded authors' intentions a different role in determining each. I am a moderate actual intentionalist about interpretative fictive content. I take authors' intentions to prompt audiences to engage in imaginings with certain contents to determine the interpretative fictive content of the works they produce only under certain conditions. In particular, the fictive utterances they employ to do so must comprise a means of prompting audiences who lack independent knowledge of their intentions to engage in those imaginings. If they do not, their intentions do not determine interpretative fictive content.

By contrast, I am an anti-intentionalist about the contents of fictive utterances, if anti-intentionalism is construed simply as the denial that the contents of fictive utterances are ever determined by authors' intentions that their utterances have certain contents. Nevertheless, I allow authors' intentions certain roles in determining the contents of their fictive utterances. Authors' intentions play a categorial role by determining whether their utterances are governed by the content-determining rules of fiction institutions and thus whether they are fictive utterances. An utterance is a fictive utterance only if there is an institutional practice of fiction to which audiences' responses to the whole series of utterances of which it is a part are intended to conform. Moreover, which rule of a fiction institution governs a particular fictive utterance can depend on the effects it is intended to elicit in its audience. However, the intentions at issue here are intentions to convey contents (whatever they might be) in a particular *manner*, rather than intentions to convey contents of particular kinds.

The content-determining rules of fiction institutions can also incorporate a counterfactual conditional role for reasoning about intentions, in virtue of the way in which they specify the imaginings they prescribe in response to fictive utterances with certain features. Certain fictive utterances of representations are governed by rules that prescribe imagining the contents that non-fictive utterances of those representations would communicate, if they were made in certain contexts. Such rules have some affinity with one version of hypothetical intentionalism. Hypothetical intentionalism about the contents of fictive utterances can be construed in either one of two ways. It can be construed as claiming that their contents are determined by appropriate readers' hypotheses regarding the intentions with which authors produce their *fictive utterances*. Interpreted in this way, it fails for the same reasons the intentionalist accounts considered in Sections 3.2 and 3.3 fail. It relies on the existence of some method by which audiences can form justified hypotheses regarding the intentions with which such utterances are produced, and no such method is available. Alternatively, it can be construed as claiming that the contents of fictive utterances are determined by appropriate audiences' hypotheses regarding the intentions with which authors' fictive utterances would have been produced, had they been ordinary, non-fictive utterances produced by a person of a certain kind. On this construal, it is not subject to the same complaint, because, depending on the kind of person at issue, audiences plausibly do have the resources required to identify the intentions with which those people would have produced the relevant utterances.

My account of rules of the kind in question has clear similarities to the latter construal of hypothetical intentionalism. Nevertheless, the account I have presented is *not* a form of hypothetical intentionalism about the contents of fictive utterances. Hypothetical intentionalism is a holistic account of content determination. That is, it claims that the contents of the whole series of fictive utterances involved in producing a work of fiction are determined by appropriate audiences' hypotheses regarding the intentions of a single utterer. By contrast, on my account, each of the different fictive utterances involved in the production of a single work of fiction can be governed by different rules. Not all of these rules specify the contents of fictive utterances of representations by appeal to what hypothetical utterers would communicate by non-fictive utterances of those representations. Moreover, even when they do, the different rules may prescribe interpreting the utterances whose contents they govern as if they were produced by speakers of different kinds. Consequently, there need not be any single hypothetical utterer by reasoning about whose intentions audiences can identify the contents of all the fictive utterances by which a work of fiction was produced.

References

Austen, J. (1882). *Emma*. Steventon edition. London: Richard Bentley.

Austen, J. (2014). *Pride and Prejudice*. Minneapolis: First Avenue Editions.

Bach, K. (2006). 'On What it Takes to Refer', in Ernest Lepore and Barry Smith (eds), *The Oxford Handbook of Philosophy of Language*. Oxford: Oxford University Press, 516–54.

Bach, K., and Harnish, R. (1979). *Linguistic Communication and Speech Acts*. Cambridge, MA: MIT Press.

Beardsley, M. C. (1981). 'Fiction as Representation', *Synthese*, 46/3: 291–313.

Byrne, A. (1993). 'Truth in Fiction: The Story Continued', *Australasian Journal of Philosophy*, 71/1: 24–35.

Carroll, N. (1990). *The Philosophy of Horror: Or, Paradoxes of the Heart*. New York: Routledge.

Carston, R. (2002). *Thoughts and Utterances: The Pragmatics of Explicit Communication*. Oxford: Blackwell.

Chandler, R. (1984). *The High Window*. London: Hamish Hamilton.

Cortázar, J. (2001). 'Continuidad de los Parques', in *Cuentos Completos*, i. Madrid: Alfaguara.

Crane, T. (2013). *The Objects of Thought*. Oxford: Oxford University Press.

Currie, G. (1985). 'What is Fiction?', *Journal of Aesthetics and Art Criticism*, 43/4: 385–92.

Currie, G. (1990). *The Nature of Fiction*. Cambridge: Cambridge University Press.

Davies, D. (2007). *Aesthetics and Literature*. London: Continuum.

Davies, M. (1987). 'Tacit Knowledge and Semantic Theory: Can a Five Per Cent Difference Matter?', *Mind*, 96/384: 441–62.

Davies, M. (1995). 'Two Notions of Implicit Rules', *Philosophical Perspectives*, 9: 153–83.

Davies, M. (2015). 'Knowledge—Explicit, Implicit and Tacit: Philosophical Aspects', in J. D. Wright (ed.), *International Encyclopedia of Social and Behavioral Sciences*. 2nd edn. Oxford: Elsevier.

Dickie, G. (1969). 'Defining Art', *American Philosophical Quarterly*, 6: 253–6.

Dickie, G. (2000). 'The Institutional Theory of Art', in N. Carroll (ed.), *Theories of Art Today*. Madison: University of Wisconsin Press.

Epstein, B. (2015). *The Ant Trap: Rebuilding the Foundations of the Social Sciences*. New York: Oxford University Press.

Evans, G. (1973). 'The Causal Theory of Names', *Proceedings of the Aristotelian Society*, suppl. vol., 47: 187–208.

Everett, A. (2005). 'Against Fictional Realism', *Journal of Philosophy*, 102/12: 624–49.

Everett, A. (2013). *The Non Existent*. Oxford: Oxford University Press.

Fielding, H. (1825). *The History of Tom Jones: A Foundling*, vol. 1. London: Baynes and Son.

Forrester, J. (2010). 'The Lying Art of Historical Fiction', *Guardian*, 6 August, goo.gl/icmHj7.

Forster, E. M. (1927). *Aspects of the Novel*. Orlando: Harcourt.

Fowles, J. (2012). *The French Lieutenant's Woman*. London: Vintage Books.

Friend, S. (2007). 'Fictional Characters', *Philosophy Compass*, 2/2: 141–56.

Friend, S. (2008). 'Imagining Fact and Fiction', in K. Thompson Jones and K. Stock (eds), *New Waves in Aesthetics*. Basingstoke: Palgrave Macmillan, 150–69.

Friend, S. (2012). 'Fiction as a Genre', *Proceedings of the Aristotelian Society*, 112/2: 179–209.

Friend, S. (2014). 'Notions of Nothing', in Manuel García-Carpintero and Genoveva Marti (eds), *Empty Representations: Reference and Non-Existence*. Oxford: Oxford University Press.

Friend, S. (2017). 'The Real Foundation of Fictional Worlds', *Australasian Journal of Philosophy*, 95/1: 29–42.

García-Carpintero, M. (2007). 'Fiction-Making as a Gricean Illocutionary Type', *Journal of Aesthetics and Art Criticism*, 65/2: 203–16.

García-Carpintero, M. (2018). 'Co-Identification and Fictional Names', *Philosophy and Phenomenological Research*.

Gaut, B. (2003). 'Creativity and Imagination', in B. Gaut and P. Livingston (eds), *The Creation of Art: New Essays in Philosophical Aesthetics*. Cambridge, Cambridge University Press, 148–73.

Goldman, A. (1995). *Aesthetic Value*. Boulder, CO: Westview.

Grice, H. P. (1957). 'Meaning', *Philosophical Review*, 66/3 (July), 377–88.

Grice, H. P. (1989). *Studies in the Ways of Words*. Cambridge, MA: Harvard University Press.

Guala, F. (2016a). *Understanding Institutions*. Princeton: Princeton University Press.

Guala, F. (2016b). 'Epstein on Anchors and Grounds', *Journal of Social Ontology*, 2/1: 135–47.

Hardy, T. (2016). *Tess of the D'Urbervilles*. New York: Open Road.

Hawley, K. (2017). 'Comments on Brian Epstein's *The Ant Trap*', *Inquiry*, DOI: 10.1080/0020174X.2017.1289694.

Hindriks, F. (2009). 'Constitutive Rules, Language, and Ontology', *Erkenntnis*, 71/2: 253–75.

James, H. (1883). *The Portrait of a Lady*. London: Macmillan.

James, P. D. (2010). *A Certain Justice*. London: Faber and Faber.

Kafka, F. (1961). *Metamorphosis and Other Stories*, trans. Willa and Edwin Muir. Harmondsworth: Penguin.

Köppe, T., and Kindt, T. (2011). 'Unreliable Narration with a Narrator and without', *Journal of Literary Theory*, 5/1: 81–94.

Kripke, S. (1980). *Naming and Necessity*. Cambridge, MA: Harvard University Press.

Lamarque, P., and Olsen, S. H. (1994). *Truth, Fiction and Literature*. Oxford: Oxford University Press.

Legge, K. (2008). 'Truly Helen', *Australian*, 29 March, goo.gl/1qQP8a.

Lepore, E., and Stone, M. (2015). *Imagination and Convention: Distinguishing Grammar and Inference in Language*. Oxford: Oxford University Press.

Levinson, J. (1992). 'Intention and Interpretation: A Last Look', in G. Iseminger (ed.), *Intention and Interpretation*. Philadelphia: Temple University Press, 221–56.

Lewis, D. (1969). *Convention*. Oxford: Blackwell Publishing.

Lewis, D. (1975). 'Languages and Language', in Keith Gunderson (ed.), *Minnesota Studies in the Philosophy of Science*. Minnesota: University of Minnesota Press, 3–35.

Lewis, D. (1983a). 'Truth in Fiction', *Philosophical Papers*. Oxford: Oxford University Press, 1: 261–75.

Lewis, D. (1983b). 'Postscripts to Truth in Fiction', *Philosophical Papers*. Oxford, Oxford University Press, 1: 276–80.

Lodge, D. (1992). *The Art of Fiction*. London: Penguin.

Lodge, D. (2004). *Author, Author*. London: Secker and Warburg.

Marcus, R. B. (1961). 'Modalities and Intensional Languages,' *Synthese*, 13: 303–22.

Matravers, D. (2014). *Fiction and Narrative*. Oxford: Oxford University Press.

Phillips, J. (1999). 'Truth and Inference in Fiction', *Philosophical Studies*, 94/3: 273–93.

Rhys, R. (2019). *Good Morning, Midnight*. London: Penguin Classics.

Sainsbury, R. M. (2015). 'The Same Name', *Erkenntnis*, 80: 195–214.

Salmon, N. (1998). 'Nonexistence', *Nous*, 32/3: 277–319.

Schiffer, S. (1996). 'Language-Created Language-Independent Entities', *Philosophical Topics*, 24/1: 149–67.

Searle, J. (1969). *Speech Acts*. Cambridge: Cambridge University Press.

Searle, J. (1979). *Expression and Meaning: Studies in the Theory of Speech Acts*. Cambridge: Cambridge University Press.

Searle, J. (1995). *The Construction of Social Reality*. London: Penguin.

Searle, J. (2010). *Making the Social World: The Structure of Human Civilization*. Oxford: Oxford University Press.

Shakespeare, W. (1958). *Othello*, ed. M. R. Ridley. Arden Edition. London: Methuen.

Shakespeare, W. (1971). *As You Like It*, ed. Arthur Quiller-Couch and John Dover Wilson. Cambridge: Cambridge University Press.

Siegel, J. and Shuster, J. (1938). 'Superman', in *Action Comics No. 1*. New York: DC Comics.

Smith, M. (1995). 'Film Spectatorship and the Institution of Fiction', *Journal of Aesthetics and Art Criticism*, 53/2: 113–27.

Spark, M. (1963). *The Comforters*. Harmondsworth: Penguin.

Spark, M. (2001). *The Complete Short Stories*. London: Viking.

Sperber, D., and Wilson, D. (1995). *Relevance*. 2nd edn. Oxford: Blackwell.

St Aubyn, E. (2012). *Never Mind*. London: Picador.

Stevenson, R. L. (2014). *The Strange Case of Dr. Jekyll and Mr. Hyde*. Minneapolis: Lerner Publishing Group, First Avenue Classics.

Stock, K. (2011). 'Fictive Utterance and Imagining', *Proceedings of the Aristotelian Society*, suppl vol., 85: 145–61.

Stock, K. (2017). *Only Imagine: Fiction, Interpretation and Imagination*. Oxford: Oxford University Press.

Strawson, P. F. (1964). 'Intention and Convention in Speech Acts', *Philosophical Review*, 73/4: 439–60.

Thomasson, A. (1999). *Fiction and Metaphysics*. Cambridge: Cambridge University Press.

Thomasson, A. (2001). 'Ontological Minimalism', *American Philosophical Quarterly*, 38/4: 319–31.

Thomasson, A. (2003a). 'Realism and Human Kinds', *Philosophy and Phenomenological Research*, 67/3: 580–609.

Thomasson, A. (2003b). 'Fictional Characters and Literary Practices', *British Journal of Aesthetics*, 43/2: 138–57.

Thomasson, A. (2003c). 'Speaking of Fictional Characters', *Dialectica*, 57: 205–23.

Thomasson, A. (2007). *Ordinary Objects*. New York: Oxford University Press.

Tolstoy, L. (1965). *Anna Karenina*, trans. Louise and Aylmer Maude. London: Oxford University Press.

Tolstoy, L. (2010). *War and Peace*, trans. Louise and Aylmer Maude, ed. Amy Mandelker. Oxford: Oxford University Press.

Walton, K. (1990). *Mimesis as Make-Believe*. Cambridge, MA: Harvard University Press.

Weisberg, D. S. and Goodstein, J. (2009). 'What Belongs in a Fictional World?', *Journal of Cognition and Culture*, 9/1: 69–78.

Wood, J. (2008). *How Fiction Works*. London: Jonathan Cape.

Zipfel, F. (2011). 'Unreliable Narration and Fictional Truth', *Journal of Literary Theory*, 5/1: 109–30.

Index

For the benefit of digital users, indexed terms that span two pages (e.g., 52–53) may, on occasion, appear on only one of those pages.

Lightning Source UK Ltd.
Milton Keynes UK
UKHW020232110822
407160UK00003B/190